35⁰⁰

PARLIAMENTS IN WESTERN EUROPE

PARLIAMENTS IN WESTERN EUROPE

Edited by

PHILIP NORTON

FRANK CASS

First published 1990 in Great Britain by
FRANK CASS & CO. LTD.
Gainsborough House, Gainsborough Road,
London E11 1RS, England

and in the United States of America by
FRANK CASS
c/o International Specialized Book Services, Inc.,
5602 N.E. Hassalo Street,
Portland, Oregon 97213

British Library Cataloguing in Publication Data
Parliaments in Western Europe.
1. Western Europe. Parliaments
I. Norton, Philip II. West European politics,
ISSN 0140-2382
323.3094

ISBN 0-7146-3407-7

Library of Congress Cataloguing in Publication Data
Parliaments in Western Europe / edited by Philip Norton.
  p.   cm.
"First appeared in a special issue . . . of West European
politics, vol. 13, no. 3 (July 1990)"--T.p. verso.
ISBN 0-7146-3407-7
1. Legislative bodies--Europe. I. Norton, Philip.
JN94.A72R65 1990
328.3'094--dc20
90-36573
CIP

This group of studies first appeared in a Special Issue on 'Parliaments in
Western Europe' of *West European Politics*, Vol. 13, No. 3 (July 1990), published by
Frank Cass & Co. Ltd.

Typeset by Selectmove Ltd, London
Printed and bound in Great Britain by
Antony Rowe Ltd, Chippenham

Contents

Notes on Contributors

Audrey Arkins is Lecturer in Politics in the Department of Political Science and Sociology, University College, Galway. Her research interests include parliamentary reform, political communications and the mass media. She has published on Irish parliamentary select committees and, with M. Laver, in *How Ireland Voted: the 1989 General Election*, based on research at the Centre for Irish Elections, University College, Galway.

David Arter is Head of the North and East European Office at Leeds Polytechnic. He has written widely on legislative politics in Scandinavia, including *The Nordic Parliaments: A Comparative Analysis* (1985) and *One Thing Too Many: The Shift to Unicameralism in Denmark* (1990). He is currently working on a study of Åland's *Landsting*.

John Frears is Reader in Politics at Loughborough University. He is the author of *Political Parties and Elections in the Fifth Republic* (1977, 2nd ed. 1990), *France in the Giscard Presidency* (1981), and other books and articles on government and politics in France.

Paul Furlong is Lecturer in Politics at the University of Hull. He is the author of several articles on Italian government and politics, including 'The Constitutional Court in Italian Politics', *West European Politics*, July 1989, and is currently completing a book on the Italian Parliament.

Ken Gladdish is Head of the Department of Politics at the University of Reading. He has published widely on Dutch politics, including articles in *Parliamentary Affairs, Government and Opposition* and *Acta Politica*, and is author of the forthcoming *Governing from the Centre: Politics and Policy-Making in the Netherlands*.

Philip Norton is Professor of Government at the University of Hull. His many books include *Dissension in the House of Commons* (2 vols., 1975, 1980), *The Commons in Perspective* (1981), *The Constitution in Flux* (1982), *The British Polity* (1984, 2nd ed. 1990), *Parliament in the 1980s* (ed., 1985) and *Legislatures* (ed., 1990). He is an officer of the Study of Parliament Group and President of the British Politics Group in the USA.

Thomas Saalfeld is a political scientist at the University of the Bundeswehr in Munich. His publications include *Das britische Unterhaus 1965–1986* (1988). He is currently writing a study on voting cohesion in the Bundestag, 1949–90.

Parliaments: A Framework for Analysis

Philip Norton

Legislatures are remarkable institutions. They are remarkable because they are ubiquitous. They span the globe. Of countries listed in *The Statesman's Year Book*, less than 15 per cent are without one. The number of countries that have never had one (predominantly in the Middle East) can be counted on one's fingers. Legislatures predominate on every continent. Indeed, wherever there is an inhabited land mass, there is usually a legislature. Even Pitcairn Island, with fewer than 100 inhabitants, has one.

They are remarkable also because of their variety. That variety extends to their name, size and functions. They exist under a variety of nomenclatures: parliaments, congresses and (by far the most popular) assemblies. Some are remarkably large bodies. The British House of Lords leads the way with more than 1,100 members. A number are tiny, with fewer than twenty members. The tasks they perform vary considerably. They have one core-defining function: they give assent, on behalf of a political community that extends beyond the executive authority, to binding measures of public policy. Beyond that, they differ considerably. For some, the task of giving assent – what Packenham has characterised as manifest legitimisation[1] – constitutes the sole or virtually the sole task they perform. In such instances, the legislature usually meets for only a few days in a year. Other legislatures, the majority, do other things and so convene frequently and for substantial periods of time. They are usually functionally adaptable bodies. The tasks they perform not only vary from one political system to another but also vary over time. The tasks at present being fulfilled by the Supreme Soviet of the USSR or the Polish *Sejm*, for example, are not the tasks they were fulfilling a decade ago.

Just as legislatures are remarkable, so too is the study of them. It is remarkable for being skewed. There is a mass of literature on particular legislatures. We know a great deal, though not as much as some observers appear to believe, about legislatures in Western countries. The US Congress is especially well served by the literature. So too, though to a lesser extent, is the British Parliament and the assemblies of other West European nations. Yet we know relatively little about legislatures as a particular species of institution. Country-specific knowledge has not been assimililated on any comprehensive and systematic basis to allow a substantial body of generalisations to be drawn. Few truly comparative studies have been published. Of journals that encourage comparative legislative studies, such as *Legislative Studies Quarterly* in the USA and *Parliamentary Affairs* in Britain, the bulk of material submitted is country-specific and, indeed, insular; that is, it is not offered within a broader comparative framework. Indeed, in the case of *Legislative Studies Quarterly*, it is usually specific to the USA, accounting for almost 60 per cent of all articles published, a product of supply rather than editorial demand.

That there is such an imbalance in the literature is not surprising. Legislatures exist in a variety of societal contexts. Wrenching them from those contexts for the purpose of comparison is a mammoth undertaking. It is compounded by differences of language and sometimes by similarities of language. (To take a very simple illustration of confusion generated by use of the same words for different things: in the US Congress, to 'table' a motion means precisely the opposite of what it means in the UK Parliament; in the former it means killing a motion, in the latter the beginning of a deliberative process.) It is further compounded by disparity in the quantity of data available. A great deal is known about some systems, virtually nothing about others. Unavailability of data may be a consequence, for example, of a closed and uncommunicative legislature. It may reflect the limited academic means available to research and transmit the data. In some countries, there are no political scientists to undertake such research. In other cases, a problem is generated by the data being mediated through different intellectual media. Different conclusions about legislatures may be the product of different ways of looking at them. The result is that those who attempt a comparative study are dependent on a range of disparate sources.[2] The resources to undertake an exhaustive, original study do not exist.

The study of legislatures is remarkable also for operating largely within a restrictive paradigm. That paradigm derives from two propositions. The first, established since at least the seventeenth century, is that the principal task of legislatures is that of 'law making' or 'law giving', hence their generic name. The identification of this task was central to the works of both Locke and Montesquieu.[3] The second, equally long-standing proposition, though popularised especially in the literature of the nineteenth century, is that the 'best' form of legislature is one composed of men of independence, both in thought and means, able to deliberate free of vested interests and the restrictive demands of an uninformed mass. Both Bagehot and Mill bemoaned the likely consequences of a mass suffrage and the later studies of Ostrogorski, Lowell and Bryce appeared to give some empirical credence to their worst fears.

The work of the scholar-statesman Lord Bryce, in particular, has had a seminal influence. He titled Chapter 58 of his *Modern Democracies* 'The Decline of Legislatures', and the appellation stuck. Such a 'decline' had been detected earlier by scholars such as Lawrence Lowell, but Bryce popularised the concept among the thinking classes. 'Writing just after the First World War, Bryce at once summarised the view of an entire generation of observers of representative institutions and provided a dogma for a new generation of disillusioned democrats.'[4] From the perspective of such liberal thinkers, the nineteenth century marked the high point of legislatures, notably but not exclusively in Europe. Most assemblies, with the exception of the British,[5] were reduced to subservience during the period of the French Revolution. In the early years of the nineteenth century, they witnessed a revival; they grew both in number and political significance. The significance was not uniform. Germany, unlike Britain, witnessed no 'golden age' of Parliament. As Bryce himself recognised, one or two legislatures had little to decline from. None the less, as Kurt Sontheimer has noted, parliamentarianism was a feature of the century.[6] Yet no sooner had this been recognised than doubts as to its future began to find expression. Bryce, in his magisterial survey, confirmed the fears. Bryce's perception of decline was qualified, but in so far as it was taking place he proffered five 'chronic ailments' to account for it: the principal culprit was the growth of party.

Hence, early in the twentieth century the liberal paradigm was established: that of law-making bodies in a spiral of decline. This paradigm has had a notably debilitating effect on the subsequent study of legislatures by political scientists. First, it has resulted in a study focused largely upon legislatures in relation to the making of public policy, or what Packenham would term their 'decisional' functions. This focus has largely served to confirm the liberal perception of 'decline'. Public policy has increasingly been initiated and formulated – in effect, 'made' – elsewhere, usually by the executive; legislatures have been transformed from law-making to what David Olson has aptly described as 'law-effecting' institutions.[7] Second, it has rendered legislative studies to be one of the poor relations in the discipline. Recognising that power – at least in pluralist terms – has shifted away from legislatures, political scientists have generally shifted their attention to where they have detected that power now to be. In what Somit and Tanenhaus termed the middle years of American political science, for example, attention was focused on bureaucracy and the executive; in the early years of the subsequent behavioural revolution, the focus shifted decisively away from institutions.[8] In the emergent period of British political science in the 1960s, legislative studies were likewise left behind in the rush to analyse the decision-making process.[9]

The study of legislatures has not yet moved to a new paradigm. There remains an emphasis on executive-legislative relations: in other words, on the impact of the legislature on policy making by the executive. The concept of 'decline' remains current, both in comparative and country-specific literature. It has been a consistent feature of literature on the British Parliament, from Bryce to Crick. So great a hold does it have that two recent writers even suggested that what little attention was given to Parliament was too much. The rationale for this assertion was that Parliament had not only declined but was in a state of continuing decline. 'While Britain has busied itself with parliamentary reforms, the importance of Parliament . . . has been diminishing.'[10] University dons in Britain whose principal research specialisation is Parliament number fewer than a dozen.

However, advances have been made. During the past twenty years there has been a significant increase in the quantity – and quality – of material on legislatures, collectively as well as individually.[11] In the sphere of executive–legislative relations, valuable analytical frameworks have been generated by Anthony King and Malcolm Shaw;[12] Jean Blondel has introduced the concept of 'viscosity' in an attempt to facilitate cross-national measurement of legislative behaviour.[13] However, for our purposes what has been most significant have been the various attempts to widen the study of legislatures beyond that of their observable impact on the making of public policy. The attempts have not been systematic, but rather the product of pioneering work by individual political scientists. The cumulative effect of their work has been to sensitise us to the potential significance of legislatures as more than mono-functional bodies.[14] Legislatures variously fulfil significant regime-support functions. Study of these functions shifts the focus away from that of the relations of legislature to executive to that of legislature to the citizenry. Packenham, drawing upon Brazilian experience, has identified eleven functions (defined as consequences for the political system) grouped under the three heads of legitimation; recruitment, socialisation and training; and political decision-making or influence.[15] As he recognised, these functions will vary in importance from legislature to legislature. This variation has allowed a number of scholars, Nelson Polsby and Michael Mezey in particular, to generate valuable taxonomies.[16] Mezey's is especially useful for the purposes of this volume. Combined with the functional analysis of Robert Packenham, his work provides a useful framework for the analysis of legislatures in Western Europe.

MEZEY'S TYPOLOGY

In *Comparative Legislatures*, published in 1979, Mezey produced a six-box classification of legislatures based on (a) the degree of policy-making power and (b) the extent of support accruing to the institution. He distinguished three layers of policy-making power: 'strong' (capable of modifying and rejecting policy proposals), 'modest' (capable of modifying but not rejecting policy proposals) and 'little or no policy-making power' (lacking the capacity to modify or reject). Support he defined as 'a set of attitudes that look to the legislature as a valued and popular political institution' and distinguished, simply but sensibly (given the data available), between 'more supported' and 'less supported' legislatures. His resulting matrix – with five of the six boxes occupied – is reproduced as Table 1.

One qualification is necessary for analytic purposes. Mezey's definitional distinction between 'strong' and 'modest' policy-making power misses, to

TABLE 1

MEZEY'S TYPOLOGY OF LEGISLATURES

Policy-making Power	Less supported Legislatures	More supported Legislatures
Strong	Vulnerable legislatures	Active legislatures
Modest	Marginal legislatures	Reactive legislatures
Little or none		Minimal legislatures

my mind, the essential difference. Strong policy-making power must surely encompass the capacity to formulate, to 'make', policy. The power to reject, especially if only occasionally exercised, does not render a legislature a policy 'making' body. Hence, we are better served by re-defining Mezey's categories of 'strong' and 'modest': the first may be defined as the capacity to modify and reject policy as well as substitute policy of one's own (policy-making); the second as the capacity to modify or reject but not to substitute policy of one's own (policy influencing).[17] This provides a sharper, more useful distinction while retaining Mezey's six-box typology.

The principal value of Mezey's work is that it alerts us to the need to explore a dimension of legislative activity beyond that of, but not excluding, policy-making. Distinguishing the policy-making strength of legislatures is a valuable exercise. Knowing that the legislatures of most countries of Western Europe fall within the same broad category, enjoying 'modest' power in the policy cycle,[18] is both a strength and a limitation. A strength in that we are able to compare like broadly with like. There is a sufficiency of literature to demonstrate that the legislatures discussed in this volume are not policy-making bodies. We are also sufficiently well-informed to know why this is so. Without the political culture of what Martin Seymour Lipset termed 'the first new nation', the United States, and the constitutional framework generated eventually by that culture, the legislatures of Western Europe have been unable to withstand the pressures that have favoured executive dominance in the policy cycle. Industrialisation and the advent of mass suffrage have taken their toll. Political parties have served to aggregate the demands of the electorate and, consequently, constrain the freedom of individual action by members of a legislature. Increasing group demands have generated the need for an extensive policy-making, implementing and regulating executive. The more extensive, and the more complex, the measures of public policy, the greater the difficulty of a mass-member, popularly-elected assembly, *But LDP?* meeting on a non-continuous basis, maintaining an effective involvement in the policy process. Political parties have served as the conduits for the transfer of policy-making power from legislatures to executives; corporatist pressures have pushed the locus of policy-making further away. Hence, in studying the legislatures of Western Europe, we are seeking to identify to what extent they retain the capacity to exert a modest influence in the policy cycle; we are not attempting to locate the category within which each falls.

The limitation derives from the focus provided by such a concentration. Assessing the relative policy-influencing strength of legislatures known to fall within the same broad category is useful but does not take us as far as it might. There is more to legislatures than their relationship to the executive in the policy cycle. There is, as already noted, the relationship of the legislature to the citizenry. Hence the value of Mezey's emphasis upon support. Contemporary West European legislatures, with the exception of the Italian Parliament, are classified among the 'more supported' legislatures. Though there is empirical evidence to justify this classification, the reasons for that support – and the extent of it – are less

TABLE 2
PACKENHAM'S LEGISLATIVE FUNCTIONS

LEGITIMATION

Latent (through meeting regularly and uninterruptedly)
Manifest (giving the formal stamp of approval)
'Safety valve' or 'tension release' (outlet for tensions in the system)

RECRUITMENT, SOCIALISATION
AND TRAINING

Recruitment
Socialisation
Training

DECISIONAL OR INFLUENCE
FUNCTIONS

Law-making
'Exit' function (resolving an impasse in the political system)
Interest-articulation function (giving voice to public interests)
Conflict resolution
Administrative oversight and patronage
functions (keeping check on the administration and
undertaking 'errand-running' – casework – for constituents)

---

well known. This volume provides us with an opportunity to consider the nature and extent of that support and to assess to what extent it has been maintained during the past two decades, a time of increasing pressure on the political structures of the countries under review.

PACKENHAM'S DELINEATION OF FUNCTIONS

It is in analysing the nature of support that the work of Packenham is especially helpful. Published in 1970, and based upon a study of the Brazilian National Congress, Packenham's article identified a total of eleven consequences (functions) which the congress had for the political system. These are listed in Table 2. Evidence from other political systems suggested that they were consequences not confined to the Brazilian example. The empirical study of the Brazilian Congress was important primarily in determining the rank ordering of the functions – those at the top of the list had the greatest consequences for the political system, those at the bottom the least. The decisional and influence functions – those on which most observers focus – were of limited impact. They would clearly rank higher in any analysis of the US Congress but, as Packenham notes, 'what knowledge we have suggests that the Brazilian case is much closer to the mode than the US Congress'.[19] For Packenham, it is the other functions that merit attention. 'In fact, even if it had no decision-making power whatsoever, the other functions which it performs would be significant.'[20]

The Brazilian Congress, with its discontinuous history, ranks among Mezey's 'less supported' legislatures. Packenham's research demonstrated none the less that its existence and activity have had consequences for the political system. They have been essentially supportive consequences, albeit inadequate to provide popular protection against periods of military rule. A delineation of those consequences is useful for comparative purposes. They can be utilised in analysing the consequences of other legislatures for their respective political systems. The legislatures of Western Europe have a modest decisional, that is law-making, function but how important are the other functions? What mechanisms exist, and to what extent are they used, for 'tension release' and 'errand running', for example? And to what extent have they been able to cope at times of increased pressure on the political system as a whole?

With Mezey, Packenham thus draws our attention to the broader role of legislatures, beyond that of 'law-making', and it is this wider perspective that informs our study of West European legislatures and provides us with our essential hypothesis.

ANALYSING THE LEGISLATURES OF WESTERN EUROPE

This volume focuses on seven legislatures – those of the UK, France, Italy, West Germany, Ireland, the Netherlands, and Sweden – and their relationship to their respective executives in the twenty years from 1970 to 1990. It takes that relationship, though, in its wider context, encompassing the support functions that underpin the legitimacy of the political system and, hence, the authority of the executive to act. It addresses two vital questions: to what extent has each legislature declined – or been reinforced – as a policy-influencing body and to what extent has it served to maintain the popular legitimacy of government?

These are important questions at any time. They are especially important in the context of the past two decades. At the beginning of the 1970s, the countries of Western Europe were facing significant economic problems. These were exacerbated by the Arab oil embargo of 1973, which pre-cipitated a recession. Growth was slowed; in some countries there was no growth at all. Recovery was hit at the end of the decade by a second increase in oil prices. Governments had to take hard and sometimes drastic measures in order to cope with the changed circumstances. Some decisions were implemented by executive *fiat*; legislatures were asked to ratify what was already in force. There was a growing tendency among governments to resort to a corporatist model of decision-making, incorporating representatives of business and labour into the early stages of the policy cycle.[21] The Single European Act, ratified by the member states of the European Community, induced a further shift of the locus of policy-making in certain sectors from a national to a supra national level. The effect of these developments, one would hypothesise, would be to limit further the role of legislatures as agents of policy influence. Though still retaining the essential properties of bodies with 'modest' power in the policy cycle, their power would be expected to be markedly more modest than before. Hence the perception, for example, of the continuing 'decline' of the British Parliament.

Yet at the same time one would hypothesise that legislatures would be more significant as agents of regime support. Economic problems were variously exacerbated by social and core–periphery tensions. Political systems were consequently placed under strain. At times of strain, the non-decisional functions of legislatures assume greater significance. The tension release, conflict resolution and 'errand running' functions are of special importance; though Packenham lists them under different heads, they are all significant in helping maintain the health of the political system. By legitimising the system of government, legislatures serve also to legitimise the authority of the executive to act. Though governments may ostensibly not pay much regard to legislatures, the essential truth is that they need them. This is not to assert that the legislatures under review have fared especially well as agents of regime support in recent years. Rather, our observations suggest the need to investigate to what extent they have served effectively to maintain the health of the political system.

By addressing this wider question, while not neglecting that of influence in policy-making, the contributors to this volume are thus able to explore a much richer analytic seam than is normally explored. By so doing, they provide a much clearer explanation – central to any understanding of political systems in Western Europe – of why legislatures actually matter.

NOTES

1. R. Packenham, 'Legislatures and Political Development', in A. Kornberg and L.D. Musolf (eds.), *Legislatures in Developmental Perspective* (Durham NC: Duke University Press, 1970).
2. Probably the best work which draws together existing data is M. Mezey, *Comparative Legislatures* (Durham NC: Duke University Press, 1979). For a comment on the insular nature of works on European legislatures, see M. Pedersen, 'Research on European Parliaments: A Review Article on Scholarly and Institutional Variety', *Legislative Studies Quarterly*, Vol.9 (1984), pp.505–29.
3. See J. Locke, *Of Civil Government: Second Treatise* (1689), Ch. 13; Baron de Montesquieu, *The Spirit of the Laws* (1748), bk. XI.
4. G. Loewenberg (ed.), *Modern Parliaments: Change or Decline?* (Chicago: Aldine-Atherton, 1971), p.7.
5. See A. R. Myers, *Parliaments and Estates in Europe to 1789* (London: Thames and Hudson, 1975).
6. K. Sontheimer, 'Parliamentarianism in Modern Times – A Political Science Perspective', *Universitas*, Vol.26 (1984), p.1.
7. D. Olson, *The Legislative Process: A Comparative Approach* (New York: Harper & Row, 1980), p.12.
8. A. Somit and J. Tanenhaus, *The Development of Political Science: From Burgess to Behavioralism* (Boston, MA: Allyn & Bacon, 1967), parts III and IV.
9. J. E. S. Hayward and P. Norton, (eds), *The Political Science of British Politics* (Brighton: Wheatsheaf Books, 1986), Chs. 8 and 13.
10. A. G. Jordan and J. J. Richardson, *British Politics and the Policy Process* (London: Allen & Unwin, 1987), p.65.
11. See the introduction to P. Norton (ed.), *Legislatures* (Oxford: Oxford University Press, 1990). On advances in country-specific literature – in this instance, the UK Parliament – see S. C. Patterson, 'Understanding the British Parliament', *Political Studies*, Vol.37 (1989), pp.449–62.
12. A. King, 'Modes of Executive-Legislative Relations: Great Britain, France, and West

Germany', *Legislative Studies Quarterly*, Vol.1, No. 1, 1976, pp.37–65; M. Shaw, 'Conclusion', in J. D. Lees and M. Shaw (eds.), *Committees in Legislatures* (Oxford: Martin Robertson, 1979), pp.361–434.
13. J. Blondel *et al.*, 'Legislative Behaviour: Some Steps towards a Cross-National Measurement', *Government and Opposition*, Vol.5 (1970), pp.67–85.
14. See the introduction to Norton, *Legislatures*, pp.1–16.
15. Packenham.
16. N. W. Polsby, 'Legislatures', in F. I. Greenstein and N. W. Polsby (eds.), *Handbook of Political Science*, Vol.5 (Reading MA: Addison-Wesley, 1975), pp.257–319; Mezey, *Comparative Legislatures*.
17. See P. Norton, 'Parliament and Policy in Britain: The House of Commons as a Policy Influencer', *Teaching Politics*, Vol.13 (1984), pp.198–221.
18. 'Most' in that Mezey places Italy in the 'strong' policy-making category. However, in the context of the relatively weak policy-making environment in which the Italian Parliament operates, this would seem an incorrect classification. I have therefore treated it as falling into the same category as its neighbours. This judgement is borne out by Paul Furlong's contribution to this volume.
19. Packenham.
20. Packenham.
21. See A. Cox (ed.), *Politics, Policy and the European Recession* (London: Macmillan, 1982).

Parliament in the United Kingdom: Balancing Effectiveness and Consent?

Philip Norton

'Nothing more decidedly separates the United Kingdom from other nations of Western Europe than the nature of its parliamentary institutions.'[1] So declared the parliamentary historian and former Member of Parliament Enoch Powell in 1989. The Westminster Parliament enjoys a distinctiveness that is historical and, partly as a consequence of that history, constitutional.

Parliament enjoys a longevity unmatched by most other national assemblies. Norman kings were advised by a court, the *Curia Regis*, comprising principally churchmen, earls and chief barons. In the thirteenth century, knights and burgesses were also summoned to give assent to the levying of additional taxes (aids). From this addition to the king's court emerged a Parliament: the term was first used in that century. At various times in the fourteenth century, the representatives of the local communities deliberated separately and so there emerged the two Houses, the barons and churchmen coming to constitute the House of Lords, the representatives of the local communities (the *communes*) the House of Commons. Though the development of the institution has not been steady, or, in the case of the House of Lords, unbroken[2] Parliament has endured as a national assembly, able to claim a history spanning seven centuries.

The country's principal constitutional upheavals – the civil war of the sixteenth century and the Glorious Revolution of the seventeenth – pre-dated the emergence of written constitutions. Britain lacks a formal, codified constitution; what it has is a part-written, uncodified one, aptly described by Nevil Johnson as an 'unformalised' constitution.[3] The constitutional position of Parliament is thus not enumerated in one single, authoritative document. Its position in the system of government – and the relationship between its component parts – is now embodied in part in statute, notably the Bill of Rights of 1689 and the Parliament Acts of 1911 and 1949, but the doctrine that asserts the supremacy of statute law – parliamentary sovereignty – derives from common law.[4] Lacking, or rather not taking when offered, the opportunity to create a constitution from first principles, the country has acquired a national assembly that, in its origins and patchy development, is the consequence of political expediency – 'the product', as Ronald Butt describes it, 'of practical politics, not an artefact of constitutional theory'.[5] Packenham, in his discussion of functions, defines functions as consequences for the political system. It is a definition that is particularly apt in the context of the Westminster Parliament. The functions commonly listed in texts on the subject are derived essentially from what Parliament does rather than from authoritative prescriptions of what it should be doing.

The distinctiveness of Parliament's history and constitutional practice is relevant to any study of the present position of the institution in the British polity. The relevance, in the context of other West European legislatures, lies in helping explain differences of degree rather than of kind. In most typologies of legislatures, Parliament is grouped with other West European – and most major Commonwealth – legislatures. Like other Western legislatures, it has not been able to withstand the pressures – identified in the introduction – favouring executive dominance in policy-making. However, according to various observers, Parliament's capacity to withstand those pressures has been notably weaker than that of its continental neighbours. Historical and constitutional factors are important in explaining why that is so. Those factors can usefully be drawn out in looking at the consequences which Parliament has – in other words, its functions – for the political system.

PARLIAMENT: A FUNCTIONAL ANALYSIS

Drawing on the work of Robert Packenham in particular, and – for identifying other specific functions – that of Samuel Beer and Michael Mezey, it is possible to identify ten functions that may be ascribed to Parliament. These can be grouped, following Packenham, under three heads: the provision of government ministers, legitimisation, and policy affect.

Provision of Government Ministers

By convention, ministers are drawn from and remain within Parliament. For politicians ambitious for office, the route thus lies through Parliament, principally the House of Commons. The chances of an MP in the government party who has served five to ten years in the House being appointed as a parliamentary private secretary (PPS) or offered a ministerial post are almost one in two.

Both Houses provide important testing grounds for potential ministers and careers can be made or broken in the chamber. This recruitment and training function is far from problem-free. Candidates are selected by a closed party process from, usually, a particular socio-economic background (MPs are now overwhelmingly middle-class)[6] and, given limited pay and resources, not always from the ranks of those considered most able to run an administrative body (a government department). However, remedies that are offered to change the situation are geared predominantly to improving the supply of candidates available rather than changing the route to office. Parliament thus retains a virtual monopoly on the provision of ministers. That makes it important as a recruiting agency. As we shall see, it also limits it as a policy-influencing body.

Legitimisation

The various legitimising functions overlap and interact with those of policy affect. In terms of significance for the political system, *manifest legitimisation* and *latent legitimisation* deserve pride of place. Legitimisation is the oldest function of the House of Commons. It is also the one that renders Parliament powerful in terms of Steven Lukes' third dimension of power.[7]

Parliament is a powerful body in that there is popular acceptance, at both élite and mass level, that measures of public policy are not legitimate unless approved by Parliament. The legitimising authority of Parliament has been strengthened by virtue of longevity – there is no recollection, no recognisable history of any alternative form of legitimisation – and by virtue now of the election of the lower House. Indeed, as Ralph Miliband has noted, the elected nature of the House of Commons now renders illegitimate any radical alternative, 'for it suggests that what is required above all else to bring about fundamental change is a majority in the House of Commons'.[8] Parliament is thus important not only because it gives formal approval to measures but also, and most crucially, because it constitutes the institution at the heart of a *process* which enjoys acceptance by citizens as the sole authoritative process for rendering legitimate government and measures of public policy which are to be binding.

Three other functions may be subsumed under the rubric of legitimisation: those of *tension release* (Packenham's 'safety valve' function), *integration* and *support mobilisation*. Parliament provides an authoritative forum through which the grievances of individuals, groups and unorganised bodies of citizens may be channelled. Those grievances are expressed to Members of Parliament (MPs) through various media (political parties, correspondence, constituency 'surgeries') and MPs themselves have at their disposal a variety of means for representing them to government (parliamentary questions, motions, correspondence, and – most hallowed of all – debate on the floor of the House). The extent to which Parliament has actually proved efficient in giving voice to citizens' complaints is problematic. Party hegemony and limited resources have been seen by critics as contributing to limited effectiveness. Given the pressures on the political system in recent years, it is a function that one would expect to assume greater importance. The extent to which it has (or has not) done so will form a good part of our investigation.

The House of Commons also has an integrative role. It is the one body that is nationally elected and one in which, to compensate for the absence of their own assemblies, Scotland and Wales are allocated a greater number of seats than their populations justify in proportional terms.[9] An integrative role may also be played by the MP-constituency relationship and through political parties. Insofar as parties play an integrative function, it is possible to contend that this in part is carried out through Parliament: the main parties are national parties and the policies they espouse and, if in government, seek to give effect to through Parliament are national in outlook and (usually) application. The impact of this function, though, is limited, partly because the parties themselves provide a rather blunt mechanism for integration and partly because of limited parliamentary means for encouraging integration. The nature of the parliamentary system itself has militated against the development of mechanism for group integration: Members of Parliament are returned to represent individual citizens grouped together on a geographical basis, while peers are deemed formally to represent no one but themselves. MPs are returned by constituencies; writs of summons to peers are personal to them.

The function of mobilising support has been identified by Samuel Beer as the raising of public support for the specific programmes formulated by government in between elections.[10] The importance of this function one would expect to increase as government policies become redistributive. However, it is a task that Parliament has not been particularly well able to carry out. Party government has produced a situation in which government has tended to be closed and to take its parliamentary support for granted. It has thus not been inclined to take Parliament into its confidence, or support the generation of the internal mechanisms through which Parliament could better inform itself, with the consequence that Parliament has not been sufficiently well informed in order to mobilise support for particular policies. Again, it is a function one would expect to assume greater significance as pressures on the political system increase and government has to take a greater number of hard decisions.

Policy Affect

Policy affect (Packenham's decisional and influence function) encompasses *interest articulation* and *conflict resolution* as well as the more traditionally studied *administrative oversight* and *law-making*. Interest articulation overlaps with that of tension release. It is fulfilled by parties and by individual MPs and the means employed are generally those employed for expressing grievances. The limitations are similar. Interests not aggregated within parties have generally had difficulty in finding an outlet for expressing and pursuing their particular needs. Even in seeking such outlets, Parliament has rarely been an avenue of first resort. Larger interests, especially sectional interest groups, have generally been able to make their case directly to government rather than through the intermediary of Parliament. As a secondary avenue, Parliament has provided some opportunity for various, especially non-economic interests to be pursued and to have some policy affect; this has been the case especially with moral issues through the medium of Private Members' legislation.[11] Even so, the success of such legislation has generally been dependent on government support.

In terms of conflict resolution, Parliament offers a legitimate forum in which parties can express conflicting views and, by so doing, may help reduce the likelihood of physical conflict or the need for citizens to take to the streets. However, as a body for actually resolving existing or new conflicts, it clearly labours under several constraints. Party polarisation is seen by critics to encourage conflict rather than consensus and party norms and procedures are viewed as exacerbating such polarisation. Even if the political will was present, the procedures that would facilitate conflict resolution have generally been lacking.

Similarly, with law-making (in effect now, influencing measures of public policy) and administrative oversight, Parliament's impact is limited. That this should be so is not surprising. The political culture of the country has favoured a strong executive, certainly throughout most of the seven centuries of Parliament's history. Strong, but not unbounded: Parliament constitutes the body that provides the bounds within which the executive (originally the Crown, now a government of ministers) operates. Parliament has never been a policy-making body on any *continuous* basis. Rather, it has operated as a reactive body, waiting for the executive to submit measures for deliberation and approval.

The concentration of policy-making power in the executive has been reinforced by the pressures identified in the introduction. Various features of the British system have, to some degree, rendered Parliament more vulnerable than other legislatures. Perceptions of this vulnerability have been exaggerated by contrasting the position with that of the early to mid nineteenth century.

For a brief period in the nineteenth century, Parliament exhibited some of the characteristics of a policy-making legislature. The 1832 Reform Act had the effect of loosening the grip of the aristocracy, and the ministry, on seats in the Commons (they were less easy to purchase) without at the same time creating the need for extensive party organisation. In the new situation, MPs demonstrated both the will and the ability – since issues of public policy were few and easy to comprehend – to participate with ministers in shaping measures, to force the ministry to divulge information, and on occasion to turn the government out. The period was short-lived. The 1867 Reform Act and subsequent measures created an electorate of such a size that contact was possible only through extensive organisation. The Liberal and Conservative parties were transformed into complex, mass membership parties. To attract the votes of the new electors – with the passage of the 1884 Representation of the People Act, a majority of working men had the vote – promises had to be made, and for those promises to be fulfilled parties had to be cohesive in their parliamentary voting behaviour. By the end of the century, cohesion was a marked feature of parliamentary life.[12]

Constitutional, institutional and environmental factors combined to ensure that the pressures generated by the changed electoral conditions resulted in a Parliament with low policy affect. With Britain lacking both a federal structure and a formal separation of powers and personnel, political power was concentrated at the centre; consequently, parties became highly centralised, with power flowing on a 'top-down' rather than a 'bottom-up' basis. The plurality (first-past-the-post) electoral system facilitated, if not always produced, the return of a party with a majority of seats. Given that the government was drawn from and remained within Parliament, the electoral fortunes of MPs depended primarily on the success or failure of that government. Government was dependent upon its parliamentary supporters for the passage of measures and for its own continuation in office. Failure of government backbenchers to vote for their own side could result in the loss of promised measures or, on a vote of confidence, the fall of the government. It was not a prospect that government backbenchers relished.

Party pressures also encouraged deference. Local parties, usually loyal to the national leadership, held the power of political life and death over 'their' members. Constitutional practice also proved crucial. There were no alternative career channels in Parliament to that of government office, and a place in government was dependent upon the Prime Minister. The convention of collective responsibility also facilitated a growing trend toward government secrecy. Cabinet deliberations were secret: only the conclusions were revealed. The convention of individual ministerial responsibility provided a protective cloak for the internal deliberations of departments.

Parliament increasingly was not privy to what was going on within government but also had difficulty coping with the measures submitted to it. As the tasks of government increased, so legislation became not only greater in bulk but also more complex in nature. An 'amateur' Parliament, the emphasis on the generalist MP deliberating in plenary session, militated against sustained and informed scrutiny of bills. The potential for influence was also limited by parliamentary structures and procedure. Since the sixteenth century, bills had been subject to approval in plenary session (second reading) before being sent to committee for detailed consideration. Malcolm Shaw's research suggests that where bills are referred first to committee, the greater the influence of the legislature.[13] A bifurcation of standing committees (for legislative scrutiny) and select committees (for particular enquiries) is another historical inheritance which helps limit parliamentary affect. Government control of a parliamentary majority has also been used to extend structures that facilitate the passage of government measures and to limit those that may enhance parliamentary scrutiny and influence. Thus, standing committees – allowing government bills to be considered simultaneously – have become standard in the twentieth century; select committees, until recently, have not.

By 1970, Parliament thus exercised a limited role in the policy cycle, occupying the place shown in Figure 1. The locus of policy-making had shifted further and further away and the two Houses had limited resources to influence the outcome of closed policy deliberations. Influence took place on occasion: government wished to retain the goodwill of its own supporters. The developments outlined above facilitated what Anthony King has described as the opposition mode of executive-legislature relations on the floor of the House. Off the floor of the House, the intra-party mode remained important: government backbenchers were able to exploit party meetings in order to influence ministers.[14] The occasions were sufficient for Parliament to be classified as a legislature with modest policy-making power (or, in my terminology, a policy-influencing legislature) but, as such, it was one of the weaker legislatures occupying the category. The policy-making power was very modest indeed. As such, the institution was a focus for continuing criticism. Has much changed since?

TWO DECADES OF CHANGE

During the 1960s Britain's economic fortunes began to decline. By the early 1960s, it was apparent that the country was lagging behind the performance

FIGURE 1

THE POLICY PROCESS IN BRITAIN

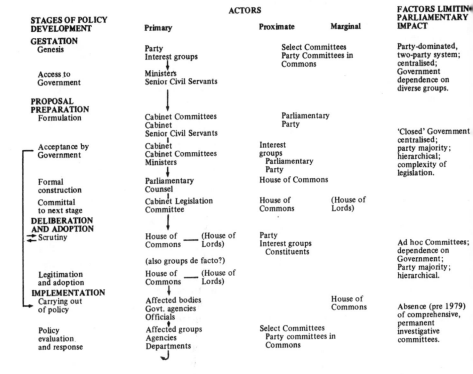

of its main European neighbours. The difficulties were exacerbated in the 1970s, especially in the wake of the Arab oil embargo that killed Edward Heath's dash for growth. Political problems compounded the economic difficulties: two general elections in one year (1974) and a government returned with less than 40 per cent of the popular vote. Under the Labour government of 1974–79, inflation peaked at 27 per cent. Under the succeeding Conservative government, unemployment reached historically high levels. Civil unrest also marked the 1980s, with inner-city riots in 1980, 1981 and 1985. Hence, one has the basis for the hypothesis that Parliament has been further marginalised in the policy cycle as government has had to respond to the changed conditions by taking hard, sometimes immediate, decisions; while, concomitantly, the regime support functions of the institution (tension release in particular) have assumed greater significance. In practice, the picture is more complex than the hypothesis suggests. There is evidence to support the second leg of the hypothesis (increased reliance on support functions) but much less to support the first.

FIGURE 2
CROSS-PRESSURES ON PARLIAMENT
SINCE 1970

Period	CHALLENGES	REINFORCEMENTS
1970–79	Sectorisation	More independent voting behaviour
	Membership of the European Community	Attitudinal change toward government
	Tripartism	
1979–85		Structural and procedural changes
	Centralisation of power	
1985–89		Greater constituency activity
	Single European Act	Televising of Lords' proceedings
1989–	Parliamentary overload	Televising of Commons' proceedings
		Response to Single European Act

Developments in boxed area are internal to Parliament.

More Marginalised Policy Role?

Over the past twenty years, several diverse developments have affected Parliament's capacity to influence policy. The most prominent of these are identified, and put in a time-specific context, in Figure 2. Those in the left-hand column in the figure are, with one exception, developments external to Parliament that have served to move the locus of policy-making even further away from Westminster. Those listed in the right-hand column are developments essentially internal to Parliament that have served to maintain, even strengthen, its capacity to influence policy once formulated and placed before it.

Challenges. The foremost developments – sectorisation, membership of the European Community (EC) and centralisation of power – have served to move the loci of policy-making downwards, upwards and the centre.

The greater co-option of interest groups into the process of policy formulation pre-dates the period under review. However, the period has witnessed a major growth in the number of interest groups in the UK. (Of groups listed in the 1979 edition of Peter Shipley's *Directory of Pressure Groups and Representative Organisations*, just over 42 per cent had come into being since 1960.) Incremental policy-making has become the preserve particularly of small, fluid policy communities – comprising civil servants

and representatives of affected groups – operating within each sector of
government responsibility; once agreement has been reached on some
policy adjustment, the adjustment is then sold to the rest of the department
for formal approval.[15] The problem for Parliament is that such activity
is largely beyond its purview. By virtue of the convention of individual
ministerial responsibility, scrutiny of such activity must be routed via the
responsible minister. Incremental, usually low-level policy-making thus
tends to take place at what constitutes one further remove from Parliament
(Parliament – minister – policy community); given that such activity takes
place at a sub-ministerial level, it may be described as a downward move
in the locus of policy-making.

The United Kingdom became a member of the EC on 1 January 1973.
The effect of membership was to move upward, to the ministerial and
official institutions of the Community, policy-making competence in a
number of sectors. Whereas the relationship between Parliament and the
UK government is a direct one, the relationship between Parliament and
the institutions of the Community is an indirect, indeed tenuous one. The
consequence of membership was thus to place policy-making once again
at one further remove from Westminster (Parliament – UK government –
European Community). The passage of the Single European Act (SEA),
a treaty amendment approved by Parliament under the terms of the
1986 European Communities (Amendment) Act, has further limited the
influence of both the UK government and Parliament by effecting a shift
in power relationships *between* the institutions of the member states and the
institutions of the EC and *within* the institutions of the EC. The extension
of weighted majority voting in the council of ministers limits the influence
of individual governments – and consequently national parliaments – while
the new co-operation procedure extends considerably the capacity of
the European Parliament to influence Community legislation. Weighted
majority voting has already been used to outvote UK ministers and the EC
Parliament has already had considerable effect on Community legislation
under the co-operation procedure. Though the two Houses of Parliament
have committees for scrutinising EC legislation – that of the House of
Lords being generally recognised as the more effective – the powers of
Parliament over EC legislation are fewer than those enjoyed by some of its
counterparts; the implementation of the Single European Act has served to
emphasise its necessarily limited role.

During the periods of Labour government in the 1960s and 1970s,
tripartism (or, more accurately in practice, bipartism) was a feature of
policy-making, especially economic policy. 'Beer and sandwiches' at 10
Downing Street was the euphemism for bipartite discussions between
senior ministers and leaders of the Trades Union Congress. On other
occasions, leaders of the Confederation of British Industry were brought
into the discussions. Bargains were variously struck, with Parliament being
merely a spectator at the feast. This mode of policy-making at the level
of high policy was brought to an end with the return of a Conservative
government in 1979. However, the mode of policy-making that replaced
it had similar consequences for Parliament. In order to achieve autonomy

in policy-making – considered necessary in order to force and then police a free market – the government had to mould what Andrew Gamble has termed 'the strong state'.[16] The ramparts of collectivism have had to be scaled; obstacles to achieving a free market have had to be removed. Consequently, power has had to be centralised. The effect for Parliament has been that, again, it has largely been a spectator at the feast.

These developments *by themselves* would be sufficient to bear out the first assumption of the hypothesis. However, they have to be set against those developments internal to Parliament which have had something of a countervailing effect, but which, in combination, have generated pressures which are now close to producing an overload of the parliamentary machine. Both Houses are facing greater demands – from government, from lobbyists, and from parliamentarians themselves – which make it increasingly difficult for them to function effectively. There are a number of quantifiable indicators of the growing burden: there has been a significant rise in the number of letters sent by MPs to ministers, in the number of parliamentary questions tabled, and in the number of early day motions tabled. There has been almost a 50 per cent increase in MP-to-minister correspondence in the period between 1982 and 1989. The average number of questions tabled each session, for oral and written answer, is now around 50,000; in the 1970s, it was less than 40,000. A decade ago, three or four hundred EDMs would be tabled each session: in the 1988/89 session, a total of 1,420 appeared on the Commons' order paper. These increases reflect in part the demands made of Parliament as an agent of tension release. However, their effect is to generate a significant burden for both Houses (the Lords witnessing similar pressures), a burden which limits the time and resources available to influence policy development. The problem of overload is, at present, manageable. It is likely to get worse in future years.

Reinforcements. Against these developments must be set those which I have termed reinforcements, those occupying the right-hand column in Figure 2. These often linked developments internal to Parliament have strengthened the institution as a policy-influencing body.

In 1965 Samuel Beer was able to assert that party cohesion in the House of Commons' division lobbies was so close to 100 per cent that there was no longer any point in measuring it.[17] No post-war government had been defeated as a result of its own supporters voting against it. In the Upper House, divisions were rare and, by agreement between the two front benches, did not take place on the second reading of measures promised in a government's election manifesto. The only feature to survive the 1970s was this gentlemen's agreement in the Lords.

The House of Commons witnessed a sudden and significant upsurge in cross-voting by government backbenchers in the Parliament of 1970–74. Conservative MPs voted against their own side on more occasions, in greater numbers and with much greater effect than before. On six occasions, the government was defeated as a consequence of this intra-party dissent, three of the defeats taking place on three-line whips. The triggering mechanism for this behavioural change I have identified elsewhere as being the prime ministerial leadership of Edward Heath.[18] Once released, the genie of backbench independence could not be put back in the bottle. The succeeding Labour government had to contend with a string of defeats: in the 1974–79 Parliament, it suffered over 100 defeats in standing committee or on the floor of the House. According to the analysis of John Schwarz, over 40 per cent of government bills during this period were affected by defeats, the defeats themselves taking place on 'significant policy matters, and they occurred in virtually every policy area outside foreign affairs and defence'.[19] Of defeats on the floor of the House, 23 were the consequence of Labour backbenchers voting, sometimes in considerable numbers, in the Conservative lobby; the most significant casualty was the government's policy for devolving powers to elected assemblies in Scotland and Wales.

Growing awareness of what could be achieved by such action – and a growing recognition that the consequences expected from government defeats (resignation of the government, imposition of sanctions by the whips) had not materialised – produced among many MPs a change of attitude towards government. The old deferential attitude was replaced by what Beer has characterised as a participant attitude.[20] There was a greater political will to be involved in influencing public policy.

These behavioural and attitudinal changes have continued into Parliaments of Conservative government since 1979. The effect of backbench independence has been less apparent, partly because large government majorities have been able to absorb more easily dissent by small numbers of backbenchers (hence a sign of weakness relative to the 1970s) and partly because of anticipated reaction by government – the threat of serious dissension, including the prospect of defeat, has induced action by government in advance of public deliberation on the floor of the House (hence a sign of strength relative to the 1970s).[21] Changes to government measures have been achieved in each of the Parliaments since 1979, including the withdrawal of some bills. The Leader of the House for part of this period, John Wakeham, explicitly conceived of his role as a 'fixer', aiming as far as possible for compromises acceptable to all those involved in serious disputes. Anticipation was not always the government's forte: on 14 April 1986 it became the first government this century enjoying an overall majority to lose a second reading vote, 72 Conservative MPs voting with the Labour Opposition to defeat the Shops Bill.

This greater independence on the part of MPs has also been used to increase the resources available to them, both collectively and individually. In 1979, MPs, in conjunction with the Leader of the House, Norman St. John-Stevas, ensured the creation of a near-comprehensive series of departmentally-related select committees. These committees are now a well-established part of the parliamentary landscape. They are multifunctional bodies. In terms of policy affect, they have proved significant bodies for administrative oversight – important as much for what they can do as for what they actually do: the potential for committee investigation helps keep officials sensitive to possible parliamentary reaction. In terms of enquiries actually undertaken, civil servants have been summoned to give evidence on an extensive basis: in the first two Parliaments of their existence, the committees summoned more than 3,000 official witnesses. (In the same period, there were more than 400 ministerial appearances before the committees.) The committees have had a direct effect on policy through recommendations which have variously been accepted by government. The effect is not amenable to precise quantification. However, there are a number of indicators that point to policy influence. In a parliamentary written answer in 1986, the Prime Minister listed 150 recommendations from select committees which the government had accepted in the previous twelve months.[22] A less quantifiable but probably more pervasive influence is exerted through extracting and making public material from departments and from a wide range of bodies outside government. As a result of such activity, the House itself is better informed and the media coverage given committee investigations gives them some additional political leverage.

The House has also introduced other structures and procedures as well as increasing Members' pay and facilities. In 1983, the National Audit Office (for undertaking efficiency audits of departments) was established; the government had initially opposed the bill introduced to set it up. MPs' pay was variously increased, at a level that ran counter to government advice, and in 1986 the House increased by 50 per cent Members' secretarial and research allowance, again against government advice. The creation of three Estimates Days each session has provided the means for discussing some select committee reports. Various other changes have also enhanced parliamentary capacity for scrutiny and influence.[23] The combined effect of these changes has been to strengthen, admittedly at a very modest level, the policy affect of the House of Commons.

These behavioural and structural changes have been paralleled in the House of Lords. Conservative peers were willing to use their voting power to defeat the Labour government of 1974–79 on a wide range of issues; that in itself is not surprising. What is remarkable is the extent to which those peers have been willing to exert their power under a Conservative government. By the beginning of 1990, the Thatcher government had suffered in excess of 120 defeats in the Upper House. Compared with the pre-1970 period, peers have attended the House in greater numbers, spent more time in session and voted more often. Though the House continues to take the committee stage of bills on the Floor of the House, it has made greater use of select committees both on a sessional and ad hoc basis. The select committees on the European Communities and on Science and Technology have achieved substantial reputations. The reasons for these changes have been identified by Nicholas Baldwin as the growth in the number of life peers – as a proportion of their number, much more active than hereditary peers – and the realisation, following the abandonment of the 1969 Parliament (No. 2) Bill, that reform of the House was unlikely to occur in the foreseeable future; consequently peers decided to make the most of the existing chamber.[24]

A further change has been the greater constituency activity of MPs. The past twenty years have seen a substantial increase in the time spent in the constituency, and on constituency casework, by the average member. In part, this change has been demand-led: constituents now expect more of their MPs; in part, it has been supply-led: new MPs in particular actively seeking out constituency grievances. (There is now some evidence that there may be some electoral benefit for such activity.)[25] MPs pursue casework by tabling questions, arranging meetings with ministers and – more often – by writing to ministers. This constituency work is most relevant to the function of tension release but has some policy affect. Letters from MPs to ministers act as a useful if somewhat crude barometer, indicating not only members' feelings on particular issues but, more often, problems with particular programmes.[26] Where a problem is revealed, a review and modification may follow.

Though this change is, strictly speaking, specific to the House of Commons – peers have no constituents – there is some parallel in the Upper House in that peers are the recipients of a mass of unsolicited representations and may pursue them with ministers on behalf of those making the representations. Peers, as we shall see, are a particular target for interest groups. Again, pursuit of such representations may influence government in terms of the principle and, more likely, the specific operation of a programme.

The final, rather speculative reinforcements identified in Figure 2 are those of the televising of parliamentary proceedings and the response to the Single European Act. Televised coverage of proceedings in the House of Lords began in 1985; though normally broadcast late at night, the programme 'Their Lordships' House' achieved both reputable viewing figures and a positive response. In 1988, the House of Commons approved, on an experimental basis, the televised coverage of its proceedings. The cameras began operating on 21 November 1989. Media coverage of the chamber increased, both quantitatively (especially on regional programmes) and qualitatively (Commons' proceedings achieving a higher priority than before in news bulletins), and appeared to attract a positive response. Prime Minister's Question Time – broadcast live on Tuesdays and Thursdays – established a viewing figure of around 1 million; a morning summary attracted some 250,000 viewers. Select committees also achieved some prominence. The effect of such coverage has been to make more publicly visible the deliberations of Parliament and, as such, to enhance its political leverage in relation to government. There is also a view common to many MPs that this innovation will itself generate further changes as the potential of television is more fully realised by the House. In other words, there is a growing perception that television may act as a catalyst for substantial reform in the 1990s.

Even more speculative is the inclusion of Parliament's response to the Single European Act. As we have seen, the effect of EC membership and the passage of the SEA has been to remove the locus of policy-making even further away from Westminster. However, there has been the recognition by some parliamentarians that there is also the potential offered by the SEA for Parliament to achieve some degree of influence in the sphere of EC legislation. In the past session of Parliament, the Commons' Select

Committee on Procedure investigated ways in which the House could exploit the new situation. Two principal means emerged: one was through creating new structures for scrutinising EC legislation and the other, not incompatible, proposal was to develop closer links with members of the now more-powerful European Parliament. Various specific proposals to achieve these goals were put before the committee: these included the formation of a Grand European Committee and co-opting MEPs on to Commons' committees. The committee itself, in its report published in November 1989, proposed, *inter alia*, the creation of five special standing committees to consider EC documents in particular sectors, the extension of the remit of the existing scrutiny committee to include consideration of trends in EC policy, principle and, more likely, the specific operation of a programme. floor debates before the twice-yearly Heads of Government meeting, and the generation of links wherever possible between select committees and the EC Commission and MEPs.[27] The parties at Westminster have also moved to strengthen links: both the Conservative 1922 Committee and the Parliamentary Labour Party decided to allow their respective MEPs to attend party meetings at Westminster.

The position facing Westminster was summarised by *The Economist* in commenting on the Procedure Committee's report: 'All this may sound minor, procedural pettifogging. It isn't. What is happening is that . . . Westminster is quietly adapting itself to a new world, ruled increasingly from Brussels. Indeed, Britain's Parliament is entering a curious constitutional race: if it does not learn, along with the other national parliaments, to exercise effective scrutiny over the European institutions, then the Strasbourg parliament will get the job'.[28] The extent to which Parliament adapts effectively to the new situation – it has started the learning process relatively late – remains to be seen. The relevant observation for the moment is that the potential exists; in that sense, the SEA constitutes an opportunity.

The past twenty years have thus seen considerable pressures which have moved the loci of policy-making further away from the Palace of Westminster. At the same time, developments internal to Parliament have strengthened it, relative to the pre-1970 era, as a policy-influencing body. Assessing these two forces side by side does not lead to one clear conclusion and certainly does not permit any quantifiable 'bottom line' assessment of an overall increase or decline in Parliament's capacity to affect policy. What is demonstrable is that the forces operating on Parliament have not been one-sided and that Parliament remains a policy-influencing legislature. The government's need to govern – to take hard and quick decisions – has not debilitated the institution to the extent that our hypothesis posited would be the case.

Maintaining support?

The extent to which Parliament has served to maintain support for the political system, especially through serving as a conduit for tension release and the articulation of interests (of individuals, groups and large bodies

FIGURE 3

PARLIAMENT AS A 'SAFETY VALVE'

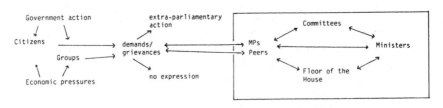

PARLIAMENTARY ACTION

of citizens), has been largely neglected yet constitutes one of the most fascinating aspects of the institution in the British political system.

The place of Parliament as a safety valve, and as a vehicle for interest articulation, is illustrated in Figure 3. Faced with greater activity on the part of government impinging on the life of citizens and with having to pursue more often redistributive policies, citizens are more likely to harbour grievances against government – either at the level of general policy (economic management) or at the level of specific effect (denial of particular benefits for example) – and to make demands of government in order to benefit from a redistribution of resources. These grievances can

TABLE 1

CITIZEN RESPONSES TO 'UNJUST' LEGISLATION

Responses to the prospect of an unjust or harmful law being considered by Parliament: hypothetical and 'most effective' actions

	Would take %	Most effective %
Personal action		
Contact MP	55	43
Speak to influential person	15	4
Contact government department	9	4
Contact radio, TV or newspaper	18	16
Collective action		
Sign petition	57	12
Raise issue in an organisation I belong to	8	2
Go to a protest or demonstration	9	6
Form a group of like-minded people	8	3
None of these	8	7

Multiple responses were possible: hence totals exceed 100%.

Source: R. Jowell and S. Witherspoon, *British Social Attitudes: The 1985 Report* (Aldershot: Gower, 1985), p.12.

be channelled through parliamentary or extra-parliamentary channels or not expressed at all. If parliamentary channels are chosen, there is a need to utilise one or more means of alerting parliamentarians and for those parliamentarians then to utilise one or more devices for representing the grievance or demand to government. To what extent, then, have such parliamentary channels been utilised in recent years? and with what effect?

For expressing grievances and demands to government, contacting one's MP is one of the most popular and judged to be effective. The British Social Attitudes Survey of 1984 found that, in a situation where an unjust or harmful measure was being considered by Parliament, a majority of respondents would contact their local MP; this constituted the most popular course of personal action (signing a petition was the most popular form of collective action) and was also considered to be the most effective (Table 1). Two years later, asked what channels they would use to influence government, contacting the MP remained the most popular course of personal action; half of all respondents judged it to be a 'very' or 'quite' effective means of influence – only contacting the media got a higher rating.[29]

How many people actually pursue such a course? In the 1986 Social Attitude Survey, 11 per cent of respondents claimed to have contacted their Member of Parliament. This is one to three per cent higher than earlier estimates. If an accurate sample, this translates into more than four million adults. Contacting the MP is thus significant as a legitimising process both in terms of recognition of its availability (a majority 'would use') and its use.

The most popular means of contact is by correspondence. There is evidence of a substantial increase over the past twenty years in the number of letters written to MPs. (A number of MPs also report a substantial increase in the number of telephone calls they receive.) A survey by the Letter Writing Bureau in 1986 found that three-quarters of MPs questioned received between 20 and 50 letters *a day*; in the 1960s, Members would be more likely to receive that number of letters in the course of a week. The increase in letter writing has been marked in the past ten years. A survey of members in 1987 found that a number were receiving approximately twice as much correspondence as they did seven years before.[30] A majority of letters come from constituents.

In addition to being the recipient of letters from constituents and groups MPs are also more proactive than before in being physically available to see constituents. In the 1940s and 1950s, some MPs paid what amounted to annual visits to their constituencies. In the 1960s, the holding of constituency 'surgeries' became common (MPs being publicly available at set times to see constituents) and MPs began to spend more time in their constituencies; the time spent on constituency business has continued to increase. The 1971 survey of MPs by the Review Body on Top Salaries found that backbenchers spent approximately 11 hours a week outside the House working on constituency business; the 1982 survey found that the average had increased to 16 hours. A 1984 survey by the Commons Reform Group found that a majority of members spent eight or more days a month in the constituency when the House was sitting: one in five spent thirteen or more days a month in the constituency. Such constituency availability is important not only in allowing members to hear grievances but also in demonstrating their availability to do so. In their analysis of constituency service in the US and the UK, Bruce Cain and his associates found that, though a greater number of American respondents had had some contact with their elected representatives than had British respondents, the British respondents were twice as likely actually to know the name of their elected representatives.[31]

Apart from the increase in contact between Members and constituents, there has also been a marked increase in the professional lobbying of Parliament. Since 1979 there has been a major growth in the number of firms of professional lobbyists. It is now common for commercial firms and interest groups to hire a firm of political lobbyists (known as political consultants) or have their own in-house staff of lobbyists. A 1985 survey of 180 sizeable UK companies found that 41 per cent of them used political consultancies and 28 per cent used public relations firms for work involving government.[32] Lobbyists help target the most relevant parliamentarians for their clients' purposes and advise on how to make an effective case. Knowledge of parliamentary rules and procedures is a particular benefit. A number of consumer groups and trade unions, with their own in-house staff, are among the bodies with a particular reputation of knowing how to get their message across to Parliament.

Once MPs have received the views or grievances of constituents and of groups with which they have some sympathy, what means do they utilise to convey them to government? For constituency cases, the most used – and judged by MPs to be the most effective – is that of writing to ministers. (The writers themselves may be ministers, writing in their capacities as constituency members.) Such letter-writing increased in the 1960s and 1970s and especially in the 1980s. A series of parliamentary answers in 1982 revealed that approximately 10,000 letters had been written by MPs to ministers in January of that year; a similar series of answer in 1989 revealed that the number had increased by roughly 50 per cent in January 1989. In the session of 1988/89 (up to the summer recess), more than 100,000 letters had been written. Whereas letters written direct to ministers by citizens normally receive replies from civil servants, MPs' letters receive priority within departments and are replied to over a minister's signature. Replies are often detailed and the correspondence takes place outside the normal framework of party conflict.

The daily half-hour adjournment debate is also frequently used by MPs to pursue constituency cases which they feel deserve a fuller and more public consideration. Other devices, less frequently used than correspondence, are those of tabling questions (more likely to be used in the event of an unsatisfactory response to a letter) and referral to the Parliamentary Commissioner for Administration (the Ombudsman). On occasion, members will also see ministers in person, either at a formal level (in the department) or, probably more often, informally (often in the division lobbies while voting). The means used are not mutually exclusive and a member determined to pursue a particular case will sometimes make use of them all.

For interest articulation, and expressing the views of large numbers of citizens, letter-writing is again often used, though other means are also employed. Private Members' bills in the Commons (and Wednesday debates in the Lords) are especially valuable as outlets for the expression of often conflicting views on issues outside the framework of party debate. This is notably the case on social, especially 'conscience', issues. Such devices have been employed in recent years as outlets, for example, for conflicting views on abortion, privacy and embryo research. Debate on such measures is valuable in itself, allowing for the expression of views in a public, authoritative forum. It is important also in that it may produce tangible results. Though an increasing proportion of successful Private Members' bills have their origins in government departments, the opportunities for measures sponsored by private members to reach the statute book provide hope for pressure groups (about 10 to 15 such bills are enacted each session); Parliament thus constitutes a magnet for such groups.[33] MPs successful in the annual ballot to introduce Private Members' bills are immediately beseiged by representatives of a large number of pressure groups imploring them to introduce bills they would like to see passed and, indeed, in some case will already have drafted.

Groups and individuals also now lobby MPs and peers extensively during the passage of government legislation. The defeat of the Shops Bill in 1986 was preceded by a massive lobbying of MPs by individuals, unions and various religious bodies, including the Church of England; MPs were inundated by letters and by constituents at their surgeries.[34] Pressure group activity during the legislative process is extensive. A 1986 survey of pressure groups found that a large majority – over 83 per cent – had been concerned by legislation in recent years. Most groups had lobbied Parliament as a consequence: almost 80 per cent of the groups contacting one or more peers and almost two-thirds circulating material to all or a large number of MPs; almost 60 per cent sent material to MPs serving on the relevant standing committee.[35]

To these well-established procedures have been added the departmentally related select committees. These constitute both important bodies for tension release as well as potential bodies for support mobilisation. The committees have acted as magnets for outside groups. Groups in particular sectors are able to concentrate on the relevant committee in their sector. The committees determine their own agenda and proceed usually by taking evidence in public session. For groups, there is thus the potential for committees to investigate matters of concern to them and for the groups to be invited to give evidence, thus allowing them to get their views on the public record. When a committee announces the topic of its next investigation, it invariably invites written submissions. Likewise with select committees in the House of Lords. The number of letters and memoranda that flow in is often considerable, sometimes running into three figures. Of witnesses summoned by committees, a majority come from outside the ranks of ministers and civil servants. More generally, the committees may also serve as safety valves through investigating matters which have given rise to public concern, as with the investigation by the Defence Committee in 1986 on the Westland affair.

By developing contact with, and being the focus of attention by, 'attentive publics' select committees are also in a position to perform an important support mobilisation role. Operating in large measure on a bipartisan basis, enjoying links with affected groups, and by being able to comment authoritatively, following investigation, on particular issues, they have the potential to mobilise or reinforce support for a policy. The committees are, after all, potential supporters – not just potential critics – of a particular policy. This potential as support mobilisers has yet to be realised on a significant scale, though there is some evidence of it and it may be enhanced considerably as a result of the televising of committee proceedings; the committees have already attracted significant coverage, including news coverage, well in advance of what many MPs had expected.

The chamber remains the ultimate forum for the expression of views and demands. The government controls the timetable for most public business, though there are outlets for debates not selected by government; these include 20 Opposition Days each session (the topic on 17 of them chosen by the Leader of the Opposition), the three Estimates Days, and Private Members' time, as well as question time preceding public business. The British Parliament is one of the most active, in terms of the time it spends sitting, of all Western legislatures. As we have seen, the behavioural and attitudinal changes of the past twenty years have produced parliamentarians more willing than before to utilise the opportunities available to express themselves. Government control of the timetable is thus not necessarily a bar to the expression of grievances and demands that the government would prefer not to be aired.

How effective has Parliament proved as a safety valve and articulator of interests? As we have seen, only a small proportion of constituents make contact with their MP. That, in itself, tells us little: there are no data currently available that would allow us to know the number with a grievance to express. What we do know from survey data is that most respondents would contact their MP if they objected to a particular measure or wished to influence government, that contacting the MP is the most used method of positive action, that the number making contact – primarily through correspondence – has increased significantly in the past twenty years, and that contacting the MP is considered by about half of all those questioned to be an effective course of action. For many constituents, writing to the MP is an end in itself: the grievance is expressed. In many cases, all that is sought is an authoritative reply: MPs are able to provide that in a way that is not otherwise possible. The effect of this on constituents is reflected in a 1978 survey finding that, of those who contacted their MP, 75 per cent reported a 'good' or 'very good' response.[36]

As an articulator of interests, allowing the expression of demands in order to have some policy affect, Parliament has developed mechanisms for such articulation at the same time as demands have increased in number. Existing mechanisms have also been used more extensively. In the legislative process, groups have been characterised as relatively inefficient but modestly effective. Of groups surveyed in 1986, most (just over 55 per cent) rated their efforts at influence as either 'very successful' or 'quite successful'. As demands have increased, Parliament has witnessed the behavioural changes which have given MPs relatively more policy affect. The select committees have also provided a major focus for group activity, supplementing the already well-established (but private) party committees. Their policy affect has already been noted; as outlets for grievances and demands, their significance is indicated by the extent of the representations made to them by groups and, in many cases, individuals. The introduction of the television cameras to the Commons also appears likely to increase the use made of MPs as agents for the expression of grievances and demands as well as enhance the potential capacity of the House to mobilise support for particular measures. The demands made of Parliament are growing – to some extent, as we have seen, dangerously so – but so far it has managed to bear them.

CONCLUSION

Parliament scores well on most of the indicators suggested by Mezey for determining a more-supported legislature. It has demonstrated impressive institutional continuity; it has not been the subject of serious attacks by the executive – in part, of course, because the executive is itself part of the institution. It is at least plausible that the institutional continuity – and the general perception of a political system that works – has helped to build a body of diffuse support[37] that has helped to maintain support for the institution at a time when the political system is under strain.

In recent years, Parliament's capacity to maintain support has been questioned. Eulogists, at least since the mid-1960s, have been overshadowed by critics. Parliament has been criticised for having lost the trust of the population.[38] Such a criticism, though, appears to derive from a false premise: that there has been a 'decline' in such trust. Distrust of politicians in Britain is longstanding.[39] And that distrust is marked at the level of the institution and the generic ('politicians'). At a more specific level – the individual MP – responses are more positive. (In this, the UK is not peculiar.)[40] In the 1970s, when trust might be expected to reach a low point, surveys found that less than 10 per cent of respondents believed that MPs did 'a bad job'.[41] What has changed in recent years has been the level of political participation, but this increased activity has been directed at Parliament rather than away from it. The 1986 Social Attitudes Survey detected a 'widespread and growing self-confidence on the part of the electorate to try to bring influence to bear on Parliament'.[42] As we have seen, the principal avenue of personal action has been contacting the Member of Parliament. And the most used collective action – signing petitions – is an intermediate one designed usually to influence the recipient of the petition: in other words,

Parliament. Parliament, as we have seen, has *so far* been able to bear the strain generated by this increased participation.

Indeed, it is possible to postulate that Parliament may in future years not only maintain but possibly enhance the extent of popular support. One variable identified by Mezey as buttressing support is that of meeting popular expectations. Survey data regularly reveal that electors expect MPs to pursue the interests of their constituencies. The more active MPs are for their constituents, the more likely is a positive perception of MPs by constituents. There is some empirical basis for this assumption in the electoral performance of constituency-active first-term incumbents in the 1987 general election.[43] If Parliament generates the means to cope with the increased demand, the more the institution is likely to maintain itself as a 'more supported' legislature.

In terms of policy affect, perceptions of 'decline' have also not been borne out in recent years. Parliament has been subject to a number of significant cross-pressures which, in combination, are peculiar to Westminster. Contrary to what we hypothesised, Parliament has avoided the extremes of marginalisation in the policy cycle. This is not to assert that Parliament has witnessed some accretion of policy-making power, nor that it is now a more effective policy-influencing assembly than some of its continental neighbours. What it does assert is that Parliament has not slipped back, and certainly not collapsed, to the extent that many critics feared. Furthermore, to focus solely on policy affect is to lose sight of the wider consequences of Parliament for the political system. The effect of Parliament as a legitimising body is difficult to exaggerate. It is this that makes the institution indispensable to government. Though successive governments have tended to take Parliament for granted, the more government is forced to divulge information and to listen to parliamentarians, the greater the benefit to the system of which it is an intrinsic part.

NOTES

1. E. Powell, book review, *New European*, Vol.2, No.2 (1989), p.49.
2. The House of Lords was abolished by fiat of the Commons in 1649 and restored in 1660.
3. N. Johnson, *In Search of the Constitution* (London: Methuen, 1980), pp.31–2.
4. A. W. Bradley, 'The Sovereignty of Parliament – in Perpetuity?' in J. Jowell and D. Oliver (eds), *The Changing Constitution* (Oxford: Oxford University Press, 1985), pp.27–32.
5. R. Butt, *A History of Parliament: The Middle Ages* (London: Constable, 1989).
6. C. Mellors, *The British MP* (Farnborough: Saxon House, 1978); M. Rush, 'The Members of Parliament', in M. Ryle and P. G. Richards (eds), *The Commons Under Scrutiny* (London: Routledge, 1988), pp.18–33.
7. S. Lukes, *Power: A Radical View* (London: Macmillan, 1974).
8. R. Miliband, *Capitalist Democracy in Britain* (Oxford: Oxford University Press, 1984), p.20.
9. For the fifty years that it had its own Parliament at Stormont, Northern Ireland had fewer seats than its population would otherwise have justified. The number of seats in Northern Ireland was increased by the House of Commons (Redistribution of Seats) Act 1979.
10. S. H. Beer, 'The British Lawmaker and the Problem of Mobilising Consent', in E. Frank (ed.), *Lawmakers in a Changing World* (Englewood Cliffs, NJ: Prentice-Hall,

1966), pp.30–48.

11. See P. G. Richards, *Parliament and Conscience* (London: George Allen & Unwin, 1970).

12. A. L. Lowell, *The Government of England*, Vol.II (New York: Macmillan, 1924), pp.76–8.

13. M. Shaw, 'Conclusion', in J. D. Lees and M. Shaw (eds.), *Committees in Legislatures* (Oxford: Martin Robertson, 1979), p.417.

14. A. King, 'Modes of Executive-Legislative Relations: Great Britain, France and West Germany', *Legislative Studies Quarterly*, Vol.1, No.1 (1976), pp.11–36.

15. See G. Jordan and J. J. Richardson, 'The British Policy Style or the Logic of Negotiation?' in J. J. Richardson (ed.), *Policy Styles in Western Europe* (London: George Allen & Unwin, 1982), pp.82–96.

16. A. Gamble, *The Free Economy and the Strong State* (London: Macmillan, 1988).

17. S. H. Beer, *Modern British Politics* (London: Faber, 1969 edition), p.350.

18. P. Norton, *Conservative Dissidents* (London: Temple Smith, 1978), Ch. 9.

19. J. Schwarz, 'Exploring a New Role in Policy Making: The British House of Commons in the 1970s', *American Political Science Review*, Vol.74, No.1 (1980), p.27.

20. S. H. Beer, *Britain Against Itself* (London: Faber and Faber, 1982), p.190.

21. See P. Norton, 'The House of Commons: Behavioural Changes', in P. Norton (ed.), *Parliament in the 1980s* (Oxford: Basil Blackwell, 1985), pp.22–47.

22. *House of Commons: Official Report*, Vol.98, cols. 396–446. See also G. Drewry (ed.), *The New Select Committees*, 2nd ed. (Oxford: Oxford University Press, 1989).

23. P. Norton, 'Independence, Scrutiny and Rationalisation: A Decade of Changes in the House of Commons', *Teaching Politics*, Vol.15, No.1 (1986), pp.69–98.

24. N. Baldwin, 'The House of Lords: Behavioural Changes', in Norton, *Parliament in the 1980s*, pp.96–113.

25. P. Norton and D. Wood, 'Constituency Service by MPs: Does it Contribute to a Personal Vote?' *Parliamentary Affairs*, Vol.43, No.2 (1990).

26. P. Norton, '"Dear Minister" . . . The Importance of MP-to-Minister Correspondence', *Parliamentary Affairs*, Vol.35, No.1 (1982), pp.65, 69–70.

27. Fourth Report from the Select Committee on Procedure, Session 1988/89: *The Scrutiny of European Legislation*, HC 622-I (London: HMSO, 1989), pp.vii–xli.

28. 'Europe Comes to Westminster', *The Economist*, 16 Dec. 1989, p.33.

29. R. Jowell, S. Witherspoon and L. Brook, *British Social Attitudes: The 1987 Report* (Aldershot: Gower, 1987).

30. C. Miller, *The Government Report* (London: Public Policy Consultants, 1987), p.9.

31. B. Cain, J. Ferejohn and M. Fiorina, *The Personal Vote* (Cambridge, MA: Harvard University Press, 1987), pp.28–9.

32. *Financial Times*, 23 Dec. 1985.

33. D. Marsh and M. Read, *Private Members' Bills* (Cambridge: Cambridge University Press, 1988), pp.45–6.

34. See P. Regan, 'The 1986 Shops Bill', *Parliamentary Affairs*, Vol.41, No.2 (1988), pp.225–8.

35. See P. Norton, 'Public Legislation', in M. Rush (ed.), *Parliament and Pressure Politics* (Oxford: Oxford University Press, 1990).

36. B. Cain, J. Ferejohn and M. Fiorina, 'The Roots of Legislator Popularity in Great Britain and the United States', *California Institute of Technology: Social Science Working Paper* (Oct. 1979), pp.6–7.

37. See J. C. Wahlke, 'Policy Demands and Systems Support: The Role of the Represented', *British Journal of Political Science*, Vol.1 (1971), pp.521–37.

38. See, e.g., V. Bogdanor, book review, *Times Higher Education Supplement*, 15 Dec. 1989, p.20.

39. *British Social Attitudes: The 1987 Survey*, p.58.

40. The same applies in New Zealand: see the Royal Commission on the Electoral System, *Towards a Better Democracy* (Wellington: Government Printer, 1986), p.118.

41. P. Kellner, 'Who Runs Britain?' *Sunday Times*, 18 Sept. 1977. See also Granada Television, *The State of the Nation* (Manchester: Granada TV, 1973), p.201.

42. *British Social Attitudes: The 1987 Survey*, p.58.

43. Norton and Wood, 'Constituency Service by MPs'.

The French Parliament: Loyal Workhorse, Poor Watchdog

John Frears

As Philip Norton says in the introduction to this volume, all the parliaments in Western Europe fall into the category of 'modest', policy-influencing rather than policy-creating, legislatures. The question is the extent to which they help to 'maintain the health of the political system'. The French Parliament in the Fifth Republic is 'modest' to the point of being inadequate but it remains a valued institution. Its most serious shortcomings are its failure to be the arena for the nation's political debate – for 'the continuous election campaign', in Bernard Crick's phrase, that characterises liberal democracy – and its incapacity to act as a check on executive power. It does, however, contribute to the health of the political system by its positive role in legislation, by the great value that the public and local communities attach to the role of their member of Parliament, and by the habit of disciplined majority support for government that has developed, thanks to the electors, and sustained political stability. Indeed, it is the emergence of a party system producing parliamentary majorities that is the most remarkable new factor in the relations between Parliament and government in the Fifth Republic. There remains one fundamental sense in which the Fifth Republic is a parliamentary system of government. Practically all its 32 years have been characterised by presidential supremacy – but this is only possible where a majority in Parliament is willing to support presidential leadership. From 1986 to 1988 there was a disciplined majority in Parliament which did not. President Mitterrand was obliged to appoint a prime minister acceptable to the new majority. Policy leadership passed to the Prime Minister, and presidential supremacy, until the electors restored it at the presidential and parliamentary elections of 1988, disappeared like morning mist.

The reasons why Parliament is so inadequate as an arena for political debate and as a check on the executive are a mixture of constitutional, procedural, historical and cultural elements. The French Parliament, in particular the directly elected National Assembly, is by tradition the institutional and ideological inheritor of the French Revolution, its powers won from the monarchy which it overthrew, its members the expression of national sovereignty. In the nineteenth century any attempt to reduce its status was regarded as an attack on republican tradition. The constitution of the Fifth Republic which did greatly reduce its status was fiercely contested by parliamentarians in the period 1958–62. Indeed when General de Gaulle proposed to submit a major constitutional revision in 1962 – the direct election of the President – directly to the people in a referendum instead of first seeking the approval of Parliament as Article 89 of the 1958 Constitution prescribes, defence of the republican tradition was the main theme of his parliamentary opponents. In the October 1962 censure debate in the National Assembly Paul Reynaud, a voice from the Third Republic, Prime Minister in 1940 no less, went so far as to declare: 'For us Republicans, France is here and nowhere else . . . The representatives of the people know that together they are the nation, and that there is no higher expression of the people's will than our votes after public debate'.

The Fifth Republic constitution, however, had already changed all that. When de Gaulle was invited, at the height of the Algerian crisis of May 1958, to 'assume the powers of the Republic', he agreed to do so on the understanding that Parliament would authorise him to present a new constitution to the French people. This new constitution was drawn up very much along the lines of a speech made by de Gaulle long before – at Bayeux in 1946. In that speech de Gaulle envisaged the separation of powers between the executive and the legislature and declared 'that it is from the Head of State, placed above parties and elected more widely than just by Parliament, . . . that executive power must proceed'. By 1958 the Fourth Republic, the epitome of a parliamentary regime, was widely considered to have failed. It had become a byword for ministerial instability – eighteen governments in twelve years – and had shown itself incapable of supporting effective government, particularly in the frequent crises that occurred, most notably the colonial wars in Indo-China and Algeria. The main theme of the new constitution, which obtained a Yes vote of 80 per cent in the referendum of 28 September, was the strengthening of the executive by the containment of Parliament. Of its 89 articles, 28 deal directly with Parliament, with its relations with the executive, and with minute details of its procedure, like the exact dates of its sessions (to keep them short) or the ways the government can intervene in the legislative process (to keep it short too, and get its way). It was even established in one of the earliest conflicts between the parliamentary opposition and the executive in the Fifth Republic that Parliament's capacity to make its own standing orders was subject to control by the Constitutional Council.

The constitutional and procedural constraints can be summarised thus: complete executive supremacy in the legislative process, severely limited opportunities for general debates criticising the government, virtually no opportunities for scrutinising executive acts and making the executive give an account of them. Not all of this is bad. It is far from indispensable for effective and democratic government that Parliament should find it too easy to remove the executive from office and to impede and harass it all the time. It is the government's job to govern, not the legislature's. The legislative process in the Fifth Republic, most observers agree, is a great improvement on what went before, and, as we shall see, Parliament makes a constructive contribution to it. But in France it goes too far: executive power is a little too immune from proper scrutiny.

PARLIAMENT AS A CHECK ON EXECUTIVE POWER

The most important role of a modern Parliament is, in Sir Kenneth Wheare's phrase, 'making the government behave'. Even in legislation its main task, certainly where the government has the support of a reliable majority, is to scrutinise, to warn, and to improve. Legislation originates for the most part from government – because of the technical complexity of running a modern state or because the government has an electoral mandate for its programme. So the democrat looks to Parliament to ensure that the executive is kept under scrutiny and prevented from abusing its powers. Questions, debates, committee hearings, parliamentary procedures for removing the executive from power – these are the usual means for doing this. There are many ways in which governments and their supporters can prevent these methods from being effective, but they cannot work at all if the opposition has no real procedural opportunity to apply real scrutiny nor if its efforts do not arouse the media of information and public opinion. This is the real problem in France. In the next section we shall look at Parliament's inadequacy as an arena for national debate, in this the lack of procedural opportunities for the opposition.

There are four types of Parliamentary Question in France: written questions, which are very numerous (around 16,000 replies a year in the National Assembly – at last since 1983 practically matching the number of questions put down – and about 5000 a year in the Senate) but almost entirely minor constituency queries destined to demonstrate that a member is looking after local interests; oral questions with debate; oral questions without debate; and *questions au gouvernement*. Oral questions with debate have disappeared from the National Assembly since the introduction of *questions au gouvernement*, but there are around 60 a year in the Senate. No vote is allowed at the end of a question so that it cannot be like the dreaded *interpellations* of earlier Republics. Oral questions without debate (150–200 a year in each Assembly) consist of a two-minute speech, a reply from the minister, a further five minutes from the author of the question, and a final reply from the minister. In other words they are rather like adjournment debates in the House of Commons, which also are not followed by a vote. They are not directed to topical issues because a considerable time elapses between the tabling of a question and its appearance on the agenda, and they tend to be technical or constituency-related, and, in the National Assembly, they take place on a Friday when everyone is absent. Topical issues are dealt with in *questions au gouvernement* (about 300 a year in the National Assembly and 100 in the Senate), a procedure introduced in the mid-1970s during the Giscard d'Estaing presidency but extended to the Senate only in 1982. The idea was to have something resembling Question Time at Westminster – short topical questions fired at ministers without prior notice with a proper share of time for the opposition. They take the form of a speech by the questioner followed by a speech in reply by the minister with no supplementary question allowed. They are an improvement – parliamentarians do regard them as a political opportunity and some sessions are broadcast by the third TV channel, though these broadcasts have an extremely limited audience and no political effect at all. The President of the Senate complained in 1983 of the 'interminable ministerial monologues' which bored the TV audience and damaged the image of the Senate. Parliamentary questions in France do not have anything like the political impact that they do at Westminster. The problem is as much cultural as procedural.

Committees in the French Parliament do not act as much of a check on the executive either. The Constitution did not intend them to – it lays down that there shall be six and only six permanent committees in each house (with excessively large memberships for any real investigation) and that they are part of the legislative process with the job of examining each legislative proposal and producing a report on it. The permanent committees in the Senate also produce periodic reports on whether the laws passed by Parliament are actually being implemented – a mild form of parliamentary control. There is also a procedure, not very often used because it requires the support of the government's majority, for establishing special ad hoc committees to examine particular legislative proposals.

The only committees whose real function is control of the executive are Committees of Enquiry and Committees of Control, which can be set up ad hoc to look into a particular matter. In the first two Parliaments of the Fifth Republic, when the executive, memories of the Fourth Republic still fresh, was at its most anti-parliamentary, requests to set up Committees of Enquiry or Control were stifled by the pro-Gaullist Laws Committee. Since the beginning of the Giscard presidency, the Laws Committee could no longer bury the requests for these Committees, and, as Table 1 shows, the requests have become much more frequent in the National Assembly. Requests for Committees of Enquiry were used by the RPR as a way of demonstrating a measure of independence within the majority under the Barre governments of 1976–81, and the Senate keeps trying to be a thorn in the side of government.

Committees of Enquiry and Control, however, are ineffective as instruments of parliamentary control for four reasons. The first is that there has to be a majority for the motion to set one up. This means that government supporters can stop any that would be too embarrassing. Most requests are rejected – although the numbers mask the fact that often a group of requests relate to a single topic. The ones that are set up either have all-party support because they relate to something general like the state of the French language or the problems of the textile industry, or else relate to things that happened under previous governments that the new majority is happy to embarrass. The best example of this was the 1984 Committee of Enquiry which looked into the 'sniffer-plane scandal' in which the previous government, under President Giscard d'Estaing, had hushed up a report on the investment of a large amount of public money into an aircraft said to to be able to detect oil deposits underground! The pro-Chirac majority in both the National Assembly and the Senate allowed Committees of Enquiry to be set up into the student demonstrations of December 1986 – but not specifically into the police handling of them as the opposition wanted, but more into the manipulation of the student movement by 'professionals of political syndicalism'. The second reason for the ineffectiveness of Committees of Enquiry and Control is that the Committee has only six months to produce a report (it used to be four). The third, and very serious, inadequacy is that ministers can refuse to co-operate

TABLE 1

COMMITTEES OF ENQUIRY AND CONTROL

Parliament	National Assembly				Senate	
	Enquiry		Control		Enquiry	Control
	a	b	a	b		
1958–62	6	0	3	1	0	1
1962–67	5	0	1	0	0	1
1967–68	6	0	1	0	0	1
1968–73	10	1	6	1	1	1
1973–78	59	7	8	2	0	1
1978–81	66	6	9	1	3	0
1981–86	61	3	2	0	1	6
1986–88	19	1	3	0	1	0

a = Committees proposed; b = Committees set up.

and instruct their officials not to attend committee hearings. If the matter can be considered remotely *sub judice* the enquiry comes to an end anyway. The fourth and in a way most serious deficiency is not procedural at all: it is the curious fact that Committee reports, even into what would appear to be bombshells like the 'sniffer-plane' affair, make absolutely no impact on public opinion whatever – a small paragraph in *Le Monde* and nothing on television. In France there are no committee hearings remotely comparable in impact with those of American Congressional Committees or even of House of Commons Select Committees.

The other important procedural means by which Parliament can act as a check on executive power are censure and confidence motions – the traditional parliamentary ways of removing a government from office. In the Third Republic *interpellations* – a demand for an explanation of government policy on an issue followed by a vote – used to bring down governments. In the Fourth Republic votes against the government following *interpellations* were damaging but not usually fatal. In the Fifth they have been outlawed completely. The only way now that National Assembly *députés* can vote against the government, other than on a mere legislative matter, is by a motion of censure which has a special procedure (Article 49 of the Constitution) and which, if successful, forces the government to resign (Article 50) – and the Senate cannot even do that. The special procedure, probably rightly, makes it very difficult but still possible to bring down the government. Constant ministerial crisis is not an indispensable requirement for democratic government. It is possible to bring down the government only if an absolute majority of the Assembly positively wants to do so. A motion of censure can be put down if the opposition wants to condemn government policy or a particular aspect of it, or in response to the government making a legislative proposal a matter of confidence (see section on legislation and Table 4). It needs the signature of one tenth of all the *députés*. They cannot sign another until the next parliamentary session (except when the government makes one of its legislative proposals a matter of confidence). There is no vote for 48 hours – so tempers can cool, arms can be twisted, and topicality can fade. Only votes in favour of censure are counted – so that absentees, including the sick, as well as all abstainers are in effect counted as supporters of the government. Motions of censure and confidence are becoming more frequent: 34 in the first twenty years of the Fifth Republic, 54 in the next ten. However, since the beginning of the Fifth Republic in 1958 there has only been one successful motion of censure. That was in October 1962 over the issue of the referendum on direct presidential elections called by General de Gaulle. The Pompidou government resigned – but de Gaulle asked it to stay in office while an election was held. At the election those who voted for the motion of censure were annihilated, and de Gaulle reappointed Pompidou! The censure motion, however, is no meaningless charade. On the contrary, it is Article 49 which ensures that France is fundamentally a parliamentary democracy. The President cannot impose a government or his own policies on the country if a disciplined majority in the National Assembly is determined to prevent it. That is why President Mitterrand had to appoint his political adversary Chirac Prime Minister in 1986 and allow him to implement the programme on which his party and its allies had won the 1986 parliamentary election.

PARLIAMENT AS AN ARENA FOR NATIONAL DEBATE

In other European countries one of the most important contributions Parliament makes to the functioning of the political system is to be a forum for the national political debate. In Great Britain there are emergency debates on grave issues, such as the attack on the Falkland Islands in 1982, and other parliamentary occasions like the Budget when one can say that the House of Commons is fulfilling this role. In West Germany there was intense interest in Berlin in the Bundestag debate on Chancellor Brandt's Ostpolitik in 1972. The whole city seemed to be listening, with knots of spectators round the windows of television retailers. Nothing like this happens in the Fifth Republic at all. Neither Parliamentary Questions nor Committees of Enquiry, as we have seen, have any impact. Censure motions are the same – the only media interest in the 1989 censure motion against the Socialist government's European policy was that it was initiated by a group of younger Gaullists contesting the leadership of Chirac. Sometimes legislative debates arouse some interest, such as the 1975 bill to legalise abortion, or the 1982 nationalisation bill. There are no other parliamentary debates at all. In the first days of the Fifth Republic the National Assembly and the Senate drafted their standing orders permitting motions and debates which could be voted upon. However, this was referred to the Constitutional Council and ruled to be unconstitutional. So there is nothing resembling 'opposition days' or emergency debates – except debates on ministerial statements (with no vote at the end) of which there were 16 in the whole 1973–78 Parliament, and 14 under the Socialist government of 1981–86. In 1988 the Rocard government made just one general statement of government policy. But there were no statements that really allowed Parliament to voice the nation's or even the opposition's concern about something that was happening. Partial exceptions include statements in 1986 about terrorism, in 1980 about a bomb outrage in Paris, or (without debate) on the Giscard–Brezhnev meeting in Warsaw in 1980 (an initiative by the French President that backfired). The sending of French paratroops to Zaire in 1978 eventually produced a government statement without debate. There was no statement about the sinking of the Greenpeace *Rainbow Warrior* by the French Secret Service in 1985.

The inadequacy of Parliament as a forum is perhaps not entirely the fault of Parliament – nor even of the executive. It is occasionally asked 'If Parliament is not the forum for the nation's political debate in France, what is?'. The answer seems to be that there is not one. It is not television or radio. France has hardly any of those panel discussions and debates on current political questions, or those constant news programmes in which government and opposition are interviewed about the latest issue – the endless probings about the health service, taxation options, housing, atomic weapons, the latest strike, or whatever it happens to be. Indeed the type of issue-centred political debate, of the kind of so familiar in the Anglo-Saxon democracies, scarcely exists in France. The question of immigration was perhaps a partial exception to this in the period round the 1988 elections, though the debate was mainly in terms of philosophical generalities like tolerance and intolerance. Political leaders are occasionally interviewed, but in a most respectful tone and only on their general 'vision' of domestic and foreign policy. What debate there is centres on personalities and the statements (*petites phrases*) they issue to the press which are analysed for clues about their ambitions and leadership chances, or about the state of alliances between parties. There appears to have been no serious debate whatever about such issues as the development of nuclear power in the 1970s, never anything serious about the annual budget (except the symbolic presence or absence of wealth tax), nothing about the serious issues mentioned above: the dispatch of paratroops to Kolwezi in 1978, or the sinking of the *Rainbow Warrior* in 1985 (though in this last instance there was a search for revelations and much discussion over who would be politically embarrassed by them). In the Fifth Republic the executive has been remarkably free to get on with the job of governing. Occasionally government has been impeded by popular protest and has backed down – indeed there are some dramatic instances such as the mass demonstrations over education reform proposals in 1984 (against the left) and 1986 (against the right) – but most of the time it acts as it thinks fit with no real compulsion to pause or to justify itself – in Parliament or elsewhere – and the only check is the fear of provoking violence or losing the next election. One of the reasons for this is that France has done very well over the last three decades and effective government has been seen as a great improvement on what went before. Let us therefore now turn to the more positive side of the balance sheet – the areas in which Parliament is a valued institution contributing to the 'health of the political system'.

PARLIAMENT'S CONTRIBUTION TO LAW-MAKING

In France the role of Parliament as legislator is circumscribed but real. As in other countries most legislation is initiated by government. In France, though, the domain of law-making is restricted by the Constitution (Article 34), the rest falling into the sphere of government regulation, and the Constitutional Council is there to ensure that Parliament does not try to legislate outside its domain. Even more importantly, the Constitution gives the government absolute mastery of the legislative process and some heavy armour to curtail discussion. Nevertheless Parliament takes its legislative role seriously, examines and improves legislation, and gives it legitimacy by final parliamentary adoption.

When the Council of Ministers decides to introduce a *projet de loi* (government bill) it is submitted to either the National Assembly or the Senate (except for the annual Finance Bill which has to go first to the National Assembly). The house that receives it first sends it to the appropriate permanent committee for examination. A *rapporteur* is appointed and he eventually presents a report to the house. The committee's, the government's, and members' amendments are discussed. The text that is adopted after this 'first reading' is transmitted to the other house. The same procedure is followed. If the two houses support an identical text the process is complete and the *projet* is adopted. If there are new amendments it goes back to the first house for reconsideration (second reading). If it is accepted there, the process is complete. If not it goes back again and so on. This procedure is known as the 'shuttle'(*navette*). In the Fourth Republic this could go on for ever; in the Fifth, as we shall see, the government has ways to stop it. Legislative proposals from members of Parliament (*propositions de loi*) follow the same procedure – except that they do not get on to the parliamentary timetable without government support. On average about 5 per cent of *propositions de loi* actually receive the government support to become law, the majority originate from government supporters, and successful *propositions* (see Table 5 below) vary between about 10 and 25 per cent of all legislation.

Executive supremacy in the legislative process is based on four main constitutional provisions. The first is priority for government *projets* (or any *proposition de loi* it supports) on each day's timetable (Article 48) – so Parliament cannot refuse to discuss legislation wanted by the government. The second is the power to intervene in the 'shuttle' and, if there is a deadlock between Senate and National Assembly, to secure the outcome it wants (Article 45). After two readings in each house (or just one if the government declares the matter urgent or if it concerns the Finance Bill) the government can call for a Joint Committee (CMP – *Commission mixte paritaire*) composed of seven members of each house designated by proportional representation of political groups. If the CMP agrees a text the government may if it wishes submit it to both houses for adoption – with no further amendment unless the government agrees. If the CMP reaches no agreement the government then has the option of asking the National

Assembly to make the final decisions usually on the basis of what it last agreed before it went to the Senate. This is a very convenient weapon to have because the Senate has been for most of the Fifth Republic much less reliable from the government's point of view than the National Assembly. General de Gaulle had difficulties with the traditional parliamentarians in the Senate – indeed he resigned when his proposal to abolish it in its existing form was defeated at the referendum of 1969. The Socialist governments of the 1980s had to contend with permanent anti-Socialist Senate majorities, and Table 2 shows how frequently in the 1981–86 Parliament it had to resort to using its own majority in the Assembly to get its way against the Senate. Article 45 means that the Senate can be overridden – and the Senate protests vigorously when this happens. If it rejects a *projet* completely, as it did with the 1990 Finance Bill for instance, the *projet* just goes back, via a CMP, to the Assembly for adoption. If it will not agree to some of the fine print, it goes back, via a CMP, to the Assembly for adoption.

The third constitutional instrument in the hands of the government is Article 44, which enables it to curtail Parliamentary discussion (rather like the 'guillotine' in the House of Commons). The government can make the Assembly or the Senate take a single 'package' vote on the whole of a *projet* instead of taking it clause by clause, amendment by amendment. No amendments are allowed except those already agreed by the government. It was used about 16 times a year in the 1960s – more peremptorily by the Pompidou government which had reliable majorities than the Debré government which did not – but only about four times a year in the 1970s. There used to be howls of anguish from the Socialist Party and parliamentary walk-outs when this blunt instrument to prevent scrutiny was used. Socialists in government have in fact used it (Table 3), but much less than their predecessors (and much less than the Chirac government which used it 22 times in 1987 alone) and mainly in the legitimate cause of preventing systematic obstruction.

TABLE 2

USE OF *COMMISSION MIXTE PARITAIRE* (CMP)

Parliament	Number	CMP Reports (no agreement)	Referred back to National Assembly
1978–81	63	2	2
1981–86	203	137	140
1986–88	48	0	0

TABLE 3

USE OF ARTICLE 44: THE 'PACKAGE VOTE' PROCEDURE

Parliament	Number of times used
1978–81 (Barre Government)	18
1981–86 (Mauroy and Fabius Governments)	3
1986–88 (Chirac Government)	43

The fourth means of executive supremacy is the most massive legislative steamroller imaginable. Under Article 49 (as we saw above under motions of censure), the government may declare a *projet de loi* to be a matter of confidence. If it does, there is no further discussion and the *projet* is considered automatically adopted unless a censure motion (involving the fall of the government and probably a new election) is successfully carried in the next two days! It is important to remember that the Fifth Republic Constitution was drawn up under the assumption that there would, as in the Fourth, never be a disciplined parliamentary majority, and this explains a lot of this machinery to prevent obstruction. Article 49 is used quite frequently – sometimes abusively – and more in the 1980s than when de Gaulle or Pompidou were President (Table 4) and memories of parliamentary indiscipline were fresher in the mind. The Chirac government used it seven times in 1986 to prevent any discussion of very important matters like changes in the electoral law or privatisation. The Barre government in 1979 and the Rocard government in 1989 used it to get their Finance Bills through. In 1979 when Chirac's RPR, though part of the government's majority, was refusing to vote for it, Article 49 was used to call their bluff. The 1981–86 Socialist government used it for each of several readings of its law on prices and incomes in 1982, and of its law on press freedom in 1984. In 1989 the Rocard government had no overall majority and had to rely either on abstention by the Centrists or the Communists abstaining to get anything through – and it normally managed with careful concessions to obtain one or the other. However, on the final vote of the budget both Centrists and Communists declared they would vote against; so Article 49 was wheeled out in the knowledge that the Communists would not vote with the right to bring down the government.

There are other means, too, which the government can use to obtain legislation without parliamentary scrutiny – indeed without the assent of Parliament. It can legislate by referendum instead of through Parliament (Article 11). This was done by de Gaulle on several occasions, but only rarely since. The most recent example was the law on the future of New

TABLE 4

LEGISLATIVE USE OF ARTICLE 49

(Bill declared by government to be a matter of confidence)

Parliament	Number of times used
1958–62	5
1962–67	0
1967–68	3
1968–73	0
1973–78	1
1978–81 (Barre Government)	12*
1981–86 (Mauroy and Fabius Governments)	10
1986–88 (Chirac Government)	8

* Almost all during the 1979 Finance Bill.

Caledonia – a troubled French territory in the Pacific – adopted by referendum, not Parliament, in 1988. The government can also, under Article 38, ask Parliament to delegate to the government the power to make laws – on a given subject and for a limited period – by ordinance or decree. In the de Gaulle period this used to happen fairly often, sometimes when unpopular measures needed to be taken for which *députés* or Senators might not have the stomach (for example, in the 'Social Scourges' measures of 1960 which tried, among other things, to stop three million farmers distilling alcohol from fruit) and sometimes when the government's majority was precarious and controversial measures were considered urgent (for instance, the changes to medical and social security provisions in 1967). The Chirac government of 1986–88, the most anti-parliamentary in its instincts since the early 1970s, used it for its series of economic and social measures (including privatisation) and its reform of the electoral law in 1986. It was in a hurry, considered it had a mandate from the people, and had only a narrow overall majority of five seats. The Socialists have used it too; for example, in 1983 authority was delegated to the government on the issue of income support for the unemployed.

Having described in lurid detail the ways by which the executive can manipulate and coerce Parliament in the legislative process, how can we justify placing Parliament's role as legislator on the positive side of the balance sheet in assessing whether Parliament helps to maintain 'the health of the political system'? The answer is that Parliament, despite everything, is still the legislature. A reasonable proportion of legislation is initiated by members of Parliament (Table 5) – even by parties considered somewhat anti-system. Both National Assembly and Senate can and do examine and amend legislation introduced by the government. Indeed Table 6 shows how assiduous all political groups are, and how seriously the Senate takes its legislative role. The reports of the legislative Committees (which of course have pro-government majorities) produce a very large number of amendments and they are taken seriously by all governments, with a 'success rate' for their amendments of over 75 per cent. As far as amendments initiated by individual members, not committees, are concerned, the table shows two other interesting things. It shows how governments favour amendments from their own supporters: over 60 per cent of Socialist amendments were successful in the 1981–86 Parliament, and Communists did best in the same Parliament when they were part of the government (1981–84). It also shows how the alternation of power from government to opposition, which occurred for the first time in the Fifth Republic in 1981, produced a new earnestness in the task of opposition. Amendments started being tabled in their thousands against controversial legislation like nationalisation or (after power changed hands again in 1986) privatisation. Notice how the anti-Socialist majority in the Senate vigorously joined in the game during the 1981–86 period.

Parliament can reject legislation if a majority of members really wants to – even though the National Assembly might have to be prepared to vote a motion of censure and face a new election if the government, abusively perhaps, makes a particular proposal a matter of confidence. The executive

TABLE 5

PROPOSITIONS DE LOI (PpL) PASSED

(Private Members' Legislation)

	PpL as % of all laws passed	Introduced in National Assembly by				Introduced in Senate
		Soc	RPR/ UDF	Comm	FN	
Fourth Republic	29					
Fifth Republic						
1958–62	7					
1962–67	14					
1967–68	19					
1968–73	16					
1973–78	23					
1978–81	16	3	26	1	0	6
1981–86	9	13	18	6	0	5
1986–88	24	1	28	1	1	12

does not always get its way: Giscard did not press for a wealth tax or the abolition of the death penalty because he felt he would not be supported by his parliamentary majority, and Mitterrand could not proceed with a proposal to amend the Constitution (to widen the scope of referenda) because constitutional revisions require the support of both assemblies, and the Senate refused. In the end the laws promulgated by the President have (except for the few adopted directly by referendum) been passed by

TABLE 6

AMENDMENTS

Government		Committee	Soc	Amendments originated by			Senate (approx)
				RPR/ UDF	Comm	FN	
Barre government							
1978–81	Tabled	2576	1173	2156	1327	–	9500
	Passed	1996	126	548	60	–	
	'Success rate'	77%	11%	25%	5%		40%
Mauroy and Fabius governments							
1981–86	Tabled	12023	1658	18706	2545	–	25000
	Passed	10490	1007	733	205	–	
	'Success rate'	87%	61%	4%	8%	-	45%
Chirac government							
1986–88	Tabled	2446	3620	1708	2566	1223	9000
	Passed	1827	103	356	23	28	
	'Success rate'	75%	3%	21%	1%	2%	33%

Parliament, reflecting, most of the time in the Fifth Republic at any rate, a majority elected by the people. Most observers agree that Parliament in the Fifth Republic has been a more productive and more responsible legislator than in the Fourth. The requirement that a modern Parliament should direct itself more to scrutinising and improving legislation than initiating or impeding it is reasonably well fulfilled in France today. The dominant role of the government in the legislative process is in keeping with what obtains in most modern parliamentary democracies. As the habit of majority support for government has become established as part of the political culture since 1962, abuse by government of its powers in its relations with Parliament has become more rare – the Chirac period of 1986–88 being something of an exception. Oppositions have become more confident and more persistent (as the tables on Committees of Enquiry and amendments show). Since the great shock of the Fifth Republic's first change of power from government to opposition in 1981, oppositions have contained former leaders of government and they (and the civil service) have known the executive to be vulnerable.

At the time of writing, the Rocard government, appointed after the June 1988 parliamentary elections, does not have an overall majority in the National Assembly nor anywhere near one in the Senate. It manages, however, to get its legislation through by judicious use of concessions to the Centrists or the Communists or to the Senate and has not had to use coercive procedures very much: in 1988 seven 'package votes', two legislative texts declared issues of confidence, 10 CMPs with eight failures to agree and reference back to National Assembly for final decision. The President of the Senate, Alain Poher, in his end-of-year message on 21 December 1989 noted with satisfaction the equitable way the government had shared out *projets de loi* between Senate and National Assembly and 'an improvement in laws covering various sectors of our national life where the dialogue between the two Assemblies has worked well' (i.e. concessions were made to the Senate). 'Naturally, on bills which are the occasion for fundamental political choice', he added, 'cleavages have been apparent – as parliamentary democracy requires'.

PARLIAMENTARIANS AND THEIR CONSTITUENTS

Most of the modern literature on Parliaments, as Philip Norton reminds us in his introduction, stresses the importance of the linkage between parliamentarian and his constituents as a vital element in support for the political system. This is certainly true in France. 'Localism' – the practice of spending more time on local issues than being a national legislator – is one of the criticisms most frequently levelled against members of the National Assembly, and the constitutional role of the Senate is actually defined (Article 24) as representing *les collectivités territoriales* (local authorities). In fact Senators are elected not by the general public but by an electoral college composed almost entirely of local councillors.

In France most *députés* and Senators are local mayors, *conseillers généraux* (county councillors), or regional councillors. Many county councils and regional councils are represented in Parliament by their president – for example, former President Giscard d'Estaing was *député* for suburban Clermont Ferrand and President of Auvergne Regional Council. Most held local office before becoming members of Parliament, and they continue to do so, or seek to do so, after their election. Even as ministers, even as Prime Minister, they continue with their role as local mayor, or president of their county council or Regional Council. There are three reasons for this. First, a regional power base is an important attribute for a national political leader. Former Prime Ministers Pierre Mauroy and Jacques Chaban-Delmas owe a great deal of their political importance to their regional political leadership and in particular to the fact that they are Mayors of Lille and Bordeaux respectively. The influence of the late Gaston Defferre was based on his long leadership of France's second city, Marseilles. This is nothing new: the legendary pre-war Radical parliamentary leader Edouard Herriot was first and foremost Mayor of Lyons.

Secondly, the *député-maire*, in local government and in the national Parliament, has a pivotal role in the French political and administrative system. Access to state power is an essential element of local power and possession of local power opens the doors of state power. The role of *député-maire*, writes Pierre Grémion, offers real possibilities of 'general political control of the political system including its local sub-system'.[1] *Députés* who do not have a local mandate soon seek one, partly for electoral advantage as we shall see, but also because they feel 'incomplete' as representatives. Two of the prominent younger Gaullists illustrate this point well. Philippe Séguin, having won the parliamentary seat of Epinal in 1978, needed to consolidate his local political leadership by winning the town hall in 1983. Michel Noir greatly strengthened his claim to national leadership by becoming Mayor of Lyons in 1989. Control of an important town hall in France also means access to considerable resources: a personal staff, a car, a chauffeur, an office, a budget, above all perhaps an opportunity to demonstrate ability to achieve.

Finally there is the electoral advantage that attaches to a local *notable*.

TABLE 7

LOCAL OFFICES HELD BY DÉPUTÉS: 1988*

Office	Party				Total	% of
	Soc	RPR	UDF/UDC	Comm		*députés*
Mayor	129	64	60	12	274	47
Conseil Général	101	50	70	2	227	39
(Presidents of						
Conseils Généraux)	(12)	(7)	(5)		(26)	
Regional Council	54	15	22	3	96	17
(Presidents of						
Regional Councils)	(2)	(2)	(5)		(9)	
Paris City Council	5	10	3		18	3

* Since the 1985 law, *députés* can hold one of these offices – two if one of them is Mayor of a town of less than 20,000 population. They can also be town councillors other than mayor.

A well-entrenched local personality has a better chance of being chosen as a candidate (or getting a good position on a list – as in the European Parliament elections or the parliamentary elections of 1986 which were fought under proportional representation), a better chance of running ahead of his allies in a 'primary' (first ballot contest) so that they will stand down in his favour at the second ballot, and a better chance of getting elected.[2] There is no great mass popular following for the group of centrist parties called the UDF, certainly no large-scale organisation, yet even in opposition they have 130 *députés*: a classic confederation of *notables*.

The reason why a prominent local role gives a politician such influence and such appeal is that 'a belief in the special power of the *notable* persists'.[3] The classic French parliamentarian in the Third Republic (a regime in which Parliament was definitely not subordinate to the executive) was a local *notable*, independent of party, constantly re-elected. He alone, in a highly centralised administrative state, had access to Paris. He alone had the 'local power to make the *Préfet* tremble'. The role of the *député* is still considered in local communities to be primarily that of interceding with central government on behalf of individuals or councils, rather than as a legislator or watchdog over executive power or debater of the great issues of the day. This tradition of clientelism explains why young technocrats from ministerial *cabinets* have been so successful in winning parliamentary seats and town halls in the Fifth Republic – they are thought to be particularly good at obtaining favours from central government. Jacques Chirac – again – made himself, while serving on the staff of Prime Minister Georges Pompidou into a *notable* in the Corrèze, a backward and traditionally left-wing rural area of the Massif Central. He became *député* and *conseiller général*. Over the years he has gone to a great deal of trouble to maintain his clientele in the Corrèze and when he became Prime Minister himself, he had a 'Corrèze bureau' in the Prime Minister's office. Though Mayor of Paris since 1977, he remains *député* for the Corrèze and is invariably re-elected outright at the first ballot. The whole exercise, according to Henri Deligny, has been a lesson in 'the conquest of an electoral fiefdom with public funds and irregular governmental favours'.[4]

Research on mail received by *députés* has shown that about 96 per cent consists of requests for some kind clientelist favour – not policy interventions, nor 'redress of grievance'.[5] The main topics raised are those in which the *député* appears as helper of the underprivileged (housing, social security, pensions, study grants, and other welfare matters), those in which he is believed to have the power of patronage (military and teaching postings and promotions, jobs in the municipal or civil service), and those which ask for favours (tax reductions, favourable examination results, decorations, interventions in judicial matters, reductions of fines, telephone installations, licences for *bureaux de tabac*). Almost all these requests (not for good examination results) are passed on to the *préfecture* or to the ministry concerned for consideration and decision. Masclet[6] has calculated that the seven most solicited ministries (Finance, Agriculture, Employment, Justice, Industry, Army, Post and Telecommunications) received an annual 40,000 requests from *députés*, for which they required considerable extra staff, and that an average-sized *préfecture* would handle 1,600 interventions a year. The *député* (and the Senator) also receives numerous demands from local councils on matters like road maintenance, school building, water supply, or flood damage. He develops clientelist links with his small villages, where the mayor can 'deliver' support, and of course he gives a special priority to showing that the town of which he himself is mayor is particularly favoured.

All this localism, of course, in a system of government in which executive power has become very strong, undermines the role of the *député* as legislator and controller of the executive. It takes most of his time – indeed most *députés* find their local mandate more satisfying and more rewarding than their national one – and this explains much of the absenteeism so prevalent in the National Assembly or the lack of interest in Questions or legislative debates. It makes him a tributary of the executive rather than its watchdog. Some reformers have even argued that the combining of local and national offices (*cumul des mandats*) should be abolished. The *cumul des mandats* has been reduced – a person may now hold only one local office (mayor of a town over 20,000, or county councillor, or regional councillor) and one national office (member of Parliament or of the European Parliament) instead of, as in the past, being able to be *député*, MEP, president of Regional Council, president of *Conseil général*, and mayor all at the same time – but the tradition of combining local and national roles is too deeply a part of the national political culture, to which the electors as well as élites are attached, to disappear.

'In the spirit of the population, especially the rural population', wrote André Chandernagor, a prominent Socialist *député*, in the 1960s,[7] 'the parliamentarian is *le pouvoir fait homme* [power in human form]. One knows Ministers are inaccessible, but one wants to know one's *député*. One wants to see him, speak to him, feel that he is at the same time approachable yet sufficiently listened to and competent that, if need be, one could appeal to him for effective help and support. And one is seldom let down.' As soon as the Estates General declared itself to be a constituent assembly in 1789, apparently, its members received a deluge of mail! Despite all the modern changes, like judicial remedies for the citizen against administrative errors or faults, or the growth of interest groups and associations, 'the preference for individual solicitation of the member of Parliament is stronger than ever'.

PARLIAMENT AND POLITICAL STABILITY

Parliament did not contribute much to the political system's stability in the Third or Fourth Republics but it has in the Fifth – certainly since 1962 when a party system producing a parliamentary majority first emerged. It has done so by providing consistent and dependable support for the government of the day and for the institutions of the Republic.

G. Loewenberg and S.C. Patterson have written about the importance of the legislature's contribution to stability and support in a variety of systems. 'It is the glory of the institution that it can both integrate the nation and express its variety'.[8] Parliaments have ceremonies and styles of speech to stress national unity, as well as 'the angry debates, the shouts and interruptions, and the divided votes . . . characteristic of all free legislatures'. In almost every assembly, local or national, in Great Britain, France, or elsewhere, there is a striking contrast between the extraordinary level of hostility between political opponents, so much so that every measure proposed by one party is met by total condemnation from the other side, and the acceptance of decisions once reached. Gordon Smith[9] throws some light on this phenomenon by analysing the intensity of opposition in terms of ideology. He draws a distinction between parties whose aims are compatible with the existing political and socio-economic orders and those who seek to replace them.

In the Fourth Republic there were important anti-system parties. In 1951 almost half the electorate voted Communist or RPF (Gaullist), both parties at that time advocating the overthrow of current political institutions. In the Fifth Republic opposition takes place within the system. The Gaullists, of course, consider themselves the embodiment of the Fifth Republic and its institutions. The Socialist Party has for a very long time been a moderate pro-system party and its periods in government have been characterised by continuity not change – not just continuity in terms of political institutions but also of the national consensus on defence and foreign policy, and of the social and economic order. There has been an abundant literature on the 'tribune' role of the Communist Party in France since the 1960s – its function of defending the less privileged groups in society through conventional union, parliamentary, and local council action – and on its attempt to win a share in government by alliance with the Socialists in the 1970s.[10] There was actual Communist participation in government from 1981 to 1984 with no accusations of subversion at all directed at their four ministers. Since 1984 their isolation has resumed to some extent and they have not experienced any Eastern Europe-style democratic revolution or *perestroika*, but they have become a very marginal political force with less than 10 per cent electoral support. The *Front National* is probably the nearest to being a real anti-system party, but it too has 10 per cent support or less, and when it had some parliamentary strength (35 *députés* 1986–88) its parliamentary group was divided between those who wanted to appear respectable and perform a conventional parliamentary role (genuine amendments, committee reports, serious *propositions de loi*) and those who wanted to riot in the Chamber.

Political parties, therefore, and in particular their parliamentary élites, have contributed greatly to the stability of the Fifth Republic. Parties have become much more important. The Gaullists in the 1960s and the Socialists in the 1980s emerged as mass parties with what the French call 'a majority vocation' – parties that could win around 35–40 per cent of the popular vote and win a parliamentary majority. These parties have seen their primary role as being to support 'their' government. This has never happened before in French republican history. Parliamentary groups are disciplined – with the possible exception today of the Centrists, who have formed their own parliamentary group outside the UDF of which they remain a component. Socialist members must clear their questions, amendments and *propositions de loi* with the group leadership, and the group remains subordinate to the party. RPR members have a little more freedom, and the parliamentary group is more independent of the party but voting discipline is firmly maintained. Coalition partners such as the UDF and RPR, allies in government and in opposition ever since the 1960s, observe the same discipline, certainly when it comes to a motion of confidence or censure. Indeed the whole period has been marked by a reluctance to create crisis by allowing a government to fall. The government maintains close relations with 'its' parliamentary majority through its Minister for Relations with Parliament, normally attached to the Prime Minister's office, and, as we have seen, helps its supporters to promote legislation and amendments.

PARLIAMENT AND EXECUTIVE RECRUITMENT

Is Parliament in France the recruiting ground for political leadership in the way that it is in Great Britain and other parliamentary democracies? We have seen that Parliament can remove the government from office by voting a motion of censure and that it can establish a government in office by providing a disciplined majority that will have no other. That was why President Mitterrand had to appoint his opponent Jacques Chirac Prime Minister in 1986. Many of the most important political leaders of the Fifth Republic, however, come from outside Parliament – indeed from outside the party system. General de Gaulle was the most important, but his successor Georges Pompidou, a former member of de Gaulle's private staff, was also from outside Parliament and totally unknown to the general public when de Gaulle appointed him prime minister in 1962. Many other political leaders have been recruited from outside Parliament – Prime Ministers Raymond Barre (1976–81) and Laurent Fabius (1984–86) are two recent examples. Indeed President Mitterrand, *député* for the Nièvre for over 30 years, is one of the very few leading politicians of the Fifth Republic to tread the traditional parliamentary road to the top. The best path to a political career in the Fifth Republic has been the National School of Administration, then entry into one of the most prestigious parts of the civil service, a *Grands Corps de l'état* like the Inspectorate of Finance or the Conseil d'Etat, followed by recruitment to a ministerial *cabinet* (private staff). Many Fifth Republic ministers have been appointed direct from the civil service (over a third in the de Gaulle and Giscard Presidencies), and especially those with service in a ministerial *cabinet*. De Gaulle's Foreign Minister, Couve de Murville, was a career diplomat as most subsequent foreign ministers have been, since successive Presidents have followed the de Gaulle tradition of being in personal charge of Foreign Affairs. Most of the key ministers in the 1986–88 Chirac government came from his entourage at Paris City Hall or had been his colleagues from the days when he and they were civil servants on Pompidou's private staff. The idea that ministers must be recruited from the ranks of the government party in Parliament has not been a feature of the Fifth Republic. Indeed one of the curious anti-parliamentary features of the Fifth Republic's constitution is the incompatibility rule (Article 23) by which ministers, if they have them, have to resign their parliamentary seats.

To set against this rather technocratic and anti-parliamentary portrait of the Fifth Republic, however, is the attraction that a seat in Parliament evidently exercises for those who aspire to political leadership, even if they were recruited from the civil service. Quermonne[11] makes a distinction between those who are appointed to government as administrative specialists and continue in that way, and those who began life in the administration but begin to feel the call to the political heights. The second group displays a strong motivation to enter Parliament. Leading examples include Giscard d'Estaing (Inspector of Finance), who by the way made a comeback to Parliament after being defeated as President, Jacques Chirac (Cour des Comptes), Michel Rocard (Inspector of Finance), Raymond Barre (former EEC Commissioner), or, from the newer political generation Philippe Séguin (Cour des Comptes). Furthermore, though ministers have to resign their parliamentary seats, they do so in the letter rather than the spirit. They continue to maintain close links with their constituencies (the electors of which expect the clientelist functions of their *député* to be even more effectively performed now that he is a minister), have a section in their *cabinet* dealing with constituency affairs, continue as local mayor or county councillor, and fight the constituency at the next election even though, if they are reappointed ministers, the seat must be resigned again. Such resignations do not involve a by-election: the minister is replaced by his *suppléant* (running mate), who, if he knows what is good for him, will loyally keep the seat warm for the minister, and resign (which in this case does make a by-election possible) if the minister leaves the government. So Parliament continues to attract the leading politicians of the nation.

CONCLUSION

How can we summarise relations between executive and Parliament in the Fifth Republic and the contribution of Parliament to the health of the political system? As in nearly all modern democracies, the executive initiates most of the legislation and dominates the legislative process – possessing in France some particularly savage means of eliminating discussion. However, both parliamentary assemblies doggedly pursue their task of trying to improve legislation and legitimising it. If recent governments, as our tables have shown, have resorted more frequently to coercive methods to curtail discussion, it is partly because oppositions today, having tasted power themselves and knowing since 1981 that power in the Fifth Republic can change hands, are more confident and assertive. The greatest weakness of Parliament is, as we have seen, as a watchdog. The procedures for controlling executive power, for scrutinising or debating or questioning executive acts, are completely inadequate. Executive power in France can do more or less as it likes – with only violence in the streets or the fear of losing the next election as a check. Despite all this, though, Parliament remains a valued institution. Parliamentary elections continue to be regarded as political events of the highest significance. In 1973 and 1978 the prospects of a Socialist/Communist parliamentary majority provoked endless discussion about a 'change of society'. In 1986 the election of the RPR/UDF majority forced 'cohabitation' upon a Socialist President and policy leadership passed from the President to his Prime Minister who had the support of Parliament. The country's leading politicians continue to want to be members of Parliament. The electors continue to regard their *député* as an intermediary of the greatest importance and the linkage between constituent and parliamentarian and parliamentarian and central government remains a vital part of the political system and of support for it. Opinion research done in the late 1960s and early 1970s indicated, despite fairly recent experience of the Fourth Republic, about one third of people wanting Parliament to play a more important role, about one third satisfied with it as it then was, but only two or three per cent wanting its role to be further reduced. General de Gaulle's referendum proposal in 1969 effectively to abolish the Senate was unpopular and its rejection brought his reign to an end. Subsequent Presidents have, on the whole, tried to extend and protect the prerogatives of Parliament. Giscard introduced a constitutional amendment to give members of Parliament the right to invoke the Constitutional Council. Mitterand refused to sign decrees when he felt the Chirac government had not allowed sufficient parliamentary discussion. The most profound change in the Fifth Republic affecting relations between executive and Parliament, though, is the transformation of the party system. Control of the legislature by government requires a disciplined majority[12] and disciplined parliamentary majorities have contributed greatly to the political stability of the Fifth Republic.

NOTES

1. In Colloque, *Les facteurs locaux de la vie politique française* (Bordeaux: Institut d'Etudes Politiques), p.94.
2. J. R. Frears and J-L. Parodi, *War Will Not Take Place* (London: Hurst, 1979), p.72, and J. R. Frears, 'The Role of the *député* in France', in V. Bogdanor (ed.), *Representatives of the People* (London: Gower/PSI, 1985), pp.105–8.
3. J-C. Masclet, *Le rôle de député et ses attaches institutionelles sous la Vème République* (Paris: Librairie générale du droit et de jurisprudence, 1979), p.199.
4. *Chirac ou la fringale du pouvoir* (Paris: Moreau, 1977), p.419.
5. M-T. Lancelot, 'Le courrier d'un parlementaire', *Revue Française de Sciences Politiques* (June 1962), pp.426–32, and Masclet, pp.195 and 201–3.
6. Masclet, pp.201–2.
7. *Un parlement, pour quoi faire?* (Paris: Gallimard, 1967), pp.147–8.
8. *Comparing Legislatures* (Boston: Little, Brown, 1979), p.4.
9. 'Party and Protest: The Two Faces of Opposition in Western Europe', in E. Kolinsky (ed.), *Opposition in Western Europe* (London: Croom Helm, 1987), p.58.
10. See J. R. Frears, *Political Parties and Elections in the Fifth Republic* (London: Hurst, 1977, 2nd ed. 1990).
11. *Le gouvernement de la France sous la Ve République* (Paris: Dalloz, 1980), p.480.
12. See E. Suleiman, 'Towards the Disciplining of Parties and Legislators', in E. Suleiman (ed.), *Parliaments and Parliamentarians in Democratic Politics* (New York: Holmes & Meier, 1986), p.82.

Parliament in Italian Politics

Paul Furlong

Relations between Parliament and the executive in Italy have not normally occupied centre stage for those whose lot it is to analyse such matters. In practice, so little had been written on Parliament (both absolutely and in comparison with other more favoured subjects) that interpretations of the institution and of its relationship with government generally have to be deduced from work which has other objectives and whose taciturnity on Parliament gives a summary indication of where Parliament figures in the pecking-order. There is a very limited number of obvious exceptions to the neglect. Even these, however, are marked by a striking disparity between the vigour with which they espouse their subject and their inability or unwillingness to hoist Parliament's status further up the flagpole. One of the major works – the only full-length English-language text – is indeed devoted to a thesis which proclaims the crisis of Parliament; the alternative view, that Parliament is now (or was for a period) central to the political system, rests on a detailed analysis of the intended scope of internal rule changes rather than on the practical activities of the legislature.[1] This article is concerned to avoid the 'pecking-order' approach, seeking rather to identify what is the general pattern of policy-making within which Parliament actually operates, to describe Parliament's relations with other major institutions, and to assess how this has changed since the end of the 1960s. After some initial discussion of the constitutional position of Parliament, the article analyses the role of Parliament in three different areas: legitimation, recruitment of ministers and policy-making.

First, a word or two about Parliament in the constitution. The Italian Constitution of 1948 is a lengthy and complex document in which a variety of different hands can be detected. The heterogeneity of its provisions and the evident lacunae are strong indications of the political pressures of the period from June 1946 to the end of 1947, when the tripartite foundation of the governing Christian Democrat (DC), Communist (PCI) and Socialist coalition was undermined and finally destroyed by international pressure and internal disagreement. A major split occurred in January 1947 between traditional Socialists (PSI) and Social Democrats (PSDI), and the PSI, excluded from government in May 1947, were not re-admitted until 1963. The Communists (PCI) were removed from government at the same time as the Socialists, and have never been re-admitted to ministerial positions. The Constitution is the product more of the earlier compromise than of the later division between the Christian Democrats and the left-wing parties. As well as reflecting party-political pressures directly, the Constitution also bears the imprint of different political traditions with their differing diagnoses of the spectacular failure of the Liberal regime in 1922 and of the 21 years of

Fascist rule.[2] One of these traditions, associated mainly with what remained of the Liberal élites, argued that the collapse of 1922 had been the result of the weakness of the structures upholding the rule of law. Hence one of their concerns was to ensure that the new constitution should be the apex of a new inclusive legal system, and that in principle all government action should fall within its framework. The tradition most opposed to this was associated with the Socialists and Communists, who tended to argue that the strongest protection against the political instability of the early 1920s lay in the spread of mass participation and in the constitutional primacy of popular sovereignty.[3] The compromise between these two intellectual and political traditions, together with the party-political tensions of the time, established a relatively rigid political framework within which Parliament has developed.

Under the Constitution, sovereignty belongs to the people, not to any political or legal structure, and is exercised by them within the framework established by the Constitution.[4] The Constitution was not subjected to any popular referendum before promulgation, though of course the Constituent Assembly which wrote it was directly elected by universal suffrage. The only subject which is constitutionally excluded from revision is the Republican form itself, which had been decided by referendum at the same time as the election of the Constituent Assembly. The procedures for constitutional revision are deliberately constructed to make the document relatively rigid, and rely on special majorities and repeated deliberations in both chambers over extended periods. The final and transitory provisions of the document declare that the constitution is the 'Fundamental Law' of the Republic. Other than the constitution itself, the principal source of law is Parliament, the two chambers acting collectively. All actions of the state are to be derived ultimately from this source – the law established by the elected chambers operating with constitutional authority. In this way, the Constituent Assembly intended to subordinate Parliament, the sole creator of law and the supreme organ of popular sovereignty, to a higher set of norms. In some respects, the Constituent Assembly showed considerable naivety or at least excessive optimism about the safeguards which the rule of law could provide – the lack of other forms of control over the judiciary, for example, has proved a serious impediment to the efficient working of the judicial process. It did not show the same optimism about Parliament. The pre-eminence of the Italian Parliament in the expression of popular constitutional sovereignty is qualified by a deliberate institutional pluralism, which ensures that no one institution can claim either a monopoly on legislative activity or the sole possession of popular legitimacy. The formal law-making functions of Parliament are shared with other institutions, in particular with the directly elected regional assemblies. These are subordinate to Parliament, but the Constitution (if not customary practice) suggests that in those areas where regions also have competence, Parliament ought to restrict itself to general laws prescribing basic principles. There is also provision for popular referenda, a procedure by which the people can repeal a law passed by Parliament – a measure which has the obvious intention of providing a limited means for popular sovereignty to check the power given to Parliament elsewhere in the document. The Constitution is protected by the constitutional court: this is entirely separate from the structures of the ordinary judiciary in that it does not act as the final court of appeal for all cases – its function is narrower and more powerful, in that for trial purposes it has the responsibility for judging in cases where the constitutionality of laws or of other norms is at issue. There is not space here to discuss the development of the relationship between the constitutional court and Parliament, but it should be observed that the structure of the Constitution does not suggest that the court was viewed as a frequent and busy source of counsel on detailed policy-making; nor does it seem to be perceived as an institution like the US Supreme Court, a necessary check on activist elected politicians. Rather its function seems initially to be envisaged as that of a lofty and detached interpreter of the high principles of the founding text, having a workload that would probably decrease over time as the principles were clarified and as law-making became gradually imbued with the ethos of the new state. Only rarely therefore would it find itself in conflict with the elected legislature, and even then on its own ground of judicial interpretation rather than on the parliamentary territory of detailed policy-making. The development of the court has actually been towards detailed analysis of the constitutionality of very specific legislation, and its workload has been both substantial and wide-ranging.[5]

In constitutional terms, relations between Parliament and the other political institutions rest on an implicit model of competitive pluralism, which is, however, always formally subject either to direct constitutional provision, in which case its contours are relatively clear or, more normally, to future parliamentary legislation, which leaves it considerably vaguer. The vagueness extends to the position of the government itself, whose powers and functions are left largely unspecified, even to the extent that the organisation of the Prime Minister's office and of the ministries is declared by Article 95 to be a matter for the legislator. The consequence of choosing in 1947 to leave large tracts of institutional organisation to Parliament (in effect, to the governing parties) was to subordinate institutional reform to the political conflicts and bitter divisions which followed. In practice, though the Constitution declares that the Prime Minister 'conducts and is responsible for the general policy of the government', and 'ensures the unity and consistency of the political and administrative programme by promoting and co-ordinating the activity of the ministers', this had had little effect in the face of the predominance of the governing parties over the policy-making process. Substantial legislative proposals as envisaged by article 95 were not actually forthcoming until 1981, when their emergence was not unconnected with the advent of the first non-Christian-Democrat Prime Minister since 1945. As a result of constitutional choices, therefore, Parliament has often seemed to lack a valid partner to talk to in a policy-making system which lacks a strong co-ordinating centre. Furthermore, the formal separation of powers is implied by the attribution of legislative authority to Parliament and of executive authority to government; intended to give government the responsibility for political direction of the affairs of state, this has the effect of maintaining an institutional barrier between government and legislature over matters such as agenda, timetable and text. Rather than talk, therefore, of the decline of Parliament, we should refer to a constitutional impasse, in which government and Parliament have been unable to develop a stable and effective working relationship precisely because of the interaction between an unreformed public administration, a loosely worded Constitution and unbalanced party-political development.

PARLIAMENT AND LEGITIMATION

This section refers mainly to the internal procedures through which governments are sustained in office by the legislature. The impact of these matters on public opinion will not be discussed, as evidence for such a discussion would be largely impressionistic. Legitimacy, in this context, means the formal and informal reliance of government on the confidence of Parliament, not the extent to which Parliament's effectiveness or ineffectiveness enhances or harms the popular support for the government or for the political system as a whole.

The instability of Italy's government is legendary, and like many legends this one relies for its power on lack of detailed understanding. There has certainly been a significant change in the phenomenon since 1968, but the responsibility of Parliament for the instability is not clear, and it is not easy to identify the impact of domestic or international policy issues directly in the changing relationship between government and other political institutions. Describing the problem is relatively straightforward. Between June 1945 and December 1989 Italy had a total of 49 governments, an average of one new government just under every eleven months. The most durable Cabinet was that of the Socialist Prime Minister Bettino Craxi, which lasted from August 1983 to August 1986, a grand total of nearly 1150 days. The next longest was the one led by the Christian Democrat Aldo Moro from February 1966 to June 1968, 739 days. In strictly formal terms, the shortest-ever government was one led by Alcide de Gasperi, the otherwise successful and widely respected post-war Christian Democrat, which lasted from 16 July to 28 July 1953.

It is clear even from these brief figures that there is a very considerable variation in how long governments last. The average duration of individual governments is just over nine months, but this figure may be misleading, as no government has ever actually fallen in its ninth month. This level of durability does seem to be more or less constant, in the sense that despite the high short-term variation, in the longer term there is no consistent trend upwards or downwards from the nine-month mean – the average life of governments has stayed between 280 and 310 days since the mid-1950s. Whatever factors are at work in determining government duration are obviously extremely stable.[6] The difference between the eleven-month average period from one government to the next and the nine-month average government life (approximately) is made up by the period of government crisis, that is the period between the fall of one government and the swearing-in of the next. In this we can undoubtedly see a marked change, in that government crises are becoming increasingly protracted. A crude indication of this is that in the first fifteen years of the Republic (up to 1963) no crisis lasted longer than 30 days, but since then the majority of crises have taken over 30 days to resolve. Hence there has been a small but significant increase in the period between one government and the next, from an overall average of about 300 days in the early 1960s to about 320 in the 1970s and 1980s. There is also an increasing likelihood of crises being resolved by fresh elections. The statutory period between elections is five years, but the last five Parliaments (every one since 1968) have been cut short by dissolution by the President of the Republic, following repeated failure of the political parties to find a new government. The crudity of the figures no doubt leaves much to be desired, but it is difficult to avoid the general conclusion that though governments are no more and no less stable now than they ever have been in the post-war period, since the 1960s and particularly since 1968 government crises have become significantly more difficult to resolve. A reason for this development might be supposed to be the increasing intensity and depth of policy disagreements between the governing parties, perhaps exacerbated by the severity of the economic problems of the 1970s. Undoubtedly Italian governments did face major challenges of adjustment to the new international order after the collapse of the dollar hegemony and the first oil crisis, and these were to some extent exacerbated by the ways in which employers and government responded to increased trade union militancy between 1968 and 1972.[7] These domestic and international policy issues prompted differing responses and considerable disagreement particularly between the Socialists and the Republicans, over issues such as levels and direction of public sector spending, tax reform and industrial policy. If this argument does not entirely convince, it may be because such disputes rarely found the largest party, the DC, strongly committed to either side, and because where such disputes did appear relevant the new governing coalition did not usually differ markedly from the overt policy stance of its predecessor. A further reason for scepticism is that some government crises are clearly inexplicable in these terms. The public explanation for the break-up of government may not even pay lip-service to policy issues but may refer directly to narrow party concerns. These may be either about the balance of power, in which case issues such as the timing of elections and referenda are at the forefront, or about the distribution of power within the parties, when party congresses and the internal cycle of meetings can determine the rhythm of government crises. In any case, the weight of such considerations in the ordinary functioning of Italian politics means that the public motivation for a crisis is often regarded by commentators and politicians alike as a shallow pretext for party-political advantage, and where this advantage is not immediately apparent cunning journalists and party officials will usually find one behind the public façade. This tactic-mongering is apparently entrenched in Italian politics, and applies to other events than government crises: the term used to describe the art of identifying the hidden motives is 'dietrologia', the science of what lies behind. Whatever the excesses of the 'dietrologists', the weakness of policy debate and its insignificance in electoral terms should deter us from giving policy disputes too much weight in understanding government crises. An underlying factor which certainly is important is the lack of any strong incentive for the governing parties to maintain government stability for its own sake. The exclusion of the Communists, who remain the second largest party, ensures that there is no practical alternative to the existing five-party coalition or some derivative of it.

The role of Parliament in the process of government formation and collapse is ensured formally by the constitutional provision that governments must 'enjoy the confidence of both Houses' (Article 94). Governments have to seek a vote of confidence from Parliament within ten days of their appointment. The same article explicitly states that 'the contrary vote of one or both Houses on a proposal made by the Government does not necessitate resignation.' It has sometimes been argued that in the Italian Republic as in the French Fourth Republic government crises are engineered by backbench deputies and Senators eager to promote their own ministerial careers.[8] There is very little evidence to support this assertion for the Italian case. On the contrary, what evidence there is points to the extra-parliamentary nature of government instability. Governments often continue in office for relatively long periods despite undergoing a series of defeats on their legislative programme; a prime example of this is the long-lasting Craxi government from 1983 to 1986. This suffered numerous defeats on its budget proposals from October 1985 to June 1986, but the government did not resign until the political conditions best suited the Prime Minister. Successive parliamentary defeats on major proposals obviously weaken a government, but they are not sufficient in themselves to cause a government resignation. While there are several instances of governments resigning after defeat on a legislative proposal in one of the Houses, there are none of governments being defeated when they attach a vote of confidence to a proposal and the issue comes to a vote. Such occasions tend to assume the otherwise misleading character of a confrontation between governing and opposition parties, and though none of the governing parties has a formal whipping system, informal pressure and residual party loyalty in the DC and the PSI have always proved sufficient to ensure government victory even at times of severest strain for intra-government relations.

The precise mechanisms and motivations which result in government resignation are too complex to be covered in detail here, but we give below a statistical summary of the main procedures. By mechanism here we mean the formal procedures which immediately preceded the provisional acceptance of the resignation of the government by the President of the Republic. This in itself is not an uncontentious categorisation, since on occasions (notoriously in 1987) presidents have accepted resignations only to withdraw their acceptance later in an effort to get the resigning government to face a vote of confidence in Parliament. Where this has happened we have taken the final provisional acceptance preceding the actual replacement of the government. Categorising the motivation for a government crisis is certainly contentious, and the categories used here

TABLE 1

MECHANISMS AND MOTIVATIONS OF GOVERNMENT CRISES

Mechanisms	Number of crises
1. Normal dissolution for elections	6
2. Ministers withdrawn from Cabinet by party	15
3. Defeat of government at initial vote of confidence	4
4. Defeat of government during ordinary business	4
5. Withdrawal of party support, without defeat in Parliament	10
6. Voluntary resignation of Prime Minister	9
Total	**48**

Motivations	
1. Normal election timetable	6
2. Inter-party dispute	17
3. Intra-party dispute	3
4. Both 2 and 3	12
5. Backbench revolt	5
6. Programmed resignation or expected defeat	5
Total	**48**

refer to the overt and quasi-official statements of senior party politicians rather than to the researcher's interpretation of the events.

The operation of the procedures and of the motivations must await further detailed explanation elsewhere. In summary, it can be argued that if government crises were predominantly intra-parliamentary in their causes and procedures, we would expect to see a preponderance of formal government defeats among the crisis mechanisms; in fact, these make up a relatively small proportion of cases (categories 3 and 4, eight cases altogether). If backbench ambition and indiscipline were the source of government instability, we would expect a preponderance of overt backbench revolt (category 5) among the motivations; but these constitute an even smaller proportion of cases (five out of the 48). What this simple descriptive statistical exercise suggests is that government crises are overwhelmingly occasioned by disputes between or within the governing parties; and that they are triggered mainly by informal mechanisms, such as declarations of withdrawal of support or declarations that ministers from the party or parties concerned will not support the decisions of the Council of Ministers and will not attend their meetings. The parties are normally loath to be seen to be using Parliament to turn governments out; the Craxi government in 1987 provides an extreme example, when after a lengthy and bitter crisis the President of the Republic asked the Prime Minister to seek a vote of confidence in Parliament, as a means of unblocking the institutional impasse. Rather than be impaled on the dilemma either of having deputies support a government the DC wanted to be rid of or of having to explain their withdrawal of support in a debate on a motion of confidence, the DC leadership declared that its ministers were formally withdrawn from the Cabinet.[9] The extra-parliamentary route had the same consequences that the parliamentary one would have, but in the political convention is preferred. Parliament – or rather, the full Assembly of the Chamber of Deputies – appears to be perceived as a public arena of confrontation. Its avoidance on such occasions tends to be justified on the grounds that its procedures compel the parties to adopt relatively fixed positions on matters of policy which will later make negotiation difficult. Rather than tie their hands in this way, so the logic goes, the parties prefer to use informal mechanisms which do not involve detailed declarations of positions.

This is not to say that Parliament has no legitimation function. The formal aspects of its role in ratifying the processes of government formation are dutifully observed by incoming governments. Very rarely the initial vote of confidence is a genuine hurdle for governments to overcome, but the party leaders seem to give overwhelming priority to avoiding surprise defeats, and such occasions are usually very predictable. When incoming minority governments are going to be defeated at this stage, the event has the appearance of being planned and programmed, its consequences anticipated.

The formal vote of confidence on the government's programme seems to be seen as a heavy blunt instrument, unsuited to the sophisticated codes and complicated manoeuvres of Italian party practice. It is also identified by the opposition parties as on occasion when the executive comes close to infringing the independence of Parliament and of parliamentarians; this is not only because of the public pressure attracted by the vote, but also because in accordance with the Constitution the voting has to be by roll-call, unlike most other votes which until the 1989 reform were secret. Similar considerations apply to the procedure by which a government may force Parliament to treat acceptance of a particular bill as an explicit vote of confidence. The practice of formally attaching confidence in the government on to a piece of ordinary legislation was certainly not unknown in previous legislatures, but its use has grown since 1983. The example was set by the first Craxi government, which showed great determination in pushing through controversial budgets by this means; despite its unpopularity, the mechanism found repeated use under the much more fragile governments which followed. It was used in particular by the Andreotti government to ensure the passage of a local government bill in January 1990 at a time of increasing dissent within the DC itself. Andreotti made himself doubly unpopular on this occasion, since attaching the vote of confidence to the measure compelled the governing parties' deputies to attend on a Friday, the day of the vote and a day when most would be safely back in their constituencies. No doubt in partial compensation (but also to encourage attendance), the government laid on military air transport to return the deputies home. In protest at the alleged misuse of constitutional procedures, all the opposition parties excluding only the neo-Fascist MSI deserted the Chamber and refused to participate in the vote. The episode is symptomatic of the increasingly conflictual relationship between government and Parliament, and of the impatience of government ministers at their incapacity to ensure the passage of the legislative programme. Governments therefore find themselves increasingly constrained (as they see it) to use the formal legitimation function in support of the practical demands of policy-making.

Governments' traditional diffidence in facing Parliament on formal votes of confidence might be interpreted to mean that Parliament is regarded as one of the solemn parts of the Constitution, not one of its efficient instruments. But the development of the instrumental vote of confidence, and the vigorous objections it provokes, indicate that parliamentary confidence is rather too powerful and final a weapon for frequent use. In a political system where the processes of government formation and dissolution are often lengthy and byzantine, Parliament applies too categorical a judgement. It is an instrument of last resort, not a household tool.

PARLIAMENT AND RECRUITMENT

The reservoir of ministerial talent in Italy is restricted by the combination of intense party-politicisation and exclusion of the second largest party from national governmental office. The rigorous control exercised by the political parties over appointments throughout the public sector follows a system known as *lottizzazione*, which means literally the sharing out of posts, usually in accordance with the relative voting strengths of the governing parties.[10] Ministers and Under-Secretaries have central functions in such appointments, and are therefore important not only for the usual reasons associated with policy implementation but also for the maintenance of party cohesion and organisational support. Far from diminishing in recent years in the wake of increasing government divisiveness, this party control of all public sector recruitment has strengthened its grip and has become one of the driving forces behind government policy and government crisis.

In view of the weakness of Parliament in other ways, it is perhaps mildly surprising that the process of ministerial recruitment in Italy is concentrated almost exclusively on Parliament. It is not unknown for non-party ministers to be appointed, usually described as 'technocrats'; it would be unusual for them not to develop a relatively strong party-political identification after taking office, and if they achieve any success at all this is likely to be translated into a parliamentary seat as soon as the election timetable allows. But genuine technocrat-ministers are in any case rare, and such that there are generally come from the para-state sector (particularly banking), not from the ranks of the senior civil service. For all serious purposes, the route to ministerial office runs through Parliament at some stage, and as we shall see, a long sojourn in Parliament is the best route of all.

For the purposes of a wider research project into the legislative process in the Chamber of Deputies, we carried out a survey of ministerial office-holding in the three legislatures beginning in 1972, 1976 and 1979. A detailed report on the results of this survey is not possible here, but some of the main findings can be summarised readily. They corroborate and amplify the results of other similar surveys.[11] There is in fact a relatively secure and well-trodden route into the ranks of junior ministers. Behind the façade of government instability, the recruitment procedures are well-established and follow a clear pattern. For all practical purposes, ministers and under-secretaries are recruited from among deputies and senators of the governing parties in accordance with selection procedures which reward longevity in Parliament, membership of the appropriate party faction, and personal vote support in the home constituency. There is a relatively high turnover of personnel in junior ministerial office, as a result of which many deputies of governing parties can expect to hold office as under-secretaries or ministers for at least a brief period at some stage in their parliamentary careers. About 40 per cent of all deputies who represented the DC or the PSI during this period had previously held office, or were ministers or under-secretaries at some time during these legislatures. For the smaller governing parties, not surprisingly, the proportion was even higher, with a peak of 59 per cent of Social Democrat deputies.

On the other hand, the ranks of senior ministers in the most influential ministries show a high degree of stability; the instability of governments masks stability of senior personnel. There is an identifiable ministerial élite, made up of a restricted group of politicians who have held office many times and over a long period. Up to 1983, 20 DC deputies and four Social Democrats had held office on ten or more occasions, and this includes four DC deputies whose offices numbered between 20 and 32 each. Apart from membership of one of two parties, this elite is distinguished mainly by its longevity. This is scarcely surprising, since even in the Italian system it takes a considerable time to build up a record of participation in more than 30 governments. The two deputies with this extraordinary career pattern are Giulio Andreotti and Emilio Colombo, both of whom were first elected in 1946. Twenty of the 24 'élite' ministers were under 40 years of age in their first legislature, and this applied also to over half of all deputies who had held ministerial office. The other characteristic of the 'élite' is that all have had preference votes in their constituencies which amount to over 40 per cent of the total list vote for the party in that constituency. Though we cannot give details here, similar considerations on a lesser scale also apply to the broader group of ministers. A result of this development of a restricted group of powerful ministers is that it is possible for the successful minister to build up a considerable if necessarily fragmented experience at Cabinet level. Though the data used here cover only the period from 1972 to 1983, they are consistent with the findings of earlier surveys, and there is no indication that this pattern, combining élite stability with a high level of junior ministerial turnover, is changing significantly. The increasing intractability of government crises since 1968 is related immediately to arguments over the position of Prime Minister and to factional disputes within the governing parties. The actual nomination of the majority of government ministers is secondary to generic agreement over the balance of power between the parties, measured in terms of the number and rank of ministries allocated.

The importance of Parliament in this function is not readily explained. Membership and seniority in Parliament are of significance not directly but rather as indicators of party influence, to an even greater extent than in other Western European systems. Parliament as such does not initiate or train in ministerial skills, and expertise in parliamentary business is not particularly relevant in the competitive intra-party career structures. On the contrary, vigorous participation in formal Parliament business is likely to preclude the kind of network-building which is required for junior members if they wish to ensure their re-election and to place themselves well in a strong faction. Election to Parliament is part of this process, and is more important for the informal access it gives to influential national figures than for the particular powers of the individual member. Election therefore is an indication of the local strength of a politician, and is a crucial first hurdle to a national career, but the important thing is to be in Parliament, not necessarily of Parliament.

PARLIAMENT AND POLICY

Finally, we have to consider Parliament's impact on the policy process. The formal powers of the legislature in law-making are comparatively strong. The two Chambers control their own timetable and agenda and can amend government proposals almost without restriction. There is considerable scope for backbenchers and for parliamentary party leaders to propose their own bills. The fourteen specialised permanent commissions which consider legislation have the power to pass certain categories of bills directly into law without further reference to the full Assembly. In practice, these powers are exercised in close consultation with government representatives. Usually the Under-Secretary to the Cabinet (in effect, the Prime Minister's factotum) has the job of overseeing relations with Parliament to maintain the flow of government business. Before 1971, parliamentary regulations which dated from the Liberal period had enabled the governing parties to exclude the opposition from influence over the organisation of parliamentary time, but amended regulations introduced in that year provided a more collegial system. Paradoxically, this was a response to the increasing difficulty governments were having in getting Parliament (including their own parties) to meet the requirements of the new planning systems which had been introduced by the centre-left governments of the period. The Communist opposition proved willing to use the procedures in the manner intended, and often formed part of unofficial majorities on commissions to help agreed legislation through. The weakness of government drafting, the lack of co-ordination between ministers and the habitual absenteeism of some government deputies make such co-operation essential; it had in fact been a characteristic of much of the legislation of the 1960s, and the 1971 regulations formalised and enhanced it. Problems in parliamentary organisation began to occur after 1976 with the emergence of parties much less committed to making Parliament work – in particular, the middle-class protest movements having a common home in the Radical Party. The regulations were modified on a variety of occasions in the 1980s to curtail the scope for filibustering, and to give majorities more effective control over the timetable. Finally, in 1989, the provision for secret voting on request for most bills was abolished as part of an effort to enforce greater discipline on the governing parties in Parliament.

The Italian Parliament undoubtedly has considerable influence over the detail of policy. This should not be seen as an assertion of parliamentary might over an embattled executive. It rather reflects characteristics of the legislative process which are particular to Italy, and it should not be imagined that Parliament's power in this area can be much extended. Parliament's capacity to change government legislation is in direct proportion to the weakness of the government's policy-making procedures. Governments often produce legislative proposals in response to multiple private member bills from the parties in Parliament, and what emerges as government policy therefore may reflect very strongly a consensus on one of the permanent commissions in Parliament which first stimulated action on the subject. Where this is not so, in other words when the government tables proposals independently of Parliament, the permanent commissions have considerable time and opportunity to make amendments. Deputies belonging to the governing parties seem as willing to amend legislation as are the opposition, and indeed the distinction between government and opposition has little meaning for the majority of the permanent commissions when they are dealing with bills which they can pass directly into law. If they have little scope for this, if government tries to impose its own text in detail either in commission or in the Assembly, the parliamentary parties are quick to complain at the government's alleged lack of respect for parliamentary autonomy. As we have seen, parliamentary regulations (even despite recent amendments) allow and even encourage all the major parties in Parliament to come to agreements over the way Parliament works. It must be emphasised that this is possible at least partly because much of the activity of Parliament goes on far removed from publicity, in the specialised commissions of a variety of sorts whose labours are rarely published in any form accessible to the wider public. When there is publicity, when agreement has not proved possible in private and debates come to the full Assembly of the Chamber of Deputies, then the lines of confrontation re-emerge as governing parties feel the need to maintain in public the exclusion of non-governing parties which their private negotiations repeatedly deny. This disparity between the consensual day-to-day functioning of Parliament and the formal public conflict between government and opposition has become increasingly obvious as internal government divisions have increased and as individual government ministers have tried to enforce reforms on reluctant governing parties.

It is possible for Parliament to function in this way partly because of the preponderance of relatively minor legislation taking up the bulk of parliamentary legislative time. As Table 2 indicates, the Italian Parliament passes very large numbers of laws in every legislature, but the majority

TABLE 2

LEGISLATIVE OUTPUT, CHAMBER OF DEPUTIES, 1948–1987

	LEGISLATURES								
	1	2	3	4	5	6	7	8	9
Government bills proposed	1168	782	758	805	494	627	797	975	754
Other bills proposed	1028	1920	2964	3333	3063	3205	2129	3344	3618
Government bills passed in Assembly	500	433	421	398	189	324	337	384	326
Other bills passed in Assembly	87	63	63	47	16	42	84	42	48
Government bills passed in Commission	1496	1006	919	861	663	617	307	477	424
Other bills passed in Commission	344	592	639	743	480	493	145	369	337
Decree Laws presented	29	60	30	94	69	124	167	477	424

Source: *Le legislature repubblicane nelle statistiche parlamentari*, and *Resoconti Sommari delle Legislature VII, VIII, e IX* (Rome: Servizio documentazione e statistiche parlamentari, Camera dei Deputati, various years)

Note: this refers only to the Chamber of Deputies. It therefore ignores the considerable (though smaller) volume of legislation first presented in the Senate. Hence also total bills passed in any legislature includes some bills first presented in the Senate.

Legislatures: 1 – 1948–53
2 – 1953–58
3 – 1958–63
4 – 1963–68
5 – 1968–72
6 – 1972–76
7 – 1976–79
8 – 1979–83
9 – 1983–87

of these could not be described as complex and wide-ranging laws; on the contrary, the typical law at least in terms of numbers passed is usually described as 'little law' (*leggine*), far removed from the original constitutional ideal of framework laws, or from the planning laws envisaged by the reforms of 1971. *Leggine* are brief pieces of legislation, usually having a very restricted scope and concerned with public sector employment or with social security, which despite their narrowness may have a significant patronage implication for specific groups of deputies.

Governments traditionally complain about the irresponsibility of Parliament and about the difficulty of getting it to co-operate with lengthy bills or with legislation which needs urgent implementation. A degree of scepticism may be in order about these complaints, as few recent governments have shown themselves masters of organisation of their own requirements. But whether it is government or Parliament which is responsible, there is no doubt that governments have increasingly had recourse to the instrument of decree-laws to ensure the speedy passage of their legislation in a form acceptable to them (see Table 2, last category). Decree-laws have the advantage for the government that they are provisional measures which can go into effect immediately. Article 77 of the Constitution states that the procedure may be used only in times of emergency and necessity. The decree-law must be presented to Parliament on the day of publication, and Parliament has to consider it within five days. The degree of urgency with which the constitution views this procedure is indicated by the provision that Parliament must reconvene to consider a decree-law even if it has been dissolved. If not converted into law within 60 days, the decree loses all effect and lapses. As Table 2 indicates, governments have had increasing recourse to this procedure since 1972 (sixth legislature), to the extent that it has become an alternative procedure, a tactical expedient rather than an emergency instrument. In response to this development, Parliament has become increasingly unwilling to give the decree-law a privileged hearing, and is prone to respond by demanding the right to give the decree-law detailed consideration at a pace of its own choosing. The use of the decree-law ensures that a government proposal gets on to the agenda immediately, and it enlists the interest and support of pressure groups favourably affected, thereby putting more pressure on Parliament. On occasions, it may be a substitute for ordinary law, when a government repeatedly re-issues a decree-law every 60 days until agreement is finally reached with Parliament or until the need passes. The outstanding example of this was in the winter of 1979 when the government reissued three times a decree-law dealing with restrictions on energy consumption; it finally passed into law eight months after its original publication. The procedure has also been used to introduce temporary macro-economic measures such as credit and exchange-rate controls.

CONCLUSION

The role of Parliament in the Italian political system is unusual among Western European legislatures. It might be summarised by saying that its strongest weapon, the vote of confidence, is hardly used at all against government, while where government might be expected to be strong, in the policy process, Parliament finds itself actually able to exert considerable influence. Parliament is widely blamed for government instability and for failures in policy, and no doubt it has some responsibility to bear. It has a degree of practical control over policy-making which some might envy, but this falls to it rather because of government weakness than as a result of its own resources. If we consider the ways in which government crises occur, it can hardly be argued to have a major role either in government crisis or in government formation; in both of these processes it is for the most part a helpless bystander, at the mercy, like the rest of the institutions, of increasingly fractious governing parties. In the period since 1968, government crises have become progressively more difficult to resolve, and have put strain particularly on the relationship between the Head of State and the political parties. Parliament has not been a leading actor in this conflict, though one or other of the protagonists has occasionally tried to stand as a defender of parliamentary rights.

Other signs of conflict and strain are also visible. Since 1972, governments have had increasing recource to decree-laws, with the apparent aim of imposing their own calendars on Parliament. The recurrence of economic crises in the 1970s provides some explanation for this, in so far as it may require government to take immediate remedial action in public spending, in credit or exchange-rate regulations. Such measures have not generally found Parliament unwilling to co-operate, but the wider use of decree-laws as a substitute for a properly organised policy programme finds Parliament unsympathetic and has engendered mistrust. This is not a conventional dispute between government and opposition, it is a long-running and intense conflict between institutions, in which the opposition parties often find themselves arguing on the same side as backbench deputies from the governing parties. The more recent increase in the use of votes of confidence to push legislation through constitutes a further escalation of the conflict, as governments use the threat of resignation (presumably unwelcome in timing) over their own supporters in Parliament. Another aspect of this, which there has not been space to deal with here, is the increasing use of popular referenda. Initially these were promoted by pressure groups, but now are being used by the opposition parties in an attempt to wrest some influence away from the governing parties, and even by the smaller governing parties (including the PSI) to score against the DC.

Underlying these difficulties lies the historic problem of the role of parties in the Italian political system. Political parties dominate all aspects of policy-making, and the major parties have very stable and loyal electorates. But the overall development of the party system has allowed the distribution of political power to be determined by increasingly arbitrary means, and has provided no mechanism for penalising governments whose performance is weak or authoritarian. The permanence of one party or group of parties in office might be an effective way of governing if the structures with which they worked were reliable and if Parliament was able to provide a constructive independent forum for approval of legislation. But neither of these holds true: public administration is not able fully to handle the pace and detail of modern legislative programmes, and Parliament cannot provide an adequate substitute for the failings of the executive. Thus Italy has neither alternation in government nor cohesive efficient coalition government. This may seem harsh; of course it is true that Italy has had major successes in the post-war period, particularly in economic and social development, and these can be attributed in part to government policy – because of it, not in spite of it, as some have argued. This can only leave one to surmise about what Italy could have achieved had its party-political development matched its development in other fields.

NOTES

The author wishes to thank the Nuffield Foundation for its support for the research at the Chamber of Deputies in 1986 on which this study is based.

1. G. Di Palma, *Surviving Without Governing – The Italian Parties in Parliament* (Berkeley: University of California Press, 1977); Andrea Manzella, *Il Parlamento* (Bologna: Il Mulino, 1977); but see also the series edited by A. Predieri, *Il Processo Legislativo nel Parlamento Italiano* (Milan: Giuffre, 1974 onwards) on which Di Palma is partly based.
2. On the development of constitutional debate in the Constituent Assembly, see E. Cheli, *Costituzione e sviluppo delle istituzioni in Italia* (Bologna: Il Mulino, 1978)
3. See D. Sassoon, 'Togliatti e la Centralita del Parlamento', *Critica Marxista*, Vol.23, No.1 (1985), pp.35–60.
4. An English translation of the constitution can be found in *The Constitution of the Republic of Italy – Rules of the Chamber of Deputies and of the Senate of the Republic* (Rome: Research Services of the Chamber of Deputies and of the Senate, 1979).
5. P. Furlong, 'The Constitutional Court in Italian Politics', *West European Politics*, Vol.11, No.3 (July, 1988), pp.7–23.
6. Historical data on the series are compiled from *I Programmi dei Governi Repubblicani dal 1948 al 1978*, (Rome: Centro Romano Editoriale, 1978), and from *Resoconti Sommari* (Rome: Camera dei Deputati, various years).
7. See P. Furlong, 'Political Underdevelopment and Economic Recession in Italy', in A. Cox (ed.), *Politics Policy and the European Recession* (London: Macmillan, 1982).
8. This is argued at some length in G. Miglio (ed.), *Verso Una Nuova Costituzione* (Milan: Giuffre, 1983, 2 vols.). See also G. Miglio, 'Onorevole o Ministro', *Il Sole–24 Ore*, 11 Feb. 1986, p.4, on Craxi's difficulties with the Budget.
9. A full description of the crisis may be found in E. Balboni, 'Who governs? The Crisis of the Craxi Government and the Role of the President of the Republic', pp.11–24, in P. Corbetta and R. Leonardi (eds.), *Italian Politics, A Review*, Vol.3 (London: Pinter Press, 1989).
10. F. Cazzola (ed.), *Anatomia del Potere DC – Enti pubblici e 'centralita democristiana'* (Bari: De Donato, 1979); G. Tamburrano, *L'Iceberg Democristiano – Il potere in Italia oggi e domani* (Milan: Sugarco, 1975); R. Orfei, *L'Occupazione del Potere – I Democristiani '45–'75* (Milan: Longanesi, 1976).
11. J. Meynaud, *Rapport sur la Classe Dirigeante Italienne* (Lausanne: Etudes de Science Politique, 1964); S. Somogyi *et al.*, *Il Parlamento Italiano 1946–1963* (Naples: Edizioni Scientifiche Italiane, 1963); M. Calise and R. Mannheimer, *Governanti in Italia – Un trentennio repubblicano 1946–1976* (Bologna: Il Mulino, 1982); M. Cotta, *Classe Politica e Parlamento in Italia* (Bologna: Il Mulino, 1979).

The West German Bundestag after 40 Years: The Role of Parliament in a 'Party Democracy'

Thomas Saalfeld

The Chancellor's position became so strong that his opponents and supporters alike complained about his authoritarian style of leadership. Indeed, cabinet stability has been bought at a high price: [. . .] While avoiding the Scylla of government instability, the Bonn regime fell into the Charybdis of a powerless parliament. Essentially, the regime is 'demo-authoritarian'. [. . .] Apart from the general elections every four years, there is no effective means to supervise the government.[1]

Karl Loewenstein's statement was made under the impression of Konrad Adenauer's strong leadership as the first West German Federal Chancellor (1949–63). His dominant position in the Cabinet and the government's domination of the Bundestag were frequently interpreted as another indication of the universal 'trend to prime-ministerial, presidential or chancellor government' in all major liberal democracies.[2] Apart from Adenauer's personal abilities as a political leader, structural factors have contributed to a strengthening of the Chancellor's position in the Bundestag. The most important constitutional pillars of chancellor democracy are the incumbent's powers to make ministerial appointments, to organise the executive branch, that is, to establish and change the number and jurisdiction of the federal departments, and to formulate guidelines of government policy (*Richtlinienkompetenz*). The Bundestag can oust a government only on the basis of a 'constructive vote of no confidence' against the Chancellor, that is, a majority must not only be willing to depose the Chancellor and his Cabinet but also must have agreed on an alternative candidate.[3] Most legislative proposals are prepared by the government or the majority parties, and since the mid-1950s between three-quarters and four-fifths of the bills passed in each Bundestag were government bills.[4] Because of stable coalitions and cohesive party voting, important government proposals are hardly ever defeated.

In addition, the relationship between the Bundestag and the executive branch of government has been influenced by 'environmental factors'. These factors did not necessarily strengthen the Chancellor within the executive branch, but they weakened Parliament's ability to scrutinise government activities. The most important external challenges to the Bundestag's role as a check on the executive were the rapid growth of government responsibilities, the tendency among governments, especially in the face of economic recessions in the 1960s and early 1970s, to resort to neo-corporatist forms of decision-making and the increasing complexity of co-ordination and bargaining processes between the Bonn government and its counterparts at the *Länder* level and in the European Communities. Although the parliamentarisation of West Germany's political system and the growth of the modern welfare state after 1949 have expanded the legislature's influence to a scope unprecedented in German history, the increasing intricacy of policy decisions – complex inter-governmental decision-making structures at the national, sub-national and supra-national level and the inherent complexity of new policy areas – has made parliamentary scrutiny more difficult. In spite of a comprehensive system of departmental committees, the 519 members of the Bundestag cannot rival the expertise and available man-hours of the federal and *Länder* bureaucracies. This gap in expertise, resources and time reduces the capability, at least of opposition members, to scrutinise government activities effectively.

This article attempts to assess the Bundestag's role in West German politics with particular reference to the changes affecting executive–legislative relations in the last two decades. Loewenstein's characterisation of the Bundestag as a 'powerless parliament' will be tested against empirical evidence. The focus will be on changes in parliamentary behaviour rather than constitutional conditions. The basic analytical dimensions that will be used were developed by Michael Mezey. Mezey has placed the Bundestag – together with most other European parliamentary democracies – into the category of 'reactive legislatures', that is, among those Parliaments characterised by modest policy-making power and relatively strong public support. The Bundestag's role in the political process is, indeed, reactive rather than initiative. Its power depends on the constraints it is capable of placing on the policy-related activities of the executive, rather than its independent policy-making capacity. According to Mezey's definition,

> a constraint is a limitation that the legislature can place upon the executive branch of government that would not make it – the legislature – directly vulnerable to dissolution, proroguing, or closure. A constraint restricts the action of the executive branch and prevents it from making policy unilaterally. Legislatures will be salient in the policy-making process to the extent that their presence and prerogatives act as a constraint on the executive. If the constraints at the disposal of the legislature are weak, then the institution will be a correspondingly weak element in the policy-making process. The existence of substantive constraints brings with it a salient policy-making role.[5]

But its policy-making role is not the only source of a Parliament's strength. The example of the Weimar *Reichstag* confirms Mezey's assumption that even a Parliament with strong formal policy-making powers may still be vulnerable, because it lacks political support. Thus we have to assess both the Bundestag's ability to constrain the government's activities and the degree of support accruing to it.

POLICY-MAKING

Anthony King has pointed out that 'it is usually highly misleading to speak of "executive–legislative relations" *tout court* and that, if we wish to understand the phenomena subsumed under this general heading, we need to identify and consider separately a number of quite distinct relationships'.[6] In the case of the West German Bundestag, he argues, four principal dimensions of executive–legislative relations must be studied: first, the bargaining processes between those parties forming a government coalition ('inter-party mode'); secondly, the behaviour of opposition parties ('opposition mode'); thirdly, the relationships between the government and its backbenchers ('intra-party mode'); and finally the co-operation between majority and minority parties, especially in parliamentary committees ('cross-party mode').

Coalition government

The Chancellor and his Cabinet are usually members of Parliament. The head of government is formally elected by the Bundestag. In office, the government's stability and political power depend on the solidity of government coalitions and the solidarity within the parliamentary majority parties. Unlike the experiences of the Weimar Republic and some contemporary multi-party systems, government coalitions in the German Federal Republic have proved to be stable. Only one of the three premature resignations of chancellors can be primarily ascribed to a coalition crisis. The erosion of Erhard's power (1966) was accompanied by a coalition crisis, but the basic problem was that he was no longer in command of his own party, the Christian Democratic and Christian Social Unions (CDU/CSU). Brandt was toppled in 1974 owing to internal tensions between leading politicians in the Social Democratic Party (SPD), while the Free Democratic Party's (FDP) leadership had continued to support his chancellorship. Only Schmidt had to resign in 1982, because the FDP had decided to discontinue the Social–Liberal coalition and enter a coalition with the CDU/CSU.[7]

The development of coalition patterns can only be sketched very briefly here. Between 1949 and 1961 the prevailing pattern was coalitions between the CDU/CSU as the dominant partner and one or more minor parties such as the FDP, the German Party (DP), or the All-German Bloc (GB/BHE).[8] In the period of 1953–61 these coalitions were oversized in terms of William Riker's minimum size criterion.[9] Even when the CDU/CSU commanded a narrow overall majority of seats in the 1957–61 Bundestag, Adenauer preferred to continue his coalition with the DP. Only for a short period from July 1960 to September 1961 was there a one-party government formed by the CDU/CSU. The intention to integrate the small bourgeois parties, the need to secure a broad majority for the passage of important amendments of the Basic Law between 1949 and 1957 and the electoral pact with the DP in parts of northern Germany appear to be Adenauer's most important motives. However, the concentration of the German party system between 1949 and 1961 made the coalitions of the Adenauer period untypical. After 1961 coalition formation was predominantly a bargaining process among CDU/CSU, SPD and FDP. Coalition-building has become a matter of winning over the FDP as a pivotal party. The 'grand coalition' of 1966–69 appears only as an interlude. Formal coalition theory offers two possible explanations for the fact that coalitions of one of the big parties with the smaller FDP have prevailed. The first refers to pay-offs in terms of portfolios which will be larger under the conditions of a minimal winning coalition. The second explanation deals with the policy distances between the parties.

> Under the assumption of a single left-right policy continuum on which the FDP as the *centre party* is located somewhere between the CDU/CSU on the right and the SPD on the left, a grand coalition does not fulfil the criterion of a *minimum-connected winning coalition* which predicts that coalitions will be formed between ideologically adjacent parties.[10]

The SPD–FDP (1969–82) and CDU/CSU–FDP coalitions (1982-) ex-hibited a higher degree of durability than the pre-1961 coalitions. This may be a result of the fact that the grave internal tensions following the FDP's changes of coalition partners in 1969 and 1982, and the danger of being stigmatised as a 'commuter party' made its leadership increasingly reluctant to dare such a step.[11]

Especially after 1961 the need to form and maintain a stable government coalition seems to be one of the most important constraints acting upon the Chancellor. Between 1953 and 1961, the CDU/CSU had dominated its small coalition partners. Adenauer enjoyed considerable manoeuvring room within the coalition; on the one hand he was able to exploit internal tensions within the smaller coalition parties to influence such parties' decisions, while on the other hand he used these parties to increase his own independence from CDU/CSU pressure in social and economic policies, where his attitudes were closer to those of the FDP and DP than to the policies favoured by the trade-union wing of the CDU/CSU. The general elections of 1961 were a watershed, for the dominance of Adenauer's 'chancellor democracy' came to an end and a period of 'coalition democracy' began. In the 1961 general election the CDU/CSU suffered heavy losses and the FDP returned to the role of a pivotal coalition partner. The number of parliamentary parties was reduced to three, and the shift of the oppositional SPD towards the political centre – symbolised by the Godesberg programme of 1959 – made coalitions with the Social Democrats feasible for the first time after 1949. The FDP's improved position was reflected in the process of coalition bargaining in 1961 which culminated in the CDU/CSU's concession that Adenauer would step down after two more years in office. From 1961 onwards both major parties – CDU/CSU and SPD – have attempted to stabilise their respective coalitions with the FDP on a long-term basis, mainly by granting a relatively high share of Cabinet seats and influence to the latter. Since 1961 no chancellor has been able to dominate his coalition partners in the manner Adenauer did between 1953 and 1961. All coalitions after 1961 have been characterised by the individual coalition parties' relatively high degree of autonomy. Adenauer's successors were no longer able to manipulate the internal conflicts of their respective coalition partners.

To sum up, coalition government has produced workable parliamentary majorities throughout the history of the Federal Republic. The need to maintain a coalition appears to be one of the major parliamentary constraints the Chancellor has to cope with. After 1961, the concentration of the party system has reduced coalition options and made the Chancellor even more dependent on a single coalition partner. The role of the parliamentary majority parties in the *formative* stages of coalition-building appears to be limited. Most important policy decisions and the distribution of ministerial portfolios between the coalition partners are agreed upon between the lifetimes of two Parliaments and are usually dominated by the leaders of extra-parliamentary party organisations. Once a coalition has been formed, its *steering* seems to involve considerably more influence of the parliamentary majority parties' leaderships. The experience of the 'grand coalition' has demonstrated that the Cabinet is unsuited to steer a coalition. Therefore, since 1969 governments have resorted to informal 'coalition talks' (*Koalitionsgespräche*). The participants in these negotiations may vary according to the nature and salience of the matters involved, but they usually consist of representatives of the Chancellor's office, the relevant ministries and the parliamentary majority parties. Within these bodies, the views of the parliamentary groups' leaders and experts carry considerable weight.

The necessity to maintain coalitions by inter-party compromises may, however, result in grave difficulties for the individual government parties to maintain their internal cohesion. This directs our attention to King's 'intra-party mode'.

Cabinet and backbenchers

Party solidarity is primarily expressed by a high degree of voting cohesion in parliamentary divisions. If the government does not command a solid majority of votes in Parliament, it will lose at least some of its capacity for action and eventually might be forced to resign. Willy Brandt's loss of authority within the SPD parliamentary party in 1972–74, his conflicts with the party's parliamentary chairman, Herbert Wehner, and Brandt's eventual resignation in 1974 serve as an example of the Chancellor's dependence on the support of his parliamentary group.

The degree of party solidarity in a Parliament is usually assessed by analysing the parties' voting cohesion in roll calls. Unfortunately, the Bundestag's official report records the voting behaviour of MPs only in a fraction of divisions. In most cases the House votes by raising of hands or by having the members stand. In these instances official records merely contain the statement 'passed', 'defeated' or a vague commentary such as 'passed with a few abstentions'. Nevertheless, in most important and controversial matters roll calls (*namentliche Abstimmungen*) are held, and the voting behaviour of every participating MP is recorded.[12] The data presented in Table 1 measure the voting cohesion in roll calls of all parties that have formed a parliamentary group for at least one Bundestag between 1949 and 1987. For this purpose the Rice index of cohesion has been calculated on the basis of 715 roll calls between 1949 and 1987.[13] The values of this index are printed in the first row of each cell. It is calculated as the 'proportion of the group comprising the group majority on a roll call *minus* the proportion comprising the group minority. If the group divides evenly, with no majority position, the index is 50/50, or 0. If all members of the group vote the same way, the index is 100/0, or 100'.[14] This index's basic deficiency as regards the West German Parliament is that it does not account for the possibility that some absences must be considered as abstentions, that is, as expressions of internal dissent.[15] Therefore, the Rice index of cohesion has been weighted, in a second step, by an index of participation, measuring the average proportion of unexcused absences.[16] The respective values are printed in the second row of each cell. In the third row, the number of dissenting votes for the 'median member of Parliament' is printed. The last column gives the number of government defeats in 'major divisions'.[17]

A first glance at Table 1 confirms the traditional assumption that voting cohesion in the Bundestag has been relatively high in comparison with the United States Congress, but hardly extraordinary if compared with other parliamentary systems such as the French National Assembly or the British House of Commons. Between 1949 and 1987 none of the three major parties had a Rice index below 0.81. If weighted by the participation rate, there was only one instance when the cohesion index for a party fell below 0.70 (0.68 for the FDP in the 1961–65 Bundestag). In spite of considerable variations from one Parliament to another, the period 1969–87 exhibits a clear tendency towards increased voting cohesion in the CDU/CSU and FDP, whether or not we control for the effects of absences. This impression is confirmed, if the number of dissenting votes cast by the 'median' CDU/CSU and FDP member are accounted for. In the periods of 1949–53 and 1957–61 the 'median' CDU/CSU and FDP member usually cast one or more dissenting votes per Parliament. After 1976 this value was reduced to nil in the CDU/CSU, while in the FDP the median member has only once in the period of 1966–87 surpassed a value of nil. The 1969–72 Parliament marks a turning point in this respect. As regards the CDU/CSU, the increase in voting cohesion since 1969 has reflected the party's efforts to return to power as quickly as possible by a reorganisation of its parliamentary working and the presentation of a coherent alternative to the 'Social-Liberal Coalition'.[18] The FDP's internal cohesion grew after a series of defections of prominent conservative party members to the CDU/CSU. On the one hand the defections reduced the scope for internal conflict, on the other hand they narrowed the government's majority to a degree that made a high level of voting cohesion necessary. The SPD has maintained its high degree of voting cohesion, which is often regarded as typical for Socialist and Social Democratic parties, until 1983. Only once, under the exceptional circumstances of the 'grand coalition' (1966–69), did the Rice index drop below 0.95. The 1983–87 Parliament witnessed an increase in dissension which, however, is only reflected by our data when the Rice index is weighted by the participation rate. The degree to which the significant increase of absences in roll calls reflects intra-party dissension

TABLE 1

VOTING COHESION AND GOVERNMENT DEFEATS
IN THE BUNDESTAG (1949–87)

Parliament	Number of Roll Calls[e]	Measures of Cohesion: 1. Rice index of cohesion 2. Weighted index of cohesion 3. Dissenting votes cast by 'median' MP						Number of Govt. Defeats in Major Divisions[f]
		CDU/CSU	SPD	FDP	DP	GB/BHE	Green party	
1949–53	135	0.88	1.00	0.86	0.84	–	–	2
		0.84	0.98	0.80	0.79	–	–	
		4	0	4	2	–	–	
1953–57	169	0.91	0.99	0.81	0.81	0.84	–	5
		0.86	0.97	0.75	0.70	0.81	–	
		3	0	5.5	2	6	–	
1957–61	46	0.94	1.00	0.95	–	–	–	2
		0.81	0.93	0.78	–	–	–	
		0	0	0	–	–	–	
1961–65	37	0.90	0.99	0.86	–	–	–	1
		0.76	0.91	0.68	–	–	–	
		1	0	1	–	–	–	
1965–66[a]	1	–[g]	–	–	–	–	–	0
		–	–	–	–	–	–	
		–	–	–	–	–	–	
1966–69[b]	23	0.88	0.93	0.98	–	–	–	1
		0.74	0.85	0.80	–	–	–	
		1	0	0	–	–	–	
1969–72	38	0.99	1.00	0.98	–	–	–	1
		0.95	0.98	0.93	–	–	–	
		0	0	0	–	–	–	
1972–76	51	0.93	0.98	0.99	–	–	–	0
		0.84	0.94	0.88	–	–	–	
		1	0	0	–	–	–	
1976–80	59	0.98	0.99	0.95	–	–	–	1
		0.94	0.97	0.91	–	–	–	
		0	0	1	–	–	–	
1980–82[c]	21	0.99	0.99	0.99	–	–	–	0
		0.97	0.98	0.97	–	–	–	
		0	0	0	–	–	–	
1982–83[d]	5	1.00	1.00	0.88	–	–	–	0
		0.98	0.98	0.80	–	–	–	
		0	0	0	–	–	–	
1983–87	132	1.00	0.97	0.98	–	–	0.93	0
		0.90	0.83	0.84	–	–	0.80	
		0	0	0	–	–	1	

Sources: The data on roll-call votes were calculated from Deutscher Bundestag, *Steno-graphischer Bericht* (Bonn: Deutscher Bundestag, 1949–87). The numbers of major Government defeats were extracted from Peter Schindler, *Datenhandbuch zur Geschichte des Deutschen Bundestages 1949 bis 1982* (Bonn: Deutscher Bundestag, 1983), pp. 779–96 and *Datenhandbuch zur Geschichte des Deutschen Bundestages 1980 bis 1987* (Baden-Baden: Nomos, 1988), pp. 702–11.

Notes:

a   Period 20 October 1965–28 October 1966 (CDU/CSU–FDP coalition under Chancellor Ludwig Erhard) and 29 October 1966–30 November 1966 (CDU/CSU minority government under Erhard).

b   Period 1 December 1966–20 October 1969 (CDU/CSU–SPD coalition under Chancellor Kurt Georg Kiesinger).

c   Period 5 November 1980–1 October 1982 (SPD–FDP coalition under Chancellor Helmut Schmidt).

d   Period 3 October 1982–29 March 1983 (CDU/CSU–FDP coalition under Chancellor Helmut Kohl).

e   In the 1972–76 Parliament one roll call was annulled by the Bundestag President because of lack of presence of MPs in the House. This vote was excluded. In the 1983–87 Parliament the 209 amendments on the Motorways Building Bill tabled by the Green Party were also excluded.

f   According to Schindler's definition (1983, p. 779), major divisions are those on bills in the second and third reading, on the budget, on motions of high political salience and on secret ballots.

g   Indices of cohesion were not calculated for one single vote.

is not entirely clear and needs further research. A more detailed analysis of the variations of voting cohesion and possible causal explanations will be presented elsewhere.[19] For our present purpose it is sufficient to notice that the parliamentary parties in the Bundestag have, through a high degree of voting cohesion, largely contributed to the overall stability of the government system. This is indicated by the remarkably low number of government defeats on important bills and motions (Table 1).

    In recent years, however, a significant minority of members under the leadership of an FDP deputy, Hildegard Hamm-Brücher, have argued that the maintenance of stability has been achieved at the expense of individual MPs' powers to scrutinise and influence government policy. Mrs Hamm-Brücher's initiative for parliamentary reform is supported by more than 180 members from all Bundestag parties. The broad support of her efforts seems to confirm the assumption that party pressure on individual MPs has increased. None the less, it would be misleading to explain the high level of voting cohesion in the CDU/CSU and FDP as having been caused solely by the increased pressure exerted by the parliamentary party leadership. At least in part it must be ascribed to careful party management. Nevil Johnson has stressed the 'internal pluralism of the German parties, even though it is combined with relatively tough discipline and party solidarity when it comes to voting in the Bundestag'.[20] Socio-economic and regional intra-party conflicts of interest are highly institutionalised within the parliamentary groups. Powerful internal factions are less likely to give in to government pressure than individual MPs. Thus, the existence of factions usually necessitates bargaining.[21] The highly differentiated organisation and working of parliamentary parties also serves to prevent a total domination of intra-party decision-making by the Cabinet. If a party is in government, the influential position of the parliamentary group leader is traditionally incompatible with formal Cabinet membership, and the parliamentary parties have considerable financial resources at their disposal. Their working groups (*Arbeitskreise*) exert significant influence on the formulation of policies. 'As a result of these factors there is a marked tendency to see policymaking as necessitating, among other things, intra-party bargaining', rather than imposing the will of the parliamentary parties' leaderships.[22] Many government proposals meet with strong resistance from the majority's backbenches. The high degree of voting cohesion exhibited by the parliamentary groups since 1969 has not only been achieved under pressure; conflicts within the government majority are settled beforehand in intra-party consultations and negotiations between coalition partners. These bargaining processes usually take place in private. They are often difficult to nail down empirically. None the less, case-studies have demonstrated that the government is occasionally forced to modify its proposals significantly.[23]

While constraints imposed on the government from within the governing parties largely determine a Parliament's strength, they usually do not ensure democratic accountability. The concessions made by Cabinet ministers in private consultations with government backbenchers are no substitute for public scrutiny. The basic check on any democratic government remains the next general election. The government is ultimately responsible to the electorate whose choice depends on information about the government's record, and on alternatives to the government's policies and personnel. Here the opposition has to play its role. While it does not usually have the power to topple a government or to dictate its own policy proposals, it is able to subject the government to public criticism. The extent to which the parliamentary opposition is willing and able to criticise the government in a kind of a continuous election campaign, will have considerable influence on Parliament's ability to link government and electorate. Even though the opposition's direct influence on policy-making is limited, it may contribute to the fulfilment of important parliamentary functions such as tension release and interest articulation, if it sets its priority on electoral competition for office rather than on the 'exercise of influence within the halls of government'.[24]

Government and Opposition

In Robert A. Dahl's terminology, relationships between government on the one hand and the major opposition parties on the other have been 'preponderantly co-operative'. The traditional hostility towards party conflict among both German élites and voters, the model of 'co-operative federalism' and the comprehensive nature of the Basic Law in combination with the system of judicial review 'serve to narrow the scope for political conflict in the Federal Republic' and favour consensual policy-making.[25] Economic and political factors have also contributed to co-operation between government and opposition. The expansion and working of the welfare state are believed to have moderated political conflict and diminished the scope for opposition in general.[26] The 'moderate pluralism' (Sartori) of West Germany's party system between 1957 and 1983 seems to have ensured that inter-party competition takes place in the political centre rather than on the extremes.[27] The need to form a coalition with the FDP provided strong incentives for political centrism on the part of the two major parties. The advent of the Green Party in 1983 has not basically changed this pattern. As the Greens draw most of their electoral support from former Social Democratic voters, the latter still have to win over one of the bourgeois parties if they want to return to the government benches. Thus, the incentives for moderation are still considerable. At present, the possible changes in case of a major destabilisation of the CDU/CSU by the right-wing Republikaner remain a matter of speculation.

The variables enumerated above have favoured a co-operative style of opposition activity, where the minority prefers to influence decision-making in the private atmosphere of parliamentary committees, inter-governmental consultative bodies or the mediation committee of Bundestag and Bundesrat (Vermittlungsausschuß) rather than challenging the government in public. Analyses of the legislative process have demonstrated the considerable degree of consensualism between government and opposition parties in law-making. Nevertheless, parliamentary opposition has not been 'vanishing' as Kirchheimer predicted in the 1960s.[28] The data presented in Table 2 point to the contrary, that is, to a relative decline of consensual legislation since 1972. While in the Bundestag of 1972–76 more than 70 per cent of all acts were passed unanimously in the third reading, this percentage steadily declined to about 50 per cent by 1983. A distinction between more important policy bills and those of minor political importance[29] shows that unanimous voting on important bills has always been lower than on bills of minor importance. Nevertheless, the overall decline of consensual law-making is reflected in Table 2, even if one makes adjustments for the relative importance of the matters voted upon. The Parliament of 1983–87 has witnessed an extremely low level of consensualism (15.6 per cent of all acts were passed unanimously in the third reading), a level which is even below the percentage of the first Bundestag (23.4 per cent) with a high number of opposition parties and its exceptionally adversarial style. This extraordinary development in the 1983–87 Bundestag seems to be largely a result of the Green Party's activity.

The opposition's decisive weapon is not to change government legislation, but its capability to scrutinise and criticise its activities or inactivity in public. As Steven Lukes has pointed out, political power is not confined to decision-making or non-decision-making. By and large, these powers rest with the government. Power is also exercised by a political actor, if he controls the agenda of politics.[30] It is an essential prerequisite of democratic accountability that the government is not allowed to monopolise the political agenda and keep potentially inconvenient issues out of politics. In this context, the parliamentary opposition has one of its most important functions.

TABLE 2

CONSENSUAL LEGISLATION IN THE BUNDESTAG (1972–87)

Parlia- ment	Total N of Acts	Unanimous Bills Total		Important Policy Bills			Bills of Minor Importance		
		N	%	N	Unanimous		N	Unanimous	
					N	%		N	%
1972–76	516	364	70.5	72	32	44.4	444	332	74.8
1976–80	354	219	61.9	46	18	39.1	308	201	65.3
1980–83	139	71	51.1	35	9	25.7	104	62	59.6
1983–87	320	50	15.6	39	4	10.3	281	46	16.4

Source: Recalculated from Peter Schindler, *Datenhandbuch zur Geschichte des Deutschen Bundestages 1980 bis 1987* (Baden-Baden: Nomos, 1988), p. 571.

The Bundestag's standing orders provide the opposition with various instruments to challenge the government on the floor of the House. Its most important weapons are the various forms of parliamentary interpellation such as *Große Anfragen*, oral questions during question time or short topic debates on current issues (*Aktuelle Stunden*). These instruments are of major importance, because – unlike debates on occasions such as the second reading of bills, the budget or the Chancellor's government declarations (*Regierungserklärungen*) – they do not have to be agreed upon in the inter-party bargaining processes of the Council of Elders. Their application does not require any majority vote in the chamber. They merely have to be tabled by an opposition party and enjoy preferential treatment in the House's timetable. Although they may on occasion serve the majority to 'plant' questions and help the government to put forward its own views, they generally appear to be the opposition's most important instruments.

A look at the percentages in Table 3 confirms that these three forms of questioning and short debate mentioned above have indeed been predominantly a 'weapon' of the opposition parties. With a few exceptions more than 50 per cent were initiated by the minority. *Große Anfragen* are one of the most important instruments for the opposition to force a debate on the floor of the House. They cannot be initiated by individual members but only by a parliamentary party, that is (according to the definition laid down in the standing orders), at least 26 MPs. They must be addressed to the government in written form. Normally they cover a particular area of government activity and may include several detailed questions. The government is expected to answer the questions within a period of three weeks time. The opposition's *primary* objective, however, is not the government's response. If it only wants its questions on a certain policy area comprehensively answered, it will prefer to address a *Kleine Anfrage* to the government. Its major interest is the possibility to discuss the matter itself and the government's answer in a major debate. According to Table 3, the use of this instrument has declined after the first Bundestag (1949–53). The 1983–87 Bundestag, however, seems to mark a turning point. The number of 175 *Große Anfragen* in a single Parliament (1983–87) had not even been reached in the first Bundestag. To a large extent, this figure has been inflated by the competitive style of the Green party whose members initiated nearly half (87) of the total 175 *Große Anfragen*. However, the Social Democrats also tabled 61 *Große Anfragen* which is considerably more than any opposition had initiated in a single Bundestag between 1957 and 1983.

TABLE 3

SHORT DEBATES AND QUESTIONS IN THE BUNDESTAG (1949–87)

Parlia-ment	Große Anfragen		Oral Questions		Aktuelle Stunden[e]	
	N	% tabled by op-position	N	% tabled by op-position	N	% tabled by op-position
1949–53	160	38.1	392	68.8	–	–
1953–57	97	52.6	1069	58.2	–	–
1957–61	49	87.7	1536	75.7	–	–
1961–65	35	68.6	4786	56.7	2	50.0
1965–66[a]	11	36.4	n.a.	n.a.	5	40.0
1966–69[b]	34	35.3	n.a.	n.a.	12	58.3
1969–72	31	80.6	11073	64.5	8	100.0
1972–76	24	75.0	18497	68.9	20	90.0
1976–80	47	70.2	23467	64.1	9	100.0
1980–82[c]	32	75.0	12069	60.6	6	66.7
1982–83[d]	0	–	2315	64.0	6	100.0
1983–87	175	84.6	22864	65.9	117	76.9

Sources: Rearranged from Peter Schindler: *Datenhandbuch zur Geschichte des Deutschen Bundestages 1949 bis 1982* (Bonn: Deutscher Bundestag, 1983), pp. 762–3; *Datenhandbuch zur Geschichte des Deutschen Bundestages 1980 bis 1987* (Baden-Baden: Nomos, 1988), p. 677.

Notes:
a Period 20 October 1965–28 October 1966 (CDU/CSU–FDP coalition under Chancellor Ludwig Erhard) and 29 October 1966–30 November 1966 (CDU/CSU minority government under Erhard).
b Period 1 December 1966–20 October 1969 (CDU/CSU–SPD coalition under Chancellor Kurt Georg Kiesinger).
c Period 5 November 1980–1 October 1982 (SPD–FDP coalition under Chancellor Helmut Schmidt).
d Period 2 October 1982–9 March 1983 (CDU/CSU–FDP coalition under Chancellor Helmut Kohl).
e This form of debate was introduced in 1965.

'Oral questions' are usually written questions addressed to the government; they are answered orally during question time, normally by the responsible parliamentary secretary of state, rarely by the minister. Unlike *Große* and *Kleine Anfragen* they can be tabled by individual members. In practice, members have to announce them beforehand in their whips' offices where questions are being co-ordinated. A look at Table 2 shows that oral questions are the most popular instrument of inquiry. In the 1983–87 Bundestag, for example, a total of 22,864 questions have been tabled for oral response. Their sheer number makes it impossible to deal with all of them during question time; therefore, questions concerning local affairs and those which could not be answered for lack of time normally receive a written reply. Some authors – academics and MPs – have doubted the efficiency of parliamentary questions as their inflationary number is believed to decrease rather than increase public attention and question time is inherently weighted in favour of the government: while MPs are restricted to short questions and a few supplementary questions, minister have ample freedom to answer, and their answers are not necessarily informative and meaningful. Since October 1988, the House has allocated half an hour per week for the spontaneous questioning of ministers after the regular Cabinet meetings every Wednesday (*Kabinettsbefragung*). According to the participation rates, this experiment, intended to make parliamentary questions more lively, does not enjoy particular attention by members.

In order to remedy some of the defects of parliamentary questions, the House introduced in 1965 short topical discussions on current affairs (*Aktuelle Stunden*). Originally these one-hour debates followed question time; they could be initiated by a parliamentary party or at least 26 MPs, if they were not satisfied by a minister's or parliamentary secretary of state's answers. *Aktuelle Stunden* could also be initiated independent of question time, but only if supported by the majority. Between 1965 and 1983 this form of short and adversarial debates did not enjoy particular popularity. In the 1983–87 Bundestag its use increased considerably: there were more *Aktuelle Stunden* than in all previous Parliaments together. More than three quarters were initiated by the opposition parties – 48 by the Social Democrats and 42 by the Green Party. This extraordinary growth in number can largely be explained by the reform of the Bundestag's standing orders in 1980, where the initiation of this form of debate was facilitated. Since 1980 it can be demanded by any parliamentary party or at least 26 members, *independent* of question time.

The Basic Law does not contain any formal recognition of the opposition's role in a modern parliamentary democracy. In practice, however, it provides the opposition with various sites to prevent or delay the implementation of parliamentary majority decisions. Because of the federal constitution, the Bundestag opposition is never completely out of power.[31] This has raised the incentives for co-operation and discouraged confrontation in government–opposition relations. Nevertheless, the 1983–87 Bundestag witnessed a significant intensification of opposition activity on the floor of the House. Reforms of the standing orders in 1969 and 1980 extended the rights of minority parties. Moreover, there has been a growing willingness of opposition parties to use the instruments for public debate available to them *qua* minority party. While the number of parliamentary questions has risen almost steadily between 1949 and 1987, the use of *Große Anfragen* and *Aktuelle Stunden* – instruments which seem to be far more effective in forcing a debate on the government than oral questions – has only grown in the 1983–87 Bundestag. Initial data on the current Bundestag indicate that the trend towards a more adversarial style of government–opposition relations is continuing.[32] This is partly due to the advent of the Green Party whose members are very active in the chamber. The competition of another opposition party may have stimulated the Social Democrats to intensify their activities as well. Compared with the parliamentary oppositions between 1949 and 1983, the SPD has clearly expanded its activities on the floor of the House. The decrease of consensual legislation since 1972 and the increasing use of short debates and questions by the opposition parties from 1983 onwards confirm the hypothesis that – at least in terms of parliamentary style on its floor – the Bundestag has moved more closely towards the competitive and adversarial model of executive–legislative relations in the 'arena' Parliament of Westminster.

Committee work

This last point, however, should not be overstated. Most MPs' parliamentary timetable is still dominated by committee work – not only in the formal Bundestag committees, but also in parallel working groups within their parliamentary parties. In the period 1949–80 the Bundestag held 1,810 sittings on its floor compared with more than 22,000 committee meetings.[33] By and large, committee work has favoured consensual relationships between government and opposition. It is possible to distinguish at least four different kinds of parliamentary committees: permanent committees specialised by subject and area of government; special ad hoc committees (*Sonderausschüsse*), investigative committees (*Untersuchungsausschüsse*) and enquiry commissions (*Enquête-Kommissionen*). A residual category comprises domestic committees like the procedure committee (*Ausschuß für Wahlprüfung, Immunität und Geschäftsordnung*), the Petitions Committee and the Council of Elders (*Ältestenrat*) which *de facto* is also a committee of the House. Investigative committees may be an effective weapon of the opposition to inquire into instances of maladministration or government wrongdoing, but they are appointed infrequently. Between 1949 and 1987 only 26 have been set up. In the same period, the Defence Committee, which has the exceptional power of constituting itself as an investigative committee in order to hold enquiries, has used its powers in only ten instances. With regard to the day-to-day scrutiny of government policies, the most important type is the permanent departmental committee. The majority of these 20 or so committees parallel one single government department, only the Appropriations and Justice Committees' terms of reference cut across the board and affect all departments. Influence and prestige of individual committees vary, but the Appropriations Committee (*Haushaltsausschuß*) is certainly the most influential one. Although it cannot make any spending decisions without government approval, it can block the provision of money, and every bill involving public expenditure has to be scrutinised here.

The departmental committees scrutinise executive activities and bills that have passed the first reading in the chamber. It is here, that a good deal of inter-party co-operation in the sense of King's 'cross-party mode' takes place. The emphasis of committee work is on technical details rather than the general principle of a bill. The high degree of government bills approved by the opposition during the 1970s (see Table 2) can be partly explained as a result of inter-party compromises at the committee stage of the legislative process where the government majority tends to make concessions in return for opposition support for the bill as a whole. The Bundestag committee system can be seen as 'one method of institutionalizing this give-and-take'.[34] The non-partisan style of committee work and the government parties' willingness to make concessions have the effect that about 60 per cent of bills are modified at committee stage. However, it would be premature to conclude that the legislative committees play an independent role. Departmental committees do not have autonomous decision-making powers.[35] They prepare recommendations which are voted upon on the floor of the House. The vast majority of amendments made at the committee stage are related to details of minor political importance, and if there are substantial amendments, they are usually initiated by the government or the Bundesrat. Committees in the Bundestag do not initiate legislation, and the parties' positions are usually determined beforehand within their working groups and plenary meetings.[36]

Although members' role conceptions and timetables are dominated by legislation and committee work, the Bundestag is not a law-*making* body. Legislation is dominated by the government working through stable coalitions and cohesive majority parties. The chamber's ability to scrutinise and influence the government largely depends on the permeability of decision-making within the majority parties and the extent to which minority rights exist and enable the opposition to fulfil its function of criticism and presentation of alternatives. Both dimensions of parliamentary scrutiny and influence require information. Committees serve to provide the necessary infrastructure for communication and information among MPs, government ministers, bureaucrats and interest group representatives. While members of the Bundestag are usually in close contact with various sections of attentive and élite publics, the House is said to have deficits as the 'central forum of the nation', linking government and mass publics. These communicative deficits are believed to affect popular confidence in Parliament. The final section will present some empirical evidence on the level of public support accruing to the Bundestag.

SUPPORT

The political institutions of the Federal Republic were established by a constituent assembly (*Parlamentärischer Rat*) in 1948–49. The Basic Law marked the fifth sharp regime change in less than 80 years (1871, 1918, 1933, 1945 and 1949). After the Second World War, a public preoccupied with the material conditions of life paid scant attention to the Basic Law that was adopted by the *Länder* legislatures without a popular referendum. In the autumn of 1949, therefore, the citizens of West Germany 'found themselves with a set of unfamiliar political institutions'.[37] This circumstance contributed to the subsequent interpretation, that 'though the formal political institutions of democracy exist in Germany [. . .] the underlying set of political attitudes that would regulate the operation of these institutions in a democratic direction is missing'.[38] In the 1950s it was unclear if and how quickly the German population would accept the rules of parliamentary democracy.

One of the most common approaches to the assessment of the legitimacy of a certain political institution is the measurement of the amount of support accruing to it. In this context, David Easton has made an important theoretical distinction between 'diffuse' support which is a product of both long- and short-term forces and refers to attitudes people develop over time as a result of extended socialisation processes, and 'specific'

TABLE 4

CONFIDENCE IN POLITICAL INSTITUTIONS IN
EIGHT WESTERN DEMOCRACIES (1981–82)

	US	Jap.	GB	Ire.	FRG	Fr.	It.	Sp.
Parliament/Congress	53	30	40	51	53	48	31	48
Police	76	67	86	86	71	64	68	63
Armed forces	81	37	81	75	54	53	58	61
Legal System	51	68	66	57	67	55	43	48
Educational system	65	51	60	67	43	55	56	50
Church	75	16	48	78	48	54	60	50
Civil service	55	31	48	54	35	50	28	38
Major companies	50	25	48	49	34	42	33	37
Press	49	52	29	44	33	31	46	31
Labour Unions	33	29	26	36	36	36	28	31

Question: 'How much confidence do you have in each of the institutions [above]: a great deal, quite a lot, not very much or none at all?' (In per cent; only positive responses were coded).

Abbreviations: US: United States of America, Jap.: Japan, GB: Great Britain, Ire.: Ireland, FRG: Federal Republic of Germany, Fr.: France, It.: Italy, Sp.: Spain.

Source: Peter H. Merkl, 'Comparing Legitimacy and Values Among Advanced Democratic Countries', in Mattei Dogan (ed.), *Comparing Pluralist Democracies: Strains on Legitimacy* (Boulder, CO: Westview Press, 1988), p.61.

TABLE 5
CONFIDENCE IN THE BUNDESTAG (1979–89)

	1979	1981	1982	1983	1984	1986	1988	1989
Per cent of respondents expressing confidence in the Bundestag	67	64	61	71	68	74	60	60

Sources: Emnid Institute surveys quoted from Suzanne S. Schüttemeyer, *Bundestag und Bürger im Spiegel der Demoskopie* (Opladen: Westdeutscher Verlag, 1986), p.251, and Heinrich Oberreuter, 'Zwischen traditionellem und aufgeklärtem Parlamentsverständnis', *Aus Politik und Zeitgeschichte,* B37–38 (1989), p.31.

support which refers to their more immediate responses to the outputs of political actors.[39] If we want to assess the stability of popular support accruing to a legislature, even under conditions of economic stress, Cabinet crises or instances of corruption, it is particularly instructive to measure the amount of diffuse support. Most instruments developed to measure institutional trust seem to be not entirely adequate. High levels of support for Parliament may, for instance, reflect generally favourable attitudes towards the state and its institutions rather than democratic values, or they may conceal indifference and low levels of knowledge about the actual functioning of Parliament. None the less, the most common indicator of a population's affective evaluation of Parliament (or any other given political institution) independent of its current output is to measure the level of 'trust' or 'confidence' accruing to it.

In 1981–82 over half the West German respondents to the European Values System Study (Table 4) expressed 'a great deal' or 'quite a lot' of confidence in the Bundestag. An equally high degree of popular trust was at this time only enjoyed by the United States Congress. Compared with the evaluation of other West German institutions, the Bundestag ranked fourth. Such a high ranking of the national Parliament was reached in no other country included in this sample.

A different set of longitudinal data shows that, some fluctuations notwithstanding, support for the West German Bundestag has considerably increased since the early 1950s. In 1951 just over one third (35 per cent) of the West German population had a 'very positive' or 'positive' opinion of the Bundestag. By 1983 the share of positive respondents had almost doubled to 66 per cent.[40] After 1986, however, the degree of popular support seems to have sharply decreased. This is reflected by the data in Table 5. Even though as many as 60 per cent of respondents have expressed their confidence in the Bundestag in 1988 and 1989, this is the lowest level measured since this question has been first included in the Emnid institute's regular surveys in 1979.

The major reasons for the increasing amount of trust in the Bundestag observed until the early 1980s seem to lie in age-cohort and socialisation effects. In 1973 Gerhard Loewenberg was able to demonstrate that support for the legislature and the political system was greatest among Germans who were politically socialised under the stable conditions of the post-Second World War period, and that support for parliamentary democracy was relatively weak among the age groups likely to have been most affected by the breakdown of parliamentary institutions in the 1920s and 1930s.[41] The decline of public support in the second half of the 1980s may be a result of three distinct developments. First, the 'silent revolution' of the 1970s has increased the demand for more direct forms of political participation, especially among the younger and better educated age-cohorts in all Western democracies. They generally exhibit more confidence in their own political effectiveness and lower levels of institutional trust or political deference.[42] The increased demand for direct forms of political participation questions the idea of representative government and rivals the role of Parliament as the dominant source of political legitimisation. The lack of trust in representative institutions among 'post-materialists' is confirmed by empirical findings about the voters of the Green Party. While in 1986 about three quarters of all respondents to the survey quoted in Table 5 expressed their confidence in the Bundestag, the respective share among voters of the Green Party was only 41 per cent. Secondly, there appears to be a certain amount of traditional anti-parliamentary attitudes on the extreme political right. In 1989, only 31 per cent of Republikaner voters expressed to have confidence in the Bundestag.[43] Thirdly, the recent electoral success of authoritarian and anti-pluralist right-wing parties, whose propaganda concentrates not only on the issues of nationalism and law and order, but also on social and economic problems such as unemployment and housing, has emphasised the vulnerabilty of democratic and parliamentary values in phases of widespread policy dissatisfaction. It is empirically difficult to disentangle the levels of diffuse and specific support accruing to a legislature, since Parliaments tend to be identified with the incumbent governments as their most salient parts. Although support for the Bundestag has been generally higher than government popularity, popular confidence in Parliament remains to a certain extent tied to people's satisfaction with the incumbent government's policies.[44] The marked reduction of popular support accruing to the Bundestag in the second half of the 1980s seems to be a result of a few but grave instances of corruption such as the Flick and Barschel affairs, dissatisfaction with incoherent government policies and the controversial nature of some legislative proposals.[45] This would confirm Gerhard Schmidtchen's conclusion that support for the West German democracy was not diffuse enough, that it was primarily a result of policy effectiveness rather than commonly accepted political symbols.[46]

CONCLUSIONS

With the benefit of hindsight, Loewenstein's conclusion that the Bundestag was a 'powerless parliament', dominated by an all-powerful Chancellor, appears to have been premature. The Bundestag is a reactive, but not a powerless legislature. Although it rarely initiates legislation and major government proposals are hardly ever defeated on the floor of the House, it does 'set certain parameters within which the government must act'.[47] The concentration of West Germany's party system has enhanced coalition stability since 1969. The informal practices of coalition management secure a permanent involvement of the leading members of the parliamentary majority parties in the decision-making process. Since the early 1970s, voting cohesion, at least on the part of the CDU/CSU and FDP, has become markedly stronger than in the 1950s and 1960s, while it has always been relatively high in the SPD. In spite of a seemingly 'iron' party discipline, the government does not normally have the power to impose its proposals on the parliamentary majority parties. Cohesive voting appears to be mainly the result of intensive intra-party bargaining processes in which the government may be forced to modify its proposals significantly. As far as executive-legislative relations are concerned, King's 'intra-party' and 'inter-party' modes seem to place the most important restrictions upon the government. Although committee work is prominent in members' timetables and role conceptions, the constraints arising from King's 'cross-party mode' are only of secondary importance. Departmental committees serve to improve members' knowledge of the decision-making process, and a majority of bills are amended at committee stage. Nevertheless, they remain subsidiary bodies of the House and the limits within which committees can modify the government's policy proposals are fixed by the majority parties.

The federal system requires inter-administrative cooperation, irrespective of the political complexions of the federal and *Länder* governments. Between 1969 and 1982, when the opposition parties in the Bundestag (CDU/CSU) commanded a majority in the Bundesrat, the Bundestag opposition was particularly powerful and the government had to make numerous concessions in the mediation committee (*Vermittlungsausschuß*) of Bundestag and Bundesrat. By and large, these conditions have favoured co-operative government–opposition relations in the chamber. After a certain degree of polarisation between 1969 and 1972, when Chancellor Brandt's Ostpolitik, his domestic reforms and the CDU/CSU's disappointment at its loss of power reintroduced some elements of adversarialism, opposition behaviour returned to a more co-operative style during the 1970s, especially after Helmut Kohl's accession to parliamentary leadership in 1976. The opposition's renunciation of competitive strategies in the chamber reflects its relatively strong influence on the policy-making process and its weakness as an element of criticism and alternatives. Only when the Green Party entered the Bundestag in 1983 did opposition become more competitive, as a result partly of the Greens' activities and partly of the SPD's efforts to achieve more political profile against a competing opposition party.

While its policy-making power is certainly one decisive criterion to assess a Parliament's strength, it is not the only one. A Parliament's stability also depends on its support by élite and mass publics. Time-series data on trust into Parliament are only available for mass publics. According to these data, confidence in the Bundestag has markedly grown in the 1960s and 1970s. Recent decreases in trust, however, confirm the assumption that support remains in part related to specific policy outputs and fragile if the government's performance declines.

NOTES

The critical comments of Bryan Dorman, Johannes Paulmann and Ekkart Zimmermann are much appreciated. Portions of this study were first presented at the meetings of the German-Austrian-Italian working group on the 'Future of Politics' in Menaggio, 19–21 October 1987 and Vienna, 16–19 June 1988. The generous support of the *Herbert-Quandt-Stiftung*, which made these and a series of further meetings possible, is gratefully acknowledged.

 1. K. Loewenstein, *Verfassungslehre* (Tübingen: Mohr, 1959), pp.93–4 (my translation).
 2. F. Ridley, 'Chancellor Government as a Political System and the German Constitution', *Parliamentary Affairs*, Vol.19 (1966), p.461.
 3. R. Mayntz, 'Executive Leadership in Germany: Dispersion of Power or "Kanzlerdemokratie"?' in R. Rose and E. N. Suleiman (eds.), *Presidents and Prime Ministers* (Washington, D. C.: American Enterprise Institute for Public Policy Research, 1980), pp.141–42. The 'constructive vote of no confidence' has been applied only twice in West German history. In 1972, an attempt by the CDU/CSU opposition to oust Willy Brandt was defeated; in 1982 Chancellor Helmut Schmidt had to resign after a successful 'constructive vote of no confidence' moved by the oppositional CDU/CSU and a majority in the FDP.
 4. P. Schindler, *Datenhandbuch zur Geschichte des Deutschen Bundestages 1949 bis 1982* (Bonn: Deutscher Bundestag, 1983), pp.681–85; *Datenhandbuch zur Geschichte des Deutschen Bundestages 1980 bis 1987* (Baden-Baden: Nomos, 1988), pp.549–50.
 5. M.L. Mezey, *Comparative Legislatures* (Durham NC: Duke University Press, 1979), p.25.
 6. A. King, 'Modes of Executive–Legislative Relations: Great Britain, France and West Germany', *Legislative Studies Quarterly*. Vol.1, No.1 (1976), p.11.
 7. K. von Beyme, 'Coalition Government in Western Germany', in V. Bogdanor (ed.), *Coalition Government in Western Europe* (London: Heinemann, 1983), pp.33–4.
 8. The DP was represented in the Bundestag from 1949 to 1961. The GB/BHE (All-German Bloc/Federation of Expellees and Dispossessed) was represented from 1953 to 1957.
 9. W.H. Riker, *The Theory of Political Coalitions* (New Haven: Yale University Press, 1962).
10. U. Hoffmann-Lange, 'Changing Coalitional Preferences Among West German Parties', in G. Pridham (ed.), *Coalitional Behaviour in Theory and Practice: An Inductive Model for Western Europe* (Cambridge: Cambridge University Press, 1986), p.46.
11. Von Beyme, 'Coalition Government in Western Germany', pp. 22–4.
12. G.L. Rueckert, 'Parliamentary Party Cohesion in the West German Bundestag', PhD dissertation, University of Wisonsin, 1962, pp.20–21.
13. S.A. Rice, *Quantitative Methods in Politics* (New York: Knopf, 1928). The total number of roll calls between 1949 and 1987 was 930. One roll call in 1976 had to be excluded because it was annulled because of lack of members in the chamber. The 209 roll calls initiated by the Green Party during the second and third reading of the Motorways Building Bill (*Fernstraßenbaugesetz*) in January 1986 were excluded, because such an unprecedented number of roll calls on a single bill would have distorted the analysis of the remaining 132 votes in the whole tenth Bundestag without adding any information. Therefore, only the final vote on this bill was included.
14. A.R. Clausen, 'Some Basic Approaches to the Measurement of Roll-Call Voting', in D.M. Freeman (ed.), *Foundation of Political Science: Research, Methods, and Scope*

(New York: The Free Press, 1977), p.338.

15. Abstentions were counted in the denominator. Of course, absences cannot be automatically treated as abstentions. A detailed analysis shows that Cabinet ministers and members of the various European assemblies have accounted for a significant share of absences. However, a study of dissenting members' personal declarations (*persönliche Erklärungen*) shows that absenteeism is a popular form of expressing one's dissent.

16. For the construction of participation indexes see H. Best, *Struktur und Handeln parlamentarischer Führungsgruppen in Deutschland und Frankreich 1948/49*, *Habilitationsschrift* (Cologne: University of Cologne: Faculty for Economics and Social Sciences, 1986), pp.312–32. We have used a variant of Best's 'P-index 3' (p.312). It was calculated by the formula: 1 – a/s, where a is the number of members voting and s is the number of members who should be present in the House according to the lists of excused absences. The 'weighted index of cohesion' is the result of a multiplication of the Rice index with the participation index.

17. According to Schindler's definition in his *Datenhandbuch zur Geschichte des Deutschen Bundestages 1949 bis 1982*, p.779, major divisions are those on bills in the second and third reading, on the budget, on motions of high political salience and on secret ballots.

18. G. Pridham, 'The Government/Opposition Dimension and the Development of the Party System in the 1970s: The Reappearance of Conflictual Politics', in H. Döring and G. Smith (eds.), *Party Government and Political Culture in Western Gemany* (London: Macmillan, 1982), pp.142–50.

19. T. Saalfeld, *Stabilisierung und Kontrolle* (forthcoming).

20. N. Johnson, 'Committees in the West German Bundestag', in J.D. Lees and M. Shaw (eds.), *Committees in Legislatures* (Oxford: Martin Robertson, 1979), p.107.

21. S.J. Eldersveld, *Political Parties: A Behavioural Analysis* (Chicago: Rand McNally, 1964), pp.6–12, 526–8.

22. Johnson, p.107.

23. Mayntz, pp.159–61. A recent example is the bill on child benefits from March 1989. Here the CDU/CSU parliamentary group refused to accept a government proposal and forced the Cabinet to modify its plans.

24. G. Loewenberg, 'The Patterns of Political Opposition in Germany', in H.S. Commager *et al.* (eds.), *Festschrift für Karl Loewenstein aus Anlaß seines achtzigsten Geburtstages* (Tübingen: Mohr, 1971), p.333.

25. W.E. Paterson and D. Webber, 'The Federal Republic of Germany: The Re-Emergent Opposition?' in E. Kolinsky (ed.), *Opposition in Western Europe* (London: Croom Helm, 1987), p.145.

26. Ibid.

27. G. Sartori, *Parties and Party Systems: A Framework for Analysis*, Vol.1 (Cambridge: Cambridge University Press, 1976), pp.178–9.

28. O. Kirchheimer, 'Germay: The Vanishing Opposition', in R. A. Dahl (ed.), *Political Oppositions in Western Democracies* (New Haven: Yale University Press, 1967), pp.237–59.

29. 'Important policy bills' are defined as bills involving substantial changes in public policy affecting large parts of the population. 'Bills of minor importance' are defined as small changes, corrections or adaptations of existing laws and policies affecting a restricted number of persons.

30. S. Lukes, *Power: A Radical View* (London: Macmillan, 1974).

31. Paterson and Webber, p.158.

32. By 22 June, 1989 there were 86 *Große Anfragen*, 12,690 oral questions and 81 *Aktuelle Stunden*. Cf. *40 Jahre Deutscher Bundestag: Daten – Namen Statistik* (Bonn: Deutscher Bundestag. Wissenschaftliche Dienste, 1989), p.118 (mimeo).

33. T. Ellwein and J.J. Hesse, *Das Regierungssystem der Bundesrepublik Deutschland* (Opladen: Westdeutscher Verlag, 1987, 6th ed.), p. 266.

34. Johnson, p.143.

35. The only committee with autonomous powers is the Committee of Selection which has the task of selecting judges for the Federal Constitutional Court.

36. H. Schulze-Fielitz, *Theorie und Praxis parlamentärischer Gesetzgebung- besonders des 9. Deutschen Bundestages (1980–83)* (Berlin: Duncker & Humblot, 1988), pp. 312–48.

37. G.R. Boynton and G. Loewenberg, 'The Development of Public Support for Parliament in Germany, 1951–59', *British Journal of Political Science*, Vol.3 (1973), pp.169–70.
38. G.A. Almond and S. Verba, *The Civic Culture* (Princeton: Princeton University Press, 1963), p.496.
39. D. Easton, 'A re-assessment of the concept of political support', *British Journal of Political Science*, Vol.5 (1975), pp.435–57.
40. The question asked of a representative sample of the West German adult population was 'What is your opinion of the Bonn Bundestag as our popular representation?' The answer categories were 'very positive', 'positive', 'not very positive', 'negative' and 'no opinion'. Schüttemeyer, *Bundestag und Bürger im Spiegel der Demoskopie*, p. 243.
41. G. Loewenberg, 'The Institutionalization of Parliament and Public Orientations to the Political System', in A. Kornberg (ed.), *Legislatures in Comparative Perspective* (New York: McKay, 1973), p.155.
42. M. Kaase, 'Political Alienation and Protest', in M. Dogan (ed), *Comparing Pluralist Democracies: Strains on Legitimacy* (Boulder CO: Westview Press, 1988), pp.122–3.
43. H. Oberreuter, 'Zwischen traditionellem und aufgeklärtem Parlamentsverständnis. Der Bundestag in einer gespaltenen politischen Kultur', *Aus Politik und Zeitgeschichte*, B37-38 (1989), p.31.
44. S. S. Schüttemeyer, 'Der Bundestag im Urteil der Bürger: Zur Parlamentarismusperzeption in der Bundesrepublik', in D. Berg-Schlosser and J. Schissler (eds.), *Politische Kultur in Deutschland: Bilanz und Perspektiven der Forschung* (Opladen: Westdeutscher Verlag, 1987), p.415.
45. Oberreuter, 'Zwischen traditionellem und aufgeklärtem Parlamentsverständnis', p.32.
46. G. Schmidtchen, 'Ist Legitimität meßbar?' In *Zeitschrift für Parlamentsfragen*, Vol.8 (1977), p.236.
47. Mezey, p.39, with particular reference to the British House of Commons.

Legislative and Executive Relations in the Republic of Ireland

Audrey M. Arkins

Ireland's historical relationship with Britain largely predetermined the nature of the political system adopted after independence in 1922. The Westminster brand of government was willingly embraced by the new political élite whose nationalist aspirations were less than revolutionary, for, as Lenin argued, 'unwillingness to be ruled in the old way is one of the hallmarks of a great revolution'.[1] Liberal-democratic government was preserved in Ireland after independence with its four characteristic features intact: representative organs which incorporate a legislature, head of state or President; an expert stabilising organ, usually the executive, which is accountable to the legislature; a system of social and economic checks and balances which curtail the activity of government; and, finally, a further restraining system of political checks and balances.[2]

In Ireland the legislature is known as the Oireachtas. This combines an upper and lower House known as Seanad Eireann and Dail Eireann respectively. It also consists of the office of an Uachtaran, the President, sometimes referred to unflatteringly as the 'third House'. All 166 members of Dail Eireann, known as Teachtai Dala (TDs), are directly elected by the Single Transferable Vote (STV) system of election. Members of the Seanad are elected along quasi-corporatist lines. Of its 60 members, 43 are elected by five vocational panels; six are elected by the universities and the remaining eleven are appointed by the Taoiseach (Prime Minister). Given that its members are not elected by universal suffrage and that elements of patronage affect its composition, the Seanad, like the British House of Lords, may not constitute a 'legislature' which by Michael Mezey's definition is an 'elected body of people. . .who hold their positions as a result of an election in which all adults are allowed to participate except those who are insane, imprisoned, illiterate, or who do not meet residence requirements, etc'.[3]

The separation of powers is weakened within the Westminster model of government by the overlap between the legislature and the executive. This occurs in Ireland where Dail Eireann elects a Taoiseach who in turn nominates a Cabinet comprising 'not less than seven and not more than fifteen members'.[4] These 'must be members of Dail Eireann or Seanad Eireann, but not more than two may be members of Seanad Eireann'.[5] In practice all are drawn from the Dail except on very rare occasions.

Although the pattern of independent government in Ireland has been stable it is not because the democratic institutions of the state have remained untested. The strongest challenge to democracy occurred in the early years of the new state when it was born into civil war, army mutiny and lingering support for extraparliamentary agitation. The preservation of British institutional structures helped counteract each political crisis as it arose. The Irish Civil War posed the greatest threat. It resulted from a fundamental split in both Sinn Fein, the nationalist party, and the Army, over the terms of the Anglo-Irish Treaty of 1921 which established dominion status for the south of Ireland. The Treaty was ratified by the then Provisional government with a vote of 64 in favour and 57 against. Those who opposed it saw the Treaty as a 'gross act of betrayal', refused to co-operate with the 'so-called Free State' and resigned from Parliament.[6] Despite obvious majority support for the Treaty in the 1922 and 1923 elections, anti-Treaty Republican deputies persevered with their policy of abstentionism, ignoring the national Parliament and other institutions of the new state. Parliamentary opposition was left to the small Labour Party and a single Independent deputy. Other small groups and Independents in the Dail supported the pro-Treaty government.

It was not until 1925 and another split in the Sinn Fein that the more pragmatic lieutenants of the anti-Treaty movement persuaded some of their colleagues to abandon the political wilderness and form an alternative parliamentary party. Fianna Fail – the Republican Party – was founded in May 1926 with the express objective of securing the political independence of a united Ireland as a Republic. Still contending that the national Parliament 'was not the legitimate parliament of the Republic' they nevertheless conceded its potential usefulness for achieving full independence.[7] Throughout their opposition to the new state, the anti-Treaty deputies never truly challenged the concept of parliamentary democracy, recognising it as an effective instrument for nation building and political integration. It is a testament to their acceptance of this principle that even while in diametric opposition to the Anglo-Irish Treaty they regrouped as a 'government-in-exile' with an elected President. Somewhat ironic also is the fact that the party which was born challenging the legitimacy of the state should come to dominate it so completely. In August 1927, after five years of abstentionism, anti-treaty deputies, now in Fianna Fail, took their seats in Parliament. By 1932, composing the largest parliamentary grouping, they formed their first Cabinet and were to govern for 43 of the last 58 years: this Fianna Fail predominance has undoubtedly influenced the nature of relations between the Executive and the Legislature.

FUNCTIONS OF THE OIREACHTAS

Despite considerable odds the legitimacy of the Oireachtas as the national legislature has never been subverted. Its resilience was due in major part to the functions performed by Dail Eireann, the lower House of the Irish legislature. Packenham delineates legislative functions over three broad categories: legitimation; recruitment, socialisation and training; and decisional.[8] Parliament legitimises the state in diverse ways. By meeting regularly and uninterruptedly, it presents itself as a permanent and integral element of the institutional make up of the state. Its very existence has symbolic value for the nation state. In Ireland, in the years preceding independence, the founding of the First Dail in 1919, albeit unofficial, added impetus to the separatist movement. It became the symbol on which nationalist energies were focused, adding a formal stamp of approval to their campaign against Britain. In more settled political circumstances the Oireachtas has acted as a formal setting or forum in which important political forces can be heard and tensions released. Confining the articulation of interests or conflict to a parliamentary setting to which all state institutions are responsive has allowed the system to dispatch its functions with minimal interruption.

The Oireachtas is formally endorsed through national elections. This indicates the extent to which support has been mobilised for the regime itself. In the 23 national elections held since 1922, average percentage electoral turnout has been 73 per cent. The lowest turnout, 61 per cent, was recorded in 1923 and the highest, 80.4 per cent, in 1933. TDs operate with a stable and proven mandate and their status as public representatives is regularly and systematically tested. Oireachtas procedure is characterised by discussions which involve a constant exchange between the government and the governed, through their elected representatives. TDs function as spokesmen for the public but also for the executive whose policies they articulate and defend. Such work undoubtedly serves as a training ground for the executive élite which recruits its personnel from the Oireachtas. Irish Cabinet ministers are members of the Oireachtas drawn predominantly from the Dail. With rare exceptions they are experienced parliamentarians having worked their way up through its ranks. Many first serve a kind of apprenticeship as parliamentary secretaries/junior ministers.

The 'Decisional' Function: Problems

Packenham's third category relates to the legislature's 'decisional' function. This has many forms including interest articulation, conflict resolution, administrative oversight and law-making. Each of these pose problems for the Irish public representative. Interest articulation in Ireland is inextricably linked to clientelism. Dail deputies tend not to group with obvious lobby interests. While some have developed strong profiles in areas such as family law reform or women's rights, for example, this type of specialisation is not a common feature of parliamentary life. Deputies cultivate the parliamentary profile most suited to their constituents. Thus they focus on constituency matters and articulate issues of interest to the local rather than the national community. This is apparent from the number and type of parliamentary questions addressed to the different government ministers.[9] Between 1970 and 1981 (more recent figures are not available), the highest number of questions, 10,250, was addressed to the Minister for Local Government/Environment. This average of 932 questions per year consisted mainly of queries about the provision of local services which included roads, traffic lights, housing grants and so on. The lowest number, 2,162, was addressed to the Minister for Foreign Affairs. This averaged 193 per year and related predominantly to government policy on Northern Ireland.

The Dail cannot exercise its accountability function with ease. In the last twenty years alone there has been an unprecedented increase in government business, which, because of its complexity, concentrates a greater volume of highly technical information within the area of the executive. In the past TDs tried to keep abreast of technically complex policy matters while dealing with an upward spiral of constituency duties. Research and advisory services were provided almost exclusively by the political parties unless a deputy was prepared to undertake or finance independent research himself. Some research assistance is now available as part of the Dail library service. Primarily this exists to provide memoranda on subjects requested by members in writing. This requires considerable advance notice. An additional information and reference service refers members to documents containing information relevant to their requests, including lists of articles from newspapers and periodicals. Advisory services are still channelled through the political parties.

The policy-formulating and law-making potential of the Dail is not highly developed. Julian Critchley's depiction of MPs in the House of Commons as powerlessly 'perched high on the back benches like so many battery hens', might also be applied to describe their Irish counterparts.[10] The legislative functions of the Dail deputy, although clearly set out in the constitution, bear little relation to his/her practical role. In theory, Parliament, the Oireachtas, exists to legislate. Article 15 (2.1) of Bunreacht na hEireann, the Constitution of Ireland, provides that the 'sole and exclusive power of making laws for the State is hereby vested in the Oireachtas: no other legislative authority has the power to make laws for the State'. In practice, the Westminster model of Parliament adopted in Ireland finds its leadership in the executive, and, over the centuries, that leadership has been strengthened within Parliament, thus eroding its law-making functions. Such was the reality when the system was adopted in 1922: TDs witnessed no 'golden age' of 'strong' Parliament, for that was already in decline in Britain long before the system was ever introduced in Ireland.

The exercise of power within the Oireachtas, therefore, has always been straightforward. The backbencher has few real powers; at no stage can he actually choose the executive, for ministers have always been promoted from a list of the deserving drawn up by the party whips. Nor does he formulate legislation. A TD may be able to amend or very occasionally influence legislation before it is formally presented to the Dail, but the drafting of Bills has always been the province of the civil service. The backbencher cannot in turn dismiss the executive or reject its proposals, for to do so would be to cultivate political and electoral repercussions which many backbench politicians might not survive.

Since accession to the EC in 1973, the Legislature in Ireland has lost additional ground to the Executive. Section 3 of the European Communities Act, 1972, confers very wide powers on Irish ministers to make regulations by way of statutory instruments in order to implement EC legislation. 'The ministerial power is unprecendented . . . effectively, the government could decide as a policy matter whether to implement European Community legislation through a Bill before the Oireachtas, or have the relevant Minister make a statutory instrument without any need for prior consultation or debate'.[11] Section 4 of the European Communities Act, 1972, provided for parliamentary scrutiny over the exercise of the power delegated to ministers under section 3 of the Act and a Joint Committee on Secondary Legislation was set up in 1973 'to consider and report on Community Laws at every stage in the policy-making process'.[12] The statutory role accorded to this committee ensures that it will be reconstituted with each new Parliament. While its performance has undoubtedly improved since accession, 'its role is still one of post facto control on secondary legislation and not of influencing ministerial negotiating positions at Council level'.[13] The Joint Committee on the Secondary Legislation of the EC has one significant power in that it may recommend that certain EC regulations be annulled. If a resolution to that effect is passed by both Houses of the Oireachtas within one year after the regulations are made than 'they shall cease to have statutory effect'.[14] Apart from the obvious technical hiccups in our relationship with the EC, however, which would be the inevitable consequence of the annulment of a particular statutory instrument, 'it is hardly realistic in Irish political terms to envisage such a motion being passed as no Government Minister would allow his party to vote on the floor of the House against a measure for which he was responsible when all he has to do is to put pen to paper and introduce an amending statutory instrument'.[15] Thus incorporating Mezey's classification of legislatures, we can conclude that Dail Eireann enjoys only 'modest' policy-making power insofar as it is capable of modifying but not rejecting policy proposals.[16]

Reform of the Dail

Writing in 1969, Basil Chubb voiced popular concern when he described the Dail as 'one of the worst organised, equipped and informed parliaments in the democratic world'.[17] At that time TDs were accommodated three and four to an office; research and secretarial facilities were provided at a ratio of one secretary to nine deputies. An informal committee on Dail reform which met in 1972 recommended 35 technical measures designed to modernise Dail Standing Orders.[18] Of those reforms which were implemented, many have 'streamlined some utterly outmoded Dail procedures'. Overall, however, the effects have been 'minor' and as 'a long term contribution towards meeting the more serious defects of Dail procedures, the Report [of the informal committee] was not a major contribution'.[19] A newly established Department of the Public Service in 1973 eventually made improvements to the administrative facilities serving TDs, including research, secretarial, restaurant and accommodation.

Since the 1972 report, demands from backbenchers for more substantial reforms in the area of policy formulation have featured frequently on the parliamentary agenda. Where single, cross-party motions for reform have been tabled in the Oireachtas – and there have been three of significance in the last 15 years – they have attracted widespread parliamentary interest, though contributions have been rambling, and unstructured.

In his 'memorandum' to the government in 1975, Barry Desmond TD, seeing the pressure for reform as 'drearily dispirited', acknowledged that it was never 'likely to receive much priority', possibly because the 'minds and actions of many Deputies and Senators will most likely be preoccupied with other more seemingly important political issues such as their prospects for re-election to the Dail'.[20]

Public representatives throughout the world undoubtedly work to ensure their own re-election, for even the loftiest policy objectives are meaningless without an electoral mandate. In Ireland, however, the STV system of election allegedly exerts additional electoral pressures on TDs who, standing in multi-seat constituencies, are required not only to compete with the opposition parties but also with their own party colleagues. Since candidates from the same party choose not to compete with each other on policy 'they must find another way of distinguishing themselves from their running mates'.[21] Hence, they spend a vast amount of time engaged in constituency work thus neglecting policy issues. Why such priority is given to constituency matters over policy formulation is not the subject of this study. It is clear, however, from other studies in the area that TDs are largely instrumental in manufacturing their own dilemma. Many actively chase constituents, not only by holding clinics to hear grievances but also by installing computerised mailshots offering unsolicited assistance to those who apply for grants, planning permission and so on. Such behaviour is hardly 'imposed' on TDs by the STV system of election. Most probably it stems from a traditional cultural tendency towards localism, brokerage and face-to-face relations. Clientelist practices undermine the legislative activity of the Dail deputy chiefly by robbing him of the time necessary for policy formulation and executive scrutiny. This is not to argue, however, that less time expended on constituency considerations would tilt the balance of decisional functions towards the Legislature away from the Executive.

The Irish deputy faces many obstacles which prevent him from having direct input into policy formulation, decision-making and law making. Towards the end of the 1970s, however, TDs, in their rhetoric at least, began to show a reluctance to accept what academics appear to take for granted: that their law-making function should be 'dropped as a necessary characteristic of a legislature'.[22] A number of backbenchers called for a new approach towards their role within the overall scheme of government. For them, a parliamentary life characterised by an increasing number of complex Bills and motions which they are obliged to pass, sheeplike, without effecting any concrete input, was increasingly unacceptable. A campaign for reform soon emerged and gathered momentum towards the end of the 1970s mostly thanks to Garret FitzGerald, the then leader of Fine Gael, a party which was formed in 1933 as a successor to the pro-Treaty Cumann na nGaedheal party. Fine Gael, the second largest party in Ireland, has always prided itself on its 'parliament-friendly' reputation which may be the result of long years spent out of government on the opposition benches. By the early 1980s Fine Gael adopted internal Dail reform as an integral feature of its programme, advocating, in particular, the use of select committees as a means of equipping the backbencher with information which could improve the range of his influence. Fianna Fail, then and today, view the prospect of an efficient committee system with suspicion, seeing it as a potential threat to the executive supremacy so inherent in the Westminster model of government. Strong select committees do not blend easily with this constitutional model, which sees the cabinet as the centre of power. In their search for information, they utilise powers of scrutiny which inevitably constrain government behaviour.

Oireachtas Select Committees

Measured against a background of feasible internal parliamentary reforms, select committees were nevertheless seen, by other Irish political parties, to have much to recommend them. It is evident from contributions to a debate on reform held in January 1983, and in the occasional policy documents addressing the issue, that the choice to extend the use of select committees in the Oireachtas was made with high expectations for their possible impact on its 'decisional' function. In summary, these were as follows:

- that the Oireachtas should be able to off-load more and more of its work to the committees, which were seen to be potentially a device for regional devolution. Here, TDs and Senators from each region could gather to discuss issues relevant to their province;
- that access to detailed information, interrogation of departmental officials and other witnesses would have an educative value for backbench members of the Oireachtas, which would effect an improvement in the quality of participation on the floor of the House, where ministers might be challenged on a near equal footing;
- that a more sophisticated form of accountability could be achieved and that the public service would in turn be seen to be directly answerable to the public, through the Oireachtas;
- that ministers would have to account for their actions doubly, i.e. not only to the Dail and Seanad, but also to committee;
- that committees would provide a forum for discussion without the party political complications which affect debates within the Oireachtas;
- that, as a consequence, the parliamentary process would take on a more professional image and public representatives would feel greater dignity and esteem in the performance of their duties.

Ultimately it was expected that in reporting and making recommendations, the committees would play a significant role in policy formulation, thus allowing TDs and Senators to fulfil their constitutional role as legislators.

The realisation of such expectations rests on a number of assumptions: such as that the executive are prepared to extend full support and co-operation starting with instant improvements in staffing and secretarial facilities. This alone would require a significant increase in the appropriation to the Houses of the Oireachtas. While this increased substantially from a sum of £30,000 in 1979 to £300,000 in 1986, it was cut to £50,000 by the new Fianna Fail administration in 1988. These figures represent only the annual expenditure estimate, however. The real costs of committees appear under a diverse group of expenditure categories ranging from research and secretarial expenses, through accommodation, to editing and publishing. Many of these remain unspecified. Beyond these lie additional hidden costs, such as those incurred by government departments which invest considerable labour in preparing evidence to deal with detailed interrogations by the committees. The effective use of a vast range of new committees also presupposes the physical/logistical availability of membership; general parliamentary support for their work; backing for recommendations and a non-partisan approach by the membership who, in turn, would require a minimum of electoral recognition for their work. Experience in legislatures abroad suggests that the hallmarks of an effective select committee is its non-partisan approach; the examination of detail; the disclosing of the facts of a case and its ability to advise members of Parliament. Usually it performs duties for which the body of the legislature – in Ireland's case, all 166 members – is unsuited to do, and it should do so in a manner which tends to mute party differences. Without the essential preconditions listed above, any attempts to develop an effective committee system would be thwarted.

Those who were instrumental in devising the new committee experiment looked to British precedent for guidance. A permanent departmentally related structure had been implemented there in 1979. This was never seriously considered for adoption in the Oireachtas, perhaps because few ministers would tolerate a single committee dogging their movements. Similarly, the nature of the relationship which might develop between a minister and a departmentally related select committee may be feared; such relationships could shift between antagonism on the one hand or sympathy and fraternity on the other. Both situations would impair a committee's ability to be impartial and exacting. Regardless of the structure actually adopted, it is clear that a select commmittee system would produce very different results in Ireland to those achieved in Britain or elsewhere. The Oireachtas is far smaller than the House of Commons, for example. Elections in Ireland are held under STV in multi-member constituencies. Elections in Britain are through the single-member plurality (SMP) system. The traditional role for MPs and TDs are dissimilar as are party demands and inter-party relationships. Career structures for MPs in Britain follow different paths from their Irish counterparts; whereas many MPs might not aspire to a Cabinet role, choosing instead to become professional parliamentarians, Irish TDs may be more aware of their prospects for promotion to the executive élite. Government machinery is more expansive in Britain than in Ireland. As a larger country it has a far greater administrative workload. The prospect of delegating small responsibilities to comittees, standing or select, in areas where there is minimum contention, is possibly welcomed by the executive in Britain, while in Ireland Cabinet supremacy is cautiously guarded against any slight erosion.

By 1983, less than a year into the Fine Gael/Labour coalition government of the 24th Oireachtas, seven completely new ad hoc select committees were at work. These covered broad areas: public expenditure, women's rights, marriage breakdown, small businesses, crime and lawlessness, the Irish language and general legislation. They joined the recently established committees on commercial state-sponsored bodies, co-operation with developing countries, public accounts, secondary legislation of the EEC, building land, as well as the statutory procedural and service committees.

Impact of Committees

The new select committees struggled against great odds. What should have begun as a modest experiment using three or four well organised select committees transformed into an uncoordinated mish-mash of ideas and investigations. Thus, their potential effectiveness was immediately undermined by their abundance. Existing facilities within Leinster House (the seat of Parliament) were already strained and those responsible for servicing Oireachtas committees cannot have welcomed the increased workload. Staffing requirements were considerable given that each committee called for a minimum of one full-time clerk and secretary. Those with a particularly heavy workload, such as the public expenditure committee, required further research and secretarial assistance. These additional pressures did nothing to inspire affection for the committees among the parliamentary staff.

Of the few select committee reports which were formally debated in the Dail, each drew small audiences which were invariably composed of the relevant committee's membership with few others in attendance. The size of an audience, however, is less a measure of parliamentary interest than of electoral pressures which cause TDs to spend most of their time outside the chamber tending constituency matters. Attending a debate on a committee's report may, in the long term, be of less value than simply reading and absorbing the findings which are set out in reports and minutes of evidence, and on the basis of the facts and recommendations contained therein, tabling parliamentary questions, motions, supporting relevant lobby groups or even submitting a private member's bill.

Evidence suggests that such initiatives were not undertaken. Certain members of the Dail appeared to be unaware of the work conducted in select committee. Even while discussing the value of extending the committee system during the January 1983 debate on Dail reform, a number of politicians referred to the need for improving administrative accountability to Parliament, especially with regard to the commercial public sector. As they spoke, more reports from the joint committee on commercial state-sponsored bodies (SSBC) were going to print without the prospect of a debate in the Dail. Few speakers during that debate made reference to the work conducted by the SSBC over the previous five years. This suggests that the Oireachtas tends to set up investigative select committees and standing committees reviewing legislation, only to ignore them.

Neglect and ambivalence aside, select committee recommendations have gradually made some impact on government policy. To suggest a direct causal relationship would be misleading, but certain factors are indisputable. Where policy has derived in some way from select committee recommendations, relevant government spokesmen have not hesitated to make a formal acknowledgement. A Department of Labour policy document, for instance, on the amalgamation of the unemployment and training agencies, formally acknowledged similar proposals contained in the PEC reports.[23]

Despite the less than adequate setting in which the select committees of the 24th Oireachtas were obliged to work, their very existence did represent a new departure in parliamentary affairs. Seven years after the launch of the new committees it would appear that many ambitious expectations were invested in them. Of all the committees set up since 1978, only three are still in existence. They are the joint committees on women's rights, the Irish language, and commercial state-sponsored bodies. The Fianna Fail governments of 1987 and 1989 have not reinstated the other committees, nor have they offered a reason for their decision. Those who saw the committees as tools of instant parliamentary reform seem now to be somewhat disillusioned.

Notwithstanding the difficulties conditioning committee inquiries, members failed to capitalise effectively on their findings by following up recommendations. Only one committee, the PEC, made a habit of contacting government departments six months after the publication of a report to monitor reaction to their recommendations. Unlike in Britain, committees do not receive a formal government response to their reports and recommendations. It remains for them to go out of their way to elicit an informal response. In this the tenacity of the PEC membership proved worthwhile. Other committees failed to adopt any such strategy. In general TDs simply did not act on valuable information at the appropriate time, whether by tabling parliamentary questions when media and political interest was high or by drafting recommendations into bills which would have provided a useful framework for public debate.

It was never a reasonable ambition to expect a fledgeling new committee system to enjoy powers of command over the executive or to become alternative machines through which backbenchers could draft and enact legislation. The function of the experiment was not to set up alternative Cabinets, but to channel informed opinion and analysis into the parliamentary chamber and to present a framework for debate which might then produce a consensus or majority support for legislation. In this it was largely successful. At no other time have members of the Oireachtas received such informed research with which to pester the executive, or to form their own opinion on complex issues. Through investigating and interrogating, the new committees produced countless opportunities for future legislative initiatives. The failure to follow-up committee work was probably caused by a combination of backbench humility in the face of a dominant party leadership and sheer lack of time, experience and motivation. Backbench experience with private members' bills, for example, has been discouraging.

Between 1970 and 1981 19 private members' bills were introduced in the Dail, of which six were withdrawn, two lapsed and eleven were rejected. Not one of these got past the second stage of legislation, and a further seven were refused introduction.[24] Only 17 private members' bills have ever been passed in the history of the Oireachtas. Five were passed in the late 1920s; a further five in the 1930s, and six more in the 1950s. The recent Judicial Separation and Family Law Reform Act, 1989, was the first private member's bill to be passed in the Oireachtas in almost 40 years.

CABINET SUPREMACY

Those within the government and civil service who resisted parliamentary reforms at the outset continue to do so today. Seen from a political perspective, those who try to obstruct change in the status quo, as with select committees for example, hold fast to their traditional respect for the Cabinet's supremacy over Parliament – a respect which the majority of those in the executive, or likely to be in the executive, strive to preserve. Speaking on a motion for Dail reform, Brian Lenihan, deputy leader of Fianna Fail and current Tanaiste (deputy prime minister), Minister for Defence and current presidential candidate, said that 'Governments are the people who must make the decisions. Whatever we do here as parliamentarians must be regarded essentially as a kind of subsidiary or advisory function. . . . It is a fundamental principle that the ultimate decision must reside in the elected Government. If we begin departing from that we will be entering a shilly-shally situation in which there is not a decision-making process working to its fulfilment'.[25] Referring specifically to the idea of select committees, Deputy Lenihan went on to say that he would 'not agree with any committee system that would in any way intrude on, or obstruct the basic decision-making process of politicians elected to Government, regardless of which party or parties may form the Government' and that he would 'be in favour of setting up a committee who know their terms of reference but not a committee set up as an alternative Government'.[26]

Put another way, select committees are acceptable as long as they know their place. Before 1983, successive governments ignored calls to extend the use of select committees, possibly because they feared that their own reforms might one day prove to have repercussions. When the coalition government introduced a wide range of select committees during the 24th Oireachtas, they did so in a somewhat disorganised and haphazard fashion. They nevertheless ensured, through carefully drafted terms of reference, that the experiment did not backfire. The infrastructure which would guarantee effective results was not forthcoming, nor were the necessary publishing and editing resources or levels of staffing and accommodation. Absent too was the essential access to the parliamentary schedule to debate committee reports. The experiment consisted, therefore, of a proliferation of disparate entities which could not properly be dubbed a 'system' of select committees. A useful system would need to rely on a solid infrastructure to maximise its potential effectiveness.

CONCLUSION

Backbenchers in Ireland complain about their formal relationship with the Executive which is a subordinate one. They play a subsidiary role in policy formulation and law-making and their scrutiny of the executive is no more than cursory. For a short period in the early 1980s the use of select committees showed a potential to change parliamentary affairs for the better. Most of those committees no longer exist, partly because some of them performed too well and sent shock waves through the system, but mostly because members of the Oireachtas sat back and let them be disbanded without demanding that they be reinstated. Little or no pressure has been exerted on the present government to initiate new reforms or even to reconstitute the old ones. If anything the Oireachtas might be seen to have reverted to its former subservience in the face of dominant and charismatic executive leadership, choosing to adopt a more informal behind-the-scenes approach to its business with the executive sooner than a confrontational one. 'At the end of the day the buck stops with the government' and perhaps it is unprofitable to enter battle in the parliamentary arena when defeat is inevitable and disputes are more easily settled or conceded 'out of court'.[27]

NOTES

1. Lenin quoted in P. Zagorin, *Rebels and Rulers 1500–1660, Volume I: Society, States and Early Modern Revolution* (Cambridge: Cambridge University Press, 1982), p.201.
2. S.E. Finer, *Comparative Government* (Harmondsworth: Penguin, 1982), p.66.
3. M. Mezey, *Comparative Legislatures* (Durham, NC: Duke University Press, 1979), p.6.
4. *Bunreacht na hEireann* (Constitution of Ireland), Article 28.1.
5. Ibid., Article 28.7.2.
6. J. A. Murphy, *Ireland in the Twentieth Century* (Dublin: Gill and Macmillan, 1975), p.42.
7. Ibid., p.68.
8. R. Packenham, 'Legislatures and Political Development', in A. Kornberg and L.D. Musolf (eds), *Legislatures in Developmental Perspective* (Durham NC: Duke University Press, 1970).
9. NO. OF PARLIAMENTARY QUESTIONS PER GOVERNMENT DEPARTMENT 1970–81

Government Department	Total Questions	Average
Environment/Local Govt.	10,250	932
Education	7053	641
Agriculture/Fisheries	6604	600
Finance	5993	545
Social Welfare	4963	451
Industry/Commerce	4915	447
Post and Telegraphs	4621	420
Health	4284	389
Justice	3435	312
Foreign Affairs	2126	193

10. *The Independent*, 8 October 1987, p.8.
11. Mary T. Robinson, 'Irish Parliamentary Scrutiny of European Community Legislation', in *Common Market Law Journal*, 1979, p. 6.
12. B. Laffan, 'Ireland and Denmark in the European Community – Political and Administrative Aspects', *Administration*, Vol. 29, No. 1 (1981), p.57.

13. Ibid., p. 59.
14. European Communities (Amendment) Act, 1973, section 4, subsection 1(b).
15. Robinson, p. 10.
16. Mezey, p.27.
17. B. Chubb, 'The Republic of Ireland', in S. Henig and J. Pinder (eds.), *European Political Parties* (London: Allen & Unwin, 1969), p.458.
18. *Report of the Informal Committee on Dail Reform* (Dublin: Stationery Office, 1972), prl.2904.
19. B. Desmond, *The Houses of the Oireachtas – A Plea for Reform: A Memorandum to the Government* (Dublin, 1975), p.3.
20. Ibid., p.1.
32. M. Gallagher, 'Does Ireland Need A New Electoral System?' in *Irish Political Studies*, Vol.2 (1987), p.31.
22. Mezey, p.4.
23. *White Paper on Manpower Policy* (Dublin: Department of Labour, 1986), prl.4306, p.18.
24. Private Members' Bills introduced in the Oireachtas between 1970 and 1981: Tobacco (Control of Sale and Advertisement) Bill, 1971; Waters Preservation Bill, 1972; Misuse of Drugs Bill, 1974; Pounds (Provision and Maintenance) Bill, 1975; Maritime Jurisdiction (Amendment) Bill, 1976; Consumer Protection Bill, 1978; Film Industry Bill, 1978; Fisheries (Amendment) Bill, 1978; Industrial Relations (National Pay Agreement) Bill, 1978; National Monuments (Amendment) Bill, 1978; Sixth Amendment of the Constitution Bill, 1978; Ombudsman Bill, 1979; Imposition of Duties (Amendment) Bill, 1979; Council for Adult Education in Ireland Bill, 1980; Law Reform (Abolition of Criminal Conversation) Bill, 1980; Local Government (Building Land) Bill, 1980; National Heritage Bill 1980; Retail Grocery Trade (Special Provisions) Bill, 1981; Travel Reserve Fund Bill, 1981.
25. *Dail Debates*, 2 February, 1983, Vol.339: column 913.
26. Ibid., col. 914–915.
27. B. Lenihan, TD and current deputy prime minister, *Dail Debates* (2 February 1983), Vol.339: col. 914.

Parliamentary Activism and Legitimacy in the Netherlands

Ken Gladdish

The inaugural problem in an essay on institutional behaviour is to provide an intelligible context for the institution's place within the political system. This is aggravated in the case of the legislature: for it forms a crucial part of the elaborate nexus which, in a mature democracy, links the electorate and the political parties via the system of representation, with the political and professional executive. Within the West European cosmos, Parliament has historically combined the representation function with the legitimation of the executive powers derived from the experience of monarchy. Whether implicitly or explicitly this normally translates into some concept of parliamentary sovereignty which, in terms of constitutional theory, places the legislature at the apex of the political and legal structure. What this means in practice clearly varies from polity to polity. One task, therefore, in any specific case, is to see how far Parliament fulfils the central functions of monitoring and legitimating the direction of the state. This requires it to be viewed in relation to the entire political process: not an easy exercise in a short account of parliamentary operations over a given period.

The typology offered by Michael Mezey in his chapter 'Classifying Legislatures',[1] which the editor has taken as a starting point for the contributions to this volume, puts the Netherlands in a populous category of systems. Its legislature is deemed to possess 'modest policy-making power', 'relatively high support', and essentially 'reactive' capacities *vis à vis* the executive.[2] In terms of an overall taxonomy of the world's legislatures this is doubtless relatively true. But it is also true that such a placing scarcely brings out the specific roles of the Dutch States-General, nor the conceptual and operational distinctions between it and, say, the Swedish Riksdag, the Danish Folketing or even the Mexican Congress.

To accomplish that vital task of differentiation involves some analysis of the main elements of the political structure. Only then is it possible to try to assess how far the Dutch Parliament since 1970 has (a) 'served to maintain the popular legitimacy of government', and (b) 'declined or been reinforced as a policy influencing body'.[3] Benchmarks in the development of political systems tend to have an arbitrary character. It so happens, however, that 1970 is a not infertile vantage-point from which to view Dutch practice, because it was a stage at which there were strenuous efforts to give it a new inflection.[4] To appreciate that requires some knowledge of the basic anatomy of the system which will be summarised under the following headings:

1. The method of national representation;

2. The character of the party system;
3. The constitution of the legislature;
4. The operations of Parliament;
5. The dynamics of government.

THE METHOD OF NATIONAL REPRESENTATION[5]

The most arresting fact about national representation in the Netherlands is that it is not based upon geographical constituencies. Since 1918, members of the Second Chamber of Parliament, the effective legislative body, have been elected by a system of nationwide proportional representation through the medium of party lists. The country is administratively divided into electoral districts and the composition of lists may vary somewhat between districts. Candidates may also have certain connections with localities, which may be utilised for party purposes, and parties have recently developed regional links through specialised spokesmen. But electors have no direct or specific relationships with individual MPs and MPs have no formal links with any particular group of electors.

This has important consequences for the character of parliamentary representation. Dutch MPs arrive in the Lower House without having been through any formal process of local selection. They owe their seats to the decisions of national and regional party committees which have put them in positions on candidate lists high enough to secure their election. Should they give up their seats in the course of a Parliament, their places will be filled from the list on which they appeared at the previous election. There is neither need nor provision for by-elections. There is also neither need nor provision for the nursing of constituencies or constituents. Once in the Second Chamber, MPs will operate in relation not to the perceived or assumed wishes of a set of clients within the electorate, but according to the decisions of their respective parliamentary group or *fractie*.

The basic reason for the adoption of nationwide PR was the state of development of the party system by the second decade of the present century. By this stage four major political groupings, two of them further sub-divided into separate parties, were contesting elections in single member constituencies, where the lack of an overall majority was settled by second ballots. The tactical difficulties of this form of competition were proving increasingly troublesome and seemed likely to be exacerbated by the introduction of universal suffrage. The solution resorted to, with the agreement of all party elites, was a system based upon the aggregate national support for each party. No threshold was applied, other than the arithmetical hurdle of securing enough votes to claim a seat in a chamber of (then) 100 members. When, in 1956, the size of the Lower House was increased to 150 seats, this hurdle was effectively reduced to 0.67 per cent of the total poll. So that large and small parties competed essentially on identical terms. The contest was open, the citizens regularly confronted a large number of lists, and in principle the system was subject to whatever volatility voters displayed. In practice the results quickly became highly predictable, not as a consequence of the electoral system but because of the solidified pattern of voter mobilisation.

THE CHARACTER OF THE PARTY SYSTEM

By the 1920s, the bulk of voters were mobilised within a pattern known as *Verzuiling*, which extended from political associations to a vast range of bodies designed to provide for the social, cultural, educational, welfare, and informational needs of each 'sub-culture'. The pattern was complex, asymmetrical and never fully comprehensive. The religious or confessional groupings, Catholic and Calvinist, catered for their followers most extensively. The secular groupings, Social Democrat and Liberal, were less comprehensive, indeed the latter was a somewhat shadowy *Zuil*. But the electoral outcomes reflected the settled allegiance of 80–90 per cent of the voters. Thus in the inter-war period the Catholics normally achieved *c*. 30 per cent of the total poll, the two major Calvinist formations (the Anti-Revolutionaries and the Christian Historicals) 20–25 per cent, the Social Democrats some 25 per cent, and the Liberals 10 per cent.

These outcomes broadly transcended the caesura of invasion and occupation from 1940 to 1945, despite changes in party organisation and nomenclature. After the 1959 election, the Second Chamber consisted of 49 Catholic MPs, 48 Labour, 26 major Calvinist and 19 Liberals. These blocs accounted for all but eight seats in the 150-member House. Changes in the pattern, however, began to surface from 1967 onwards. In that year the two leading parties, Catholic and Labour, lost seats, and newer movements gained representation. The 1971 election saw the total holding of the major groups decline as the smaller units amassed the unprecedented sum of 37 seats. The party system seemed to be in flux and over the subsequent decade would change its character; so that by 1981 a new configuration was in place. The three formerly separate major confessional parties, one Catholic and two Calvinist, had now been amalgamated into a single Christian Democratic Appeal. The Liberals had become a major party on the secular right of centre, and Democrats '66, a product of the 1960s, had emerged as the fourth largest party.

These developments had obvious repercussions upon the formation of governments, and the inter-relationship of party groups within the Chamber.

THE CONSTITUTION OF THE LEGISLATURE[6]

The origins of the modern Dutch Parliament, the States-General in The Hague, can be traced back to the first national assembly of 1798, during the relatively brief period of French domination. The term States-General stems from the Republic and indeed has its roots in the pre-independence era, though it did not then refer to an elected legislature within a unitary state. The present Parliament has a continuous history since 1814, when it was established under the constitution which restored Dutch independence and inaugurated the monarchy. The operation of a parliamentary system of government dates from the constitutional revision of 1848–49. The current mode of composition of Parliament was determined by the settlement of 1917–18, while the latest enactment of its provenance and scope was set down in the constitutional re-draft of 1983.

Although the concept is not explicitly affirmed, the Netherlands is governed by the principle of parliamentary supremacy, mitigated only by the fact that certain matters require an exceptional majority in the legislature. The Netherlands has remained an hereditary monarchy since 1814, and acts which affect the throne usually necessitate special proceedings. The political role of the monarch is essentially passive and symbolic, though the perennial need for the formation of coalition Cabinets can result in the King, or currently the Queen, having to perform an intermediary task in order to initiate this process.

Articles 50–72 of the 1983 Constitutional Statement set out the fundamental items of the provision for a parliamentary system. They assert that the State-General shall consist of two chambers, a First Chamber (the ratifying house) with 75 members, and the Second Chamber (the effective legislative house) with 150 members. The parliamentary term shall be four years, but each chamber may be dissolved before a term is completed. Each chamber shall be elected by proportional representation and by secret ballot; the First by the members of the provincial councils, and the Second directly, by all adults of and above the age of 18, with two forms of disqualification (convicted prisoners serving one year or more, and mental incompetents). No-one may sit in both chamber simultaneously; and no minister, state secretary, state councillor, state auditor or certain judicial figures can be a member of either chamber. Sittings of Parliament must be held in public, but there are provisions for sessions in camera.

There are further constitutional provisions, under Articles 81–111, which deal with parliamentary procedure and competence. In the broadest terms these are the outcome of the decisions of Parliament itself over the past 140 years. For as Article 120 roundly states 'The constitutionality of Acts of Parliament and treaties shall not be reviewed by the courts'. There is thus an express exclusion of any form of judicial review, so that it can be said, *pace* Britain, that the constitution of the Netherlands is what Parliament, over time, has decided it should be. In therefore both law and practice, the State-General is at the summit of the governmental pyramid; its powers are embodied in a written constitution, but that constitution it alone can change.

THE OPERATIONS OF PARLIAMENT

The States-General conforms to the familiar model of West European parliamentary operations, embracing the four basic functions of a democratic legislature. First, all legislation requires parliamentary enactment, without exception. This extends to the approval of treaties (Article 91) though this approval may be tacit in certain circumstances. It also extends to declarations of war and the ending of war. It includes, as one would expect, all financial provisions undertaken by the state, pre-eminently the annual budget. Legislation is enacted by a simple majority in both chambers, though matters affecting the Throne (Article 29 & 30) or the financial remuneration of MPs (Article 63) require a two-thirds majority in both chambers. Since the overwhelming preponderance of bills are introduced by the Cabinet, the legislative task of Parliament is essentially that of the discussion and, if necessary, amendment of government proposals. To accomplish this task, there is an extensive committee structure which divides the field of legislation into subject areas.

The second function of Parliament is the generation of policy proposals, which may inspire further legislation, in the form of motions. In common with most other activities, the tabling of motions has increased enormously in frequency over the past 20 years. Indeed, it could be said that this form of policy initiation has become almost a new dimension of parliamentary participation since the late 1960s.

The third function, which has also assumed far greater proportions over the same period, is that of the scrutiny of government. Procedurally, the process of scrutiny takes three possible forms: questions, interpellations and commissions of enquiry. The last, which is the most searching and elaborate of the forms, is an extremely rare operation, engaged in only when the other forms seem likely to prove inadequate. It may be regarded as the last resort in the case of massive scandals, as with the furore over government subsidies to the RSV company of Rotterdam in 1985–86, or where a major vein of public policy has to be opened, as with the Commission which sat from 1947 to 1956 to enquire into the conduct of the governments in exile during the Second World War. The rarity of this procedure is illustrated by the facts that the latter was the first Commission in 60 years, while the 1985–86 example was only the next occasion.

Interpellation, which is a grand investigation of ministerial conduct by an MP with the approval of the respective Chamber, is a more frequent affair than a commission of enquiry; unlike many other forms of parliamentary activity, its frequency has not increased greatly in recent years. By far the most common form of parliamentary scrutiny is the question addressed to ministers, and this has soared in popularity since the early 1960s. Since ministers normally only attend either Chamber when presenting or defending legislative proposals, questions are usually put and answered in writing.

The fourth and final basic function of Parliament is the elective function. Dutch Cabinets are not, as has been noted, part of the legislature; nor do they need to consist of members who have been elected to either Chamber. Nevertheless, both the formation and the survival of Cabinets are dependant upon the support of a majority in both Chambers, so that parliamentary groups play a principal role in the establishment of new governments after each parliamentary election.

The legislative process can be viewed in two perspectives: the procedural and the political. The procedural mechanisms in the Netherlands, set out in a systematic, comparative form, are available in English in the compendium *Parliaments of the World*, produced by the Inter-Parliamentary Union.[7] An in-depth historical survey, up to 1959, also in English, is provided by van Raalte.[8] There are numerous accounts in Dutch, notably those by van Schendelen,[9] Visscher,[10] and in the symposium edited by Franssen.[11] The starting point of the legislative process is normally the introduction of a bill by a minister, though measures are occasionally sponsored by an MP. Before a bill is presented to Parliament, it is usually submitted to the Council of State, a body which advises on possible constitutional implications. The Social and Economic Council is also consulted on matters which fall within its sphere of expertise.

The consideration of bills begins in the Second Chamber, where, after a first reading, they are passed to the most appropriate committee for detailed scrutiny. The committee structure of Parliament, in 1986, consisted of a framework of 30 permanent subject committees in the Second Chamber, and 20 in the First Chamber. There were in addition *c.* 60 special committees in the former (reduced to 15 in 1987), and three in the latter. If a bill falls within the ambit of a subject committee it will be directed to it. Otherwise it will be referred to either an existing or a newly-formed special committee.

The composition of committees is determined by the chairman of each Chamber with respect to the overall party arithmetic. Committees elect their own chairmen, but this too is arranged to accord with the distribution of party strengths. Committee hearings are usually open, journalists may attend, and proceedings may be broadcast, either directly or in summary form, on radio and TV. At the committee stage amendments may be proposed, discussed and incorporated in bills. When the examination of a bill by a committee is completed, the results are presented to the Second Chamber for plenary debate and discussion clause by clause. There may be a further reading if the plenary discussion has resulted in significant changes.

The processes of amendment are carefully invigilated by the minister or ministers concerned. Parliament has complete control over its treatment of legislation and sets its own agenda and timing for this.[12] Given the separation between Cabinet and Parliament, the States-General is less overtly dominated by the executive than most European states, above all Britain. But legislation is nevertheless executive-directed, and, as elsewhere, governments seek to get their measures through with a minimum of alteration in the legislature. Ministers may therefore refuse to accept amendments, and in extreme cases may prefer to withdraw a bill. Cabinets expect to be able to rely upon their supporting parties in Parliament to ensure that their proposals are not mutilated to the point of nullity; and there is extensive consultation behind the scenes to prevent this happening. The success of these consultations is revealed by the fact that virtually all government measures are eventually passed, though up to half with amendments agreed between ministers and the Second Chamber.[13] One interesting feature of the amendment process is that in each case it is a matter of whether MPs decide to endorse or reject. There is no tradition of abstention in the Dutch Parliament, though spokesmen can cover the absence of individual MPs by delivering the party vote.

Once an acceptable outcome has been achieved in the Lower House, bills are then passed to the Upper House which examines them by means of a plenary debate. The First Chamber has no powers to amend legislation. It must either accept or reject measures in their entirety, and the latter course is extremely unusual. After ratification by the First Chamber, bills are submitted for the royal assent and for counter-signature by the appropriate minister. The annual budget follows the same course as other legislation. There are standing committees in both Chambers to examine the budget, and all members receive an annual report on the economic situation prepared by the Central Planning Bureau.

The effective legislative chamber, the Second, is headed by a presidium of officers chosen from among members of the major parliamentary groups. Originally comprising a chairman and two vice-chairmen, it had expanded by 1984 to include six vice-chairmen, whose task it is to regulate the flow of parliamentary business. The pattern of parliamentary operations cannot readily be presented in terms of government and opposition forces. The parties represented in Cabinet are, of course, expected generally to support the government, but this is not a matter of ministerial fiat. Instead, it relies upon the willingness of the respective parliamentary groups to satisfy themselves that the government's policy is sustainable.

There are nine *fracties* in the current Second Chamber (as from 1989), ranging in size from over 50 members (the CDA) down to one-person groups (Janmaat and RPF). The larger groups have a collegial character and are presided over by an elected chairman. Relations between the *fracties* and their respective national parties are best described as 'semi-detached'. MPs may owe their position to party managers outside Parliament, but this is rarely allowed to detract from their sense of autonomy.[14] Discipline within the *fractie* is not imposed by party whips but depends upon group cohesion. If sanctions are needed to curb dissent they more often come from the group than from the chairman.[15] Dissent does of course occur and in extreme cases can result in the formation of breakaway groups. Usually such groups are ephemeral, though they may develop into distinct parties. Thus the PPR, formed in 1968 when three MPs broke from the Catholic People's Party, achieved a permanent identity and a national base; others, such as DS '70, a breakaway from Labour, though it served in Cabinet from 1971 to 1972, had a briefer existence and was dissolved in 1981.

It is within the plenary meetings of the *fracties* that the tactics and strategy of parliamentary operations are decided. All, regardless of size, are officially recognised and have paid staffs and resources to support their activities. Indeed the budget for the parliamentary groups rose from a modest Fl 30,000 in 1965 to a towering figure of Fl 15.8 million (c.£ 5 million) in 1985.[16] The *fracties* are thus the building blocks of all legislative behaviour and their independence imbues Parliament with a strongly self-determining character. The key point here is that the Cabinet governs, to a greater extent than in most systems, with the consent of the parliamentary groups. As a leading commentator has put it, 'Because the key to cabinet stability is in the hands of. . .the parliamentary parties, the

Netherlands has become an exceptional case of "rule by Parliament"'.[17]
He goes on to locate the core of the process as 'the political osmosis
between the parties-in-coalition and their cabinet'. But as will be evident
from the logistics of parliamentary activity, parties outside the coalition
can make a significant impact upon government policy. In March 1988,
the CDA–VVD Cabinet presented to the Second Chamber a package
of social and economic measures designed to make 'drastic reductions'
in social security benefits and to lower personal taxes. The package was
substantially amended as a result of opposition from the Labour *fractie*
which was able to wrest concessions from the government on a number of
items.

THE DYNAMICS OF GOVERNMENT

It is a truism to say that the role of a legislature is largely determined by its
relationship with the executive. In the Dutch case this relationship warrants
extensive treatment because a number of factors serve to make it distinctive.
The first is a pattern of ministerial autonomy which derives partly from
the prolongation of monarchical influence upon Cabinet-making into the
present century. The notion that portfolios were a conferment of personal
responsibility by the monarch, rather than admission to a ministerial team,
has to an extent survived as an item in the political structure. Both the
necessity for and the character of governing coalitions, which stem from
the configuration of the party system, have served to reinforce this feature.
When Cabinets are formed, and the formation process is itself a distinctive
element in the delivery of party government, the distribution of portfolios
is a vital stage in the post-election settlement. It is subject to intensive
bargaining between the coalition partners and results in a pattern of party
holdings which are not thereafter susceptible to readjustment or reshuffle.
This affects the relationship between party figures in the Cabinet and party
leaders in parliament. It also affects, though this has been increasingly
modified over the past two decades, the relationship between the Prime
Minister and his Cabinet colleagues.

     The whole development of the concept of a premier, a Cabinet leader
who could exercise all essential prerogatives in the shaping of his team
and the determination of national policy, has been a slow and intermittent
process in the Netherlands. It was not until the 1930s that the formal
existence of a Minister-President with his own office, as distinct from a
Cabinet chairman without an official title, was fully and finally recognised.
Since then the extent to which Minister-Presidents have been able to impose
themselves upon successive Cabinets has varied according to personalities
and coalition circumstances. Nowadays the Minister-President is likely to
have had the principal say in the whole process of Cabinet formation,
including the overall distribution of portfolios among the governing parties.
But it is still the case that individual ministers will have been proposed by
the parties concerned. Once the Cabinet has been formed, there is little
scope for a prime minister to reallocate responsibilities, for this would
unravel the complex package which brought the Cabinet into being.

Until the 1970s, relations between ministers and party leaders in the Parliament were, in most cases somewhat distanced. In a notable and oft-quoted analysis, Lijphart, in the 1960s, pointed out that in the long record of parliamentary government which began in 1848, almost half of all Dutch ministers had never served in Parliament.[18] Moreover, little more than a third of Cabinet members had previously served in Parliament. Parliamentary leaders and party figures, when casting their share of Cabinet portfolios, were traditionally prone to seek candidates from outside the parliamentary ranks. This approach to ministerial recruitment has undergone considerable change in the past quarter-century. But it is instructive to note that of the 14 ministers sworn in on 7 November 1989, in the latest Cabinet formation following the election of September 1989, five had never held seats in the Second Chamber.

A further dimension of singularity in the relationship between Cabinet and Parliament, relates to the practice of corporatism which through the period of post-war reconstruction, and subsequently, characterised policy-making in the Netherlands. This merits an extended exposition, but its essential consequence was that into the 1960s and beyond, a complex pattern of interest group representation and consultation resulted in public policy being shaped other than by Cabinet directives. This had effects both upon the status of ministers and the involvement of Parliament in the policy process.

It will be clear from what has already been said that relations between Cabinet and Parliament are less close than in a system such as that of Britain. Ministers and state secretaries (deputy ministers) may not be members of Parliament, do not as a matter of course attend parliamentary sessions and have no vote in Parliament. They do, however, have a right to address the Chamber and may be invited to do so. Usually, only one minister will be present at any one time and will sit not on the front bench but at a table at one end of the Chamber. The Prime Minister is a somewhat infrequent attender except when major policy is under attack.

In these circumstances a bridge between Cabinet and Parliament is vital, and this is provided by the presidium, which ensures that ministerial inputs are properly staged and that a constructive relationship is promoted. Since ministers are outside the legislature they must fight their parliamentary corners individually. They must also protect their party positions. Under the conditions of multi-party Cabinets there is a relentless need to maintain accords at both governmental and parliamentary levels. This results in a continuous imperative towards collaboration between ministers and their own parliamentary parties, between ministers and their Cabinet colleagues, and between the *fracties* in Parliament which are expected to sustain the coalition.

Having sketched the major elements which provide a context for parliamentary operations in the Netherlands, this analysis goes on to examine the dynamics of parliamentary activity over the past generation, presented under four headings:

1. Behavioural change within the political system;
2. Developments in parliamentary activity since 1970;
3. Attitudes towards Parliament;
4. The current significance of Parliament.

BEHAVIOURAL CHANGE WITHIN THE POLITICAL SYSTEM

In his classic appraisal, Lijphart characterised the Dutch system as *The Politics of Accommodation*.[19] By this he meant that the system operated according to a pattern of inter-élite co-operation, rather than opposition-ally. His assessment was made, however, on the eve of a decline of the traditional arrangements, for during the later 1960s, a sea-change was evident in Dutch politics. For some two decades after 1945 a style of national management had prevailed which reflected a broad consensus among major party formations ranging from the nature of political competition to the accepted modes of economic management. This was now challenged in a variety of ways which resulted in new parties, a decline of support for traditional parties, a critical onslaught on the political system, and, on the part of the secular movements, a desire for greater polarisation.

Within the Labour Party the challenge was in part orchestrated by a tendency known as New Left, which sought to arrest the sagging appeal of democratic Socialism and to institute a more radical approach to both electoral mobilisation and government.[20] In 1969 the Labour Party Congress resolved that there should be no further Cabinet coalitions with the Catholic People's Party. In part this was a delayed response to the humiliation of being forced out of government in 1966 by the parliamentary leader of the Catholics. In part it was a reversion to the hopes of those in the wartime generation who looked for a reorientation of political forces which would offer a clearer choice between the left and the confessional centre. In both the 1971 and 1972 elections Labour formed an alliance with two new parties, Democrats '66 and the Radicals, which was presented as an alternative government seeking office. This was a radical departure from previous strategies and amounted to a frontal attack upon centre-based politics.

In response, the major confessional parties began the long process of consolidation which would lead, in the latter 1970s, to a complete merger under the banner of the Christian Democratic Appeal. The immediate upshot was that by 1973 the Labour Party had shouldered its way back into government. But not without reluctant confessional support. The mould had not been shattered, but a new inflection had been imparted to the system which now took on a somewhat more oppositional character. In 1977 the newly formed CDA took the increasingly successful Liberal Party into Cabinet and, apart from a brief interregnum from 1981 to 1982, maintained the centre–right coalition up to the election of 1989.

All this had important consequences at the parliamentary level. As the next section discloses, there was a surprising escalation of critical activity within the Second Chamber. The former understandings between the major contenders, which had resulted in a relatively quiescent legislature, now gave way to an assertion of parliamentary autonomy in the form of a more active legislature, more willing to challenge, criticise and question ministers.

DEVELOPMENTS IN PARLIAMENTARY ACTIVITY SINCE 1970

In the mid-1970s van Schendelen produced convincing evidence that the scale and intensity of parliamentary operations had augmented dramatically over the preceding decade, prompting the conclusion that: 'the increased parliamentary activism since 1967 has been such that the Netherlands can, in a sense, be said to have got a different type of Lower House'.[21] During the parliamentary session of 1956–57, 185 bills were discussed in the Second Chamber. By 1971–72 this number had risen only slightly to 213 bills. Yet committee meetings in the Lower House had trebled in frequency by the end of that period, as had the number of amendments to bills proposed by the *fracties*. So far as policy initiatives were concerned, the number of motions tabled in the Second Chamber had increased ninefold, from 20 in 1956–57 to 176 in 1971–72. While on the scrutiny front the number of interpellations had trebled, from six to 19, and the annual total of questions put to ministers had escalated by a factor of ten, from 211 (1956–57) to 2092 (1971–72).

What is most striking about these statistics is that they do not reflect any comparable growth of governmental inputs. In seeking some explanations for this enormous increase of business over a relatively short period, therefore, van Schendelen considered three possible avenues: variables affecting the personnel of the Chamber, changes in the resources available to the *fracties*, and factors deriving from changes in the political culture. Although he discerns several features affecting what he terms the 'intra-parliamentary variables', the only persuasive factor here is that from 1966 on the number of assistants available to MPs had multiplied, as is reflected in the rising budget for facilities in the Lower House. So he is driven to allocate much of the explanation to changes in the general political climate, though this cannot readily be measured. The breakdown of the settled patterns of accommodation associated with the structures of *verzuiling* seems therefore the most likely source of an acceleration of parliamentary challenge and criticism.

More recent data on parliamentary activity have been provided by Visscher who, from the vantage point of the mid 1980s, has surveyed the range of fields in which parliamentary participation has manifestly burgeoned since the 1960s.[22] Dealing first with legislative operations, his figures show a consistent expansion of parliamentary intervention (Tables 1 and 2). On the score of policy initiatives, as reflected in the number of motions tabled in the Lower House, an enormous increase is evident, as Table 3 demonstrates.

In the realm of parliamentary scrutiny, although the number of inter-pellations increased from three in 1963–64 to 17 in 1973–74, the

TABLE 1

AMENDMENTS PROPOSED TO BILLS IN THE SECOND CHAMBER

	Submitted	Adopted
1963–4	178	62
1973–4	362	81
1983–4	800	225

TABLE 2

AMENDMENTS TO THE BUDGET PROPOSED IN THE SECOND CHAMBER

	Submitted	Adopted
1964	2	0
1974	41	5
1984	115	38

TABLE 3

MOTIONS TABLED IN THE SECOND CHAMBER

	Tabled	Adopted
1963–4	9	1
1973–4	196	61
1983–4	1214	485

TABLE 4

QUESTIONS TO MINISTERS

	Second Chamber	First Chamber
1961–2	208	12
1971–2	689	169
1981–2	1481	37

figure for 1983–84 showed no further growth. In the case of questions put to ministers, a vast increase occurred over the decade from 1961–62 to 1971–72 and continued to augment in the Second Chamber over the subsequent decade (Table 4).

The overall picture shows a startling rise in the three spheres of legislative intervention, policy initiatives and scrutiny. Van Schendelen's endeavour to explain this exceptional growth of parliamentary activism has been subsequently echoed by Daalder who regards parties as having become more sensitive to public opinion with the loss of their 'special clienteles' post-*verzuiling*.[23]

ATTITUDES TOWARDS PARLIAMENT

It is a commonplace of liberal democratic theory that representative assemblies serve, *inter alia*, to maintain the popular legitimacy of government – a principal theme of this symposium. It is, however, extremely difficult to assess operationally how far this is true, or indeed to measure it in any precise or convincing way. In the discussion in Britain preceding the televising of the proceedings of the House of Commons, much play was made of the notion that visibility would somehow enhance public satisfaction. But there was little to suggest how this might be judged.

The proceedings of the Dutch Parliament have long been televised, but there is little, if any, hard information available about how far this has contributed to feelings of closer identification with the legislature on the part of the populace.

Visibility aside, studies do exist of citizen attitudes in the Netherlands towards their national representatives, which are worth summarising. Unfortunately, the pre-1970 period is somewhat blank. The record effectively begins with a study undertaken at the University of Leiden in 1970–71 which sought to discover the extent of popular participation in policy-making.[24] One area of investigation was the degree to which citizens contacted members of the Second Chamber about issues of local or national importance. The findings were, however, largely negative. On local matters few voters thought MPs a useful target of complaint, suggestion or enquiry. On matters of national concern, the place of legislators in the public estimation of worthwhile approaches was a surprisingly lowly one. More contacts were reported with labour leaders, ministers, high civil servants and provincial officials than with individual MPs.

In 1972–73 a more extensive survey was undertaken at the University of Nijmegen, which examined citizen attitudes towards the political system as a whole.[25] In respect of the operations of Parliament, opinion was divided equally between respondents who expressed confidence in the legislature, and those who expressed the opposite. On the aptness and utility of the electoral system, 51 per cent of those canvassed were prepared to support the view that MPs should be elected on a constituency basis. More cogently from the standpoint of MP–voter relations, those sampled were asked about their experience of contacting national representatives, and their judgement was sought about how effective this had been. Over 70 per cent regarded contacting MPs, on either local or national matters, to be an ineffective way of airing problems. Representatives at municipal level were thought to respond most effectively to approaches about local issues. At national level, members of the royal family turned out to be the object of slightly more frequent contacts than individual MPs.

This evidence seems to confirm that in the absence of local constituencies, voters will be unlikely to refer to members of Parliament, since they cannot identify which MP it might be worth addressing. This does not signify an absolute lack of channels of communication between the voting mass and the presiding élite. But it does reveal something about perceptions of the role of parliamentarians. The role of MPs has received much systematic attention from Dutch political scientists. The most comprehensive study of the parliamentary universe was assembled by van Schendelen in 1981.[26] In this survey an encyclopaedic range of questions was put to members of the Second Chamber about every conceivable aspect of their duties. One of its more general findings was that the indifference of voters towards MPs as fertile objects of personal communication, was paralleled by the extremely poor opinion legislators held about the level of awareness of the citizens.

This unpropitious relationship between voters and their representatives was examined by van Schendelen in an article of the same period.[27] He believed that 'strong negative orientations towards the main elements of representation-in-action' were widespread in Western democracies. In the case of the Netherlands he had this to say:

> Only 4 per cent of the citizens have ever had any contact with an MP and less than 10 per cent of M.P.s consider individual citizens to be an important source of information for their own legislative activities. The direct linkage between Dutch electors and elected is, indeed, quite weak.

That this mutual isolation may be deepening is suggested by evidence that members of the Second Chamber in 1979 placed even less emphasis upon dealing with citizens' complaints than members of the 1972 Chamber.[28] A further detail was that MPs from the major centre and right of centre parties, the CDA and the VVD, were somewhat less impressed with the cognitive abilities of voters than their colleagues from Labour and D'66.

It is difficult to determine, without extensive cross-national comparisons, whether or not the Netherlands is exceptional in the apparent distance disclosed between legislators and the public. Some further illumination is, however, available from the findings of a study of role-perceptions on the part of Dutch, German and British parliamentarians.[29] All three contingents shared a high view of their role as policy-makers. As advocates of ideologies, however, Dutch MPs were much less enthusiastic than their counterparts, preferring to regard themselves as 'technicians'. But the most revealing disclosure, in the context of representation, was that the task of mediation between groups and individuals, an activity scored highly by British and even more highly by German MPs, was virtually ignored by the Dutch.

How far the electoral system is the fundamental reason for these phenomena is difficult to assess. But there are certainly features of the representational process which tend to distance members of Parliament from the people, and thereby to augment attitudes on the part of national legislators that their responsibilities are best fulfilled sealed off from the pressures of public sentiment.

THE CURRENT SIGNIFICANCE OF PARLIAMENT

Having presented a selection of the information available about parliamentary activity, and responses to it since 1970, we now attempt to evaluate it. The first heading – how far Parliament has declined or been reinforced as a policy-influencing body – is perhaps the easier to tackle.

It is certainly possible to argue that there has been an increase of parliamentary influence upon policy-making over the past two decades. There are three general grounds on which this contention might be based. The first is the record of much greater activism on the part of the Second Chamber, as witnessed by the statistics given in the earlier section on developments since 1970. The figures speak for themselves: a fivefold increase in proposed amendments to bills, a vast growth in budget amendments (two in 1964, 115 in 1984), a similarly exponential growth of motions (nine in 1963–64, 1,214 in 1983–84), and a sevenfold increase in the number of questions put to ministers. As important as these raw totals is the proportion of initiatives which were accepted by government, and therefore incorporated, to a greater or lesser extent, in the policy process.

The second reason for the contention is that Parliament has faced a more loosely textured canvas, in terms of the way that government and politics are orchestrated by the inner political élite. It would be an exaggeration to present the period from 1945 to the late 1960s as one in which the pattern of accommodation was so settled that upsets or legislative challenge were never possible. The bringing down of the Cals Cabinet in 1966 by the Catholic People's floor-leader is a notable illustration of this point. Nevertheless, the *verzuiling* system with its highly predictable electoral outcomes, and its associated modes of inter-élite consensus, certainly served to diminish the scope for active parliamentary intervention in the policy and governmental processes.

Since the early 1970s, however, this whole conception of a fixed (in both senses) political universe has undoubtedly given way to a more competitive and therefore less certain set of outcomes. It might, perhaps, have been thought that in the period from 1982 to 1989 a new orthodoxy had emerged in the shape of the recurrent Christian–Liberal coalition. But the 1989 election and its outcome arrested that particular development, even if the recently formed Christian–Labour Cabinet did not immediately impress as a new model of stability.

The third ground for the argument derives, somewhat paradoxically, from the assertion of greater executive control over policy which has marked the performance of Ruud Lubbers as Minister-President over the past eight years. The contrast here is between the system of corporatist inputs which created an extra-political forum of policy negotiation, and the recent development of greater ministerial control, which also opens up greater scope for parliamentary challenge.

On the second of the central themes of this exercise – the maintenance of democratic legitimacy – the picture is much less clear and much less easily assessable. There is undoubtedly a problem of linkage between the mass electorate and a geographically undivided pattern of representation. But this does not in itself necessarily undermine either the status of the legislature or the degree of popular support for it. One gross source of data is the extent of turnout in parliamentary elections. It so happens that in the period since 1970 there has been a drop in overall turnout, but this can be largely attributed to the abolition of compulsory registration at the polls. From 1946 to 1967 turnout averaged 95 per cent. Unsurprisingly, in the first election after the ending of compulsory registration, in 1971, turnout fell to 79 per cent. But it has since picked up, and over the whole period since 1972, in which there have been six parliamentary elections, the average turnout has been approximately 84 per cent, which seems a very satisfactory level in comparative West European terms.

If the question is viewed from the standpoint of countervailing sources of legitimacy, for example in terms of anti-parliamentary ideologies, then there is little to suggest any palpable degree of disaffection with parliamentary government. Both the extreme right and extreme left are less visible in the Dutch political landscape than that of almost any of its counterparts. Parties to the left of Labour have both softened their programmes recently and been compelled to combine in order to preserve some representation. To the right of the Liberals and the sectarian Calvinists, there is merely a transient 1 per cent or less of voters whose common ground is anti-immigrant rather than authoritarian.

Posed in comparative terms, that is, before and after 1970, the picture regarding legitimacy seems to have changed very little. It might perhaps be noted that whereas in the 1960s, a Poujadist movement, the so-called Farmers' Party, was able to attract up to 5 per cent of the voters, this feature disappeared in the 1970s. But this remains a marginal point. One must therefore conclude with the view that there is nothing to suggest any decrease in system legitimacy since 1970, in a polity, which by any standards, symptomatises a highly stable, extremely successful, liberal democracy.

NOTES

Parts of this analysis, as acknowledged in the following notes, are derived from the author's forthcoming book, *Governing from the Centre: Politics and Policy-Making in the Netherlands* (London: C. Hurst & Co., 1990).

1. M. Mezey, *Comparative Legislatures* (Durham NC: Duke University Press, 1979).
2. Ibid., Table 2.1, p.36.
3. Editor's briefing, 15 March 1989.
4. See K. Gladdish, 'Opposition in the Netherlands', in E. Kolinsky (ed.), *Opposition in Western Europe* (London: Croom Helm, 1987), pp.221–6.
5. For a fuller account, see K. Gladdish, *Governing from the Centre: Politics and Policy-Making in the Netherlands* (London: C. Hurst & Co., 1990), Ch.6.
6. This section and the following are taken from Gladdish, *Governing from the Centre*, Ch.7.
7. First edition, prepared by V. Herman, was published by Macmillan in 1976; the second edition was published by Gower in 1986.
8. E. van Raalte, *The Parliament of the Netherlands* (London and the Hague: Hansard, 1959).
9. M. P. C. M. van Schendelen, *Parlementaire Informatie Besluitvorming & Vertegenwoordiging* [Parliamentary Information, Decision-Making and Representation] (Rotterdam: Rotterdam University, 1975).
10. G. Visscher, in H. Daalder and C. J. M. Schutt, *Compendium of Politics and Society in the Netherlands* (Alphen aan den Rijn: Samson, 1986).
11. H. Franssen (ed.), *Het Parlement in Aktie* [Parliament in Action] (Assen: Van Gorcum, 1986).
12. Van Raalte, p.166.
13. Van Schendelen, p.60.
14. See H. Daalder, 'The Dutch Party System: from Segmentation to Polarisation – and then?' in H. Daalder (ed.), *Party Systems in Denmark, Austria, Switzerland, The Netherlands and Belgium* (London: Frances Pinter, 1987), p.203 and *passim*.
15. Van Schendelen, p.45.
16. Visscher, Compendium A 0600 – 75/6.

17. M. P. C. M. van Schendelen and R. Jackson, 'Political Crises in Parliaments', paper presented to the Conference of the International Political Science Association, 1982, p.16.
18. A. Lijphart, *The Politics of Accomodation: Pluralism and Democracy in the Netherlands*, 2nd ed. (Berkeley, CA: University of California Press, 1975), p.135.
19. Ibid.
20. See S. B. Wolinetz, 'The Dutch Labour Party: A Social Democratic Party in Transition', in W. Paterson and A. Thomas (eds.), *Social Democratic Parties in Western Europe* (London: Croom Helm, 1977).
21. M. P. C. M. van Schendelen, 'The Activism of the Dutch Second Chamber', paper presented at a workshop of the European Consortium for Political Research, 1976.
22. Compendium, A 0600 – 45/61.
23. Daalder, 'The Dutch Party System', p.258.
24. G. Irwin and H. Molleman, *Political Participation in the Netherlands* (Leiden: Leiden University, 1971).
25. L. de Bruyn and J. Foppen, *The Dutch Voter 1972–3*, 2 vols. (Nijmegen: Nijmegen University, 1974).
26. M. P. C. M. van Schendelen, *The Dutch Member of Parliament 1979–80* (Rotterdam: Erasmus University, 1981).
27. M. P. C. M. van Schendelen, 'Disaffected Representation in the Netherlands', *Acta Politica*, Vol.16 (April 1981).
28. See note 26.
29. S. Eldersveld, J. Kooiman and T. van der Tak, *Elite Images of Dutch Politics* (Ann Arbor, MI: University of Michigan, 1981).

The Swedish Riksdag:
The Case of a Strong Policy-influencing Assembly

David Arter

Contrary to one of the central hypotheses of this volume, the present analysis argues that, since the transition to unicameralism, the role of the Swedish Riksdag as an agent of policy influence has expanded. Governments that are forced to make substantial concessions to Parliament in the central area of economic management can scarcely be regarded as strong, and yet this has been the routine lot of the Social Democrats in office recently. More widely, the Riksdag is depicted as an unusually strong policy-influencing assembly, perhaps a limiting case in the West European context, in that it is able to participate effectively at all three stages of the policy process: formulation, deliberation and implementation. The Riksdag also appears to be a 'more supported' assembly in Mezey's terms – enjoying substantially more public confidence as a social institution than big business and the trade unions, although significantly less than the banks and health service.

THE CHANGING LEGISLATIVE-EXECUTIVE LANDSCAPE

Sweden shifted from a bicameral to a single-chamber Riksdag on 1 January 1971 as part of a wider process of constitutional modernisation.[1] The principal measures in this so-called 'partial constitutional reform' included an overhaul of the electoral system, the reorganisation of the parliamentary standing committees and a provision allowing the Riksdag for the first time formally to express no confidence in the government. The adoption of a new constitution in 1974 involved reforms of a more technical nature, the most important of which related to the active role of the parliamentary Speaker in the process of government-formation. The overall effect of these changes has been a formal strengthening of the Riksdag's position in relation to the executive.

The reformed Riksdag became numerically the largest assembly in the Nordic region,[2] although the abolition of the First (Upper) and Second (Lower) chambers entailed a modest decrease in the total number of parliamentary delegates. Following a dead heat between the Socialist and non-Socialist blocs at the 1973 election and the situation in which the Speaker, Henry Allard, was called upon to draw lots to determine the outcome of important votes,[3] the Riksdag's size was further reduced in 1976 to its present number of 349 members.[4]

The electoral reform that accompanied legislative reform saw the introduction of a revised PR list system (effectively precluding the possibility of Finnish-style personal preference voting) using the Saint-Laguë divisor and a 4 per cent national threshold.[5] It also introduced three-year

TABLE 1
THE VOTER-MEMBER RATIO IN THE NORDIC PARLIAMENTS

Country	Electoral Term (Years)	No of MPs	Voter-Member Ratio
Denmark	4	179	28,500
Norway	4	155	26,500
Iceland	4	40	6,000
Finland	4	200	24,000
Sweden	3	349	23,800

electoral terms – the shortest in Western Europe.[6] This has in practice vitiated the provision for an early dissolution of Parliament, although formally, unlike Norway, the government does have the right to order a premature general election.

Despite the relatively large size of the Riksdag, Sweden enjoys the type of low voter-member ratio (1:23,800) characterising the smaller West European democracies (see Table 1). Each Swedish member of Parliament may loosely be said to represent a body of electors less than half as numerous as a typical British constituency. The problem is that the precise nature of the relationship between voters and members is nowhere clearly defined. By the 1880s, the tariff controversy sounded the death-knell of orthodox Burke-style theories and heralded the emergence of a modern system of representative democracy which casts mass political parties in a central role.[7] Article 7 of the 1974 constitution vests political parties with an effective monopoly of electoral representation.

Equally, the geographical arrangement of members in the Riksdag points, as in Norway, to a strong sense in which the Swedish parliamentarian represents regional interests. This operates in a rather paradoxical way. On the one hand, there is evidence of the tendency in large multi-member constituencies for an attenuation in the voter–member relationship. This is especially so in an open system of government like Sweden where a range of alternative complaints channels (including the celebrated network of Ombudsmen) are available to citizens. On the other, Riksdag members do perceive their role to be in large part the promotion of territorial interests. 'Logrolling' or cross-party backbench coalitions on issues of common regional concern are not uncommon, nor are maverick voting and a refusal to follow the party line when crucial regional interests are at stake. The legislative initiatives tabled by members, moreover, invariably have a regional content.

From a party-political standpoint, the primary consequence of the move to a unicameral system has been that the Social Democrats, although remaining comfortably the largest single force, have lost their absolute majority in the legislature (see Table 2). Since the adoption of a single-chamber assembly there has in fact been a marked trend towards *stable minority cabinets* as the predominant mode of government. This is reflected in the numerically strong Social Democratic minority governments

TABLE 2

PARTY REPRESENTATION IN THE RIKSDAG 1976–88

Party	1976	1979	Seats 1982	1985	1988
Conservatives	55	73	86	76	66
Centre	86	64	56	44	42
Liberals	39	38	21	51	44
Social Democrats	152	154	166	159	156
Left-Communists	17	20	20	19	21
Greens	–	–	–	–	20
Total	349	349	349	349	349

between 1971–76 and 1982–90 which have been largely sustained in office by the Left-Communists. There have also been periods (1978–79 and 1981–82) of numerically weak minority government involving one or more of the bourgeois parties. These followed the collapse of two Centre–Liberal–Conservative majority coalitions under Thorbjörn Fälldin. In the first two decades of the single-chamber Riksdag, the dynamics of the party system have meant that the legislative-executive balance has tilted more in favour of Parliament, although this is not to argue that Cabinets have been of necessity weak.[9]

Throughout the unicameral years, moreover, it has not been possible narrowly to present government and opposition politics on a conventional left-right continuum. From the early 1970s, an *ecology* versus *economy* cleavage has aligned the Centre and Left-Communists against the Social Democrats, Liberals and Conservatives on controversial issues such as nuclear power, while in 1988 the Greens achieved a notable parliamentary breakthrough by winning twenty Riksdag seats. The Centre, Left-Communists and Greens have taken the lead in opposing a vocal lobby of industrialists favouring Sweden taking the Austrian road to full EC membership.[10]

Although largely encased (until recently at least) within the established party framework, there is also evidence of growing electoral volatility, especially among younger voters, and a significant drop in the strength of identification with the Social Democrats. Only 70.3 per cent of 20-year-olds voted at the 1988 general election[11] and, partly as a result of a number of public scandals, such as Ebbe's Carlsson's private investigation into the murder of Olof Palme, confidence in parties and politicians is generally low.[12]

In a wider comparative perspective, a feature of the unicameral Riksdag has been the steady increase in the extent of female representation. Largely as a result of leadership decisions to pursue a more active recruitment strategy in relation to women candidates – in some parties, central directives to the local organisations set out indicative quotas – the proportion of female delegates has risen from 23 per cent of the total assembly in 1976 to 38 per

TABLE 3

WOMEN IN RIKSDAG STANDING COMMITTEES, 1989–90

Committee	No of Women	% of Women
Constitutional	6	35
Finance	5	29
Taxation	3	18
Justice	7	41
Legal Affairs	8	47
Defence	6	35
Foreign Affairs	5	29
Social Insurance	12	71
Social Affairs	10	59
Cultural Affairs	7	41
Education	7	41
Traffic	3	18
Agriculture	4	24
Economic Affairs	3	18
Labour-Market	8	47
Housing	2	12
Total	96	35

cent in the present Parliament. Women delegates remain under-represented on several of the 'heavyweight' standing committees, however, and only in the two dealing with social policy matters do they have a majority. In the Social Insurance committee, to be sure, nearly three-quarters of the membership are women (see Table 3).

Sweden boasts one of the shortest enactment procedures of any West European Parliament. Following referral to standing committee, a bill is given only a single reading on the floor of the Riksdag. In other words, there are no *structural* checks and balances designed to essay the 'second chamber effect' of the Finnish Grand Committee or the internal legislative divisions in Norway and Iceland.[13] Nor are there special legislative provisions to protect minorities such as the Finnish qualified majority rules[14] or Article 42 of the Danish constitution which permits one-third of parliamentarians to enforce a popular referendum on a measure which has completed its Third Reading. The Danish referendum provision was inspired in large part by the Finnish qualified majority rules[15] and the latter have also attracted a number of advocates in the Riksdag.[16] They would, it is argued, militate against precipitate and ill-considered decisions.

During earlier discussions on constitutional reform, the Social Democrats, like their Danish counterparts, briefly envisaged a corporate assembly which would replace the First Chamber[17] and act as a healthy counterweight to the popularly elected Second Chamber. Although this idea was quickly abandoned, the creation in the unicameral Riksdag of sixteen[18] specialist standing committees (each comprising 17 members) afforded at least the potential for the development of a corporate identity in Loewenberg and Patterson's sense of an issue-based rather than partisan orientation towards legislative proposals.[19]

The spectacle of a deserted debating chamber has prompted the Danish jest that a delegate wishing to keep something secret need only announce it from the Folketing rostrum since nobody will then hear it! The same is broadly true in Sweden where the sparse attendance at Riksdag plenaries has prompted a vigorous exchange in the press.[20] The primary function of plenary contributions would appear to be the formal registration of a member's view which is then placed on record and is less easily misquoted. It is a fact, however, that although transmitted (often in advance) to the local press, fewer members' speeches than earlier are printed.[21]

Recent procedural reforms have endeavoured to bring the Riksdag more towards the centre stage of political debate. Regular 'party leader debates' have been instituted – on the economy, defence policy, etc. – and give the opposition the opportunity to challenge the government's track record. The rules on Question Time have been revised. In February 1988, moreover, standing committees were empowered to conduct open 'hearings' at which the Swedish television cameras are frequently present. The intense public interest in the Constitutional Committee's interrogation of ministers in connection with the 'Ebbe Carlsson affair' brought the scrutiny function of the Riksdag into people's living-rooms. Equally important has been the way the public hearings held on a range of social policy questions – *inter alia* the adequacy of regional medical provision and care for the elderly – have contributed to moulding the political agenda.

A final introductory point. Although there is no incompatibility rule as such in Sweden, deputy-members do cover for Cabinet ministers (and the Riksdag Speaker) and this appears to have shifted the centre of political gravity from parliament to the Government (Cabinet) Office. Certainly ministers are rarely seen in the Riksdag in the way they used to be.

THE RIKSDAG – A POLICY-MAKING ASSEMBLY?

A distinctive feature of legislative practice in Western Europe has been the extensive representation of Swedish parliamentarians on the network

TABLE 4

THE PROPORTION OF RIKSDAG MEMBERS WITH COMMISSION EXPERIENCE

	1985	1988
Riksdag member presently on commissions	23%	33%
Previously on commissions	53%	39%
Never sat on a commission	24%	28%*
	100	100

* The survey data were collected shortly after the 1988 general election and this figure could be expected to rise as newly-elected Riksdag members were appointed to commissions.

Source: Information kindly presented by Peter Esaisson.

TABLE 5
THE PROPORTION OF COMMISSIONS WITH RIKSDAG REPRESENTATION, 1988/89 (1)

Department	No of Commissions	Commissions with Riksdag Members
Prime Minister's Office	3	0
Justice	22	12
Foreign Affairs	12	4
Defence	8	3
Social Affairs	15	7
Communications	6	3
Finance	36	10
Education	29	8
Agriculture	2	1
Labour-Market Affairs	15	5
Housing	8	1
Industry	8	4
Civil Affairs	9	5
Environment & Energy	8	1
Total	181	64
	100%	35%

1. Included in the figures are former Riksdag members who were parliamentarians when first nominated to a commission post.

2. Exceptions to the rule of Social Democratic (governing party) chairpersons are those appointed during the years of bourgeois rule between 1976 and 1982.

Source: Compiled from *Kommittéberätelse 1989*, Kommittéernas sammansättning. Stockholm, 1988.

of commissions that are routinely engaged in the gestation and formulation of public policy. Riksdag members participate at an earlier stage in the policy process than the majority of their continental counterparts. During the 1980s, approximately one-third of Riksdag members were at any one time serving members of commissions of inquiry, *utredningar* (see Table 4) while over one-third of the commissions deliberating during the 1988–89 Riksdag session contained at least one member of Parliament (see Table 5).

Most Swedish parliamentarians have served on a commission of inquiry. At the beginning of the 1988–89 Riksdag session, nearly three-quarters of delegates boasted experience of commission work (past or present) and this figure will undoubtedly have risen by the time of the 1991 general election. Many of the veteran Riksdag members who have held a parliamentary seat throughout the unicameral period, moreover, have served on more than ten commissions. Involvement in the activities of commissions, of course, imposes a heavier schedule on parliamentarians: a chairmanship may necessitate up to two or three days a week extra work. Recent studies indicate that for an ordinary Riksdag member an average of around 5 per cent of his/her weekly programme will be taken up with commission work (or related activities)[22] and this figure has varied little over the period since the shift to unicameralism.[23]

The regular participation of Riksdag members on commissions bestows on individual parliamentarians an institutionalised role in the policy-making process that is striking in comparative perspective. True, there was significant representation of Storting members on Norwegian commissions of inquiry in the mid-nineteenth century. But the proportion of parliamentarians has declined from 18.1 per cent of all commission places in the period 1921–35, to 10 per cent in 1951 and about 1 per cent at present – approximately the same level as in Denmark.[24] In Finland in 1945 no less than one-third of all commissions contained at least one Eduskunta member – comparable with Sweden – though by 1975 this had fallen to 11 per cent and it continued to fall throughout the 1980s.[25] Elsewhere, systematic material on the participation of parliamentarians on pre-legislative commissions is lacking though it appears confined to exceptional bodies such as the Royal Commissions in the UK, Enquête Commissions in the German Federal Republic and the myriad of preparatory commissions forming part of Le Plan in the Fifth French Republic.

Characteristic of executive practice in Sweden has been a long-standing institutional bifurcation of the policy formulation and policy implementation functions. Government departments are charged with the direction of policy while a complementary structure of central boards and agencies is responsible for its supervision. Since the personnel of ministries has been relatively small, commissions have been traditionally deployed to enlist a wider policy community in the preparation of legislative proposals. Governments, of course, have sought to control the commission system. It is the responsible minister who issues a directive laying down the commission's terms of reference and he it is who determines its composition and the time schedule on its deliberations. Furthermore, when political representatives are involved it is customary for the chairman to come from the governing side. None the less, there is a long history of involving opposition parties in commission work. Though this has been true to a lesser extent elsewhere in the Nordic region, what makes Swedish practice different is that the parliamentary party groups have nominated commission members from among their own number rather than turning to representatives from outside the Riksdag.

Three obvious questions arise at this point. First, why do Swedish governments, through their allocation of commission places, explicitly involve the opposition in the formulation of public policy? Next, why should the parliamentary party groups (both government and opposition) select Riksdag members in preference to outside experts for the specialist and time-consuming work of commissions? Last, what are the implications of commission work both for individual parliamentarians and for the overall role of the Riksdag in public policy-making?

A standard Swedish response to the first question would probably be that the involvement of opposition parliamentarians on policy-generating commissions forms part of the wide-ranging consultation which has become a staple element in the nation's open style of government. Tradition,

Second, commissions can act as a career stepping-stone for parliamentarians. An assiduous commission member is able to make a signal contribution to moulding opinion within his party, especially in relation to the middle-ranking technical questions which do not readily lend themselves to a party line. In so doing, he will undoubtedly advance his own career prospects. By dint of the way they serve as a career channel, a commission place is generally viewed as a prestigious remit and few problems of recruitment are encountered.

In my book *The Nordic Parliaments*, it is suggested that parliamentarians are generally preferred to outside party experts because they are more reliable and less likely to use the commission system for personal ends.[27] It seems likely, however, that the greater reliability of Riksdag members (that is, their responsible performance on commissions) is less a function of a weaker perception of career advantage than the consequence of obvious structural constraints on their activities in commission. Put another way, there is a greater degree of control exercised through the direct accountability of parliamentary members of commissions to their parliamentary party groups.

As to the main implications of parliamentary involvement on commissions for the Riksdag's overall role in policy-making, two main points need emphasis. First, through their commission representatives, the opposition parties are in a strategic position to seek to influence the formulation of policy. Via these same representatives, opposition groups in the Riksdag are better informed about the development of legislative proposals than their counterparts in other West European assemblies.

Second, parliamentary involvement on commissions has served partly to erode the dividing line between government and opposition and with it some of the adversarialism associated with other systems. In ministerial circles elsewhere in the Nordic region, there tends to be a feeling that the regular incorporation of parliamentarians on commissions would limit the government's freedom of manoeuvre. According to a former Danish minister, Folketing involvement on pre-legislative commissions would almost certainly increase a minister's workload as his party's representatives sought out his advice and guidance. A minister might also be placed in the invidious position of having to go against his own party's stance on a commission or even find his hands effectively tied by the achievement of inter-party consensus. In Sweden in contrast it may be feasible to portray the process of policy formulation as comprising a series of policy communities to which members of the legislature, executive and corporate interests all belong.

There has, however, been a significant contraction in the commission system over the 1980s concomitant on the return to power of the Social Democrats and a recessionary climate at the beginning of the decade which dictated the need for public spending cuts. The scale of government, in short, has been pruned. In autumn 1982, the Deputy Prime Minister, Ingvar Carlsson, laid down the main guidelines for the rationalisation of the commission system. Commissions were to complete their deliberations within a substantially shorter (two-year) time span. New commissions were not to be set up in areas previously investigated and government departments were to shoulder more responsibility for the formulation of policy. Accordingly, commissions have become fewer in number and smaller in size and there is a growing preference for intra-departmental working groups. Commissions, moreover, tend to have a broader overview function and to operate under the tight control of the Treasury.

A systematic evaluation of the implications of the smaller number and size of commissions for the recruitment of Riksdag members has yet to be undertaken. It is possible that the greater premium on places will be conducive to reviving the dominant recruitment pattern of the 1960s when the more experienced parliamentarians capable of articulating a variety of interests were given preference.[28] Equally, the tendency in a number of parties to recruit from among the newer parliamentarians may become more accentuated.

A large number of Swedish commissions comprise solely civil servants and not infrequently a single official. Single-member commissions usually function more expeditiously and generally cost less than multi-member bodies including parliamentarians. Despite the cutbacks, however, parliamentary involvement on policy-formulating commissions remains a characteristic feature of the legislative culture in Sweden.

THE RIKSDAG – A POLICY-INFLUENCING ASSEMBLY?

Clearly the Riksdag is not a policy-making assembly in the sense that major public policies are routinely initiated in it. The extensive involvement of its members on commissions, moreover, does not prevent the government from governing in the sense of producing the draft proposals it wishes. Widespread consultation with the affected interests does not ultimately bind ministers to a particular form of bill and it may have the desired effect of facilitating its enactment by generating a pre-legislative body of support.

The Riksdag can, however, be depicted as an unusually strong policy influencing assembly in that it is able to exert significant influence at all three stages of the policy process – formulation, deliberation and implementation. The Riksdag, and most notably the opposition parties, have a direct impact on the gestation of policy measures through the presence of parliamentarians on commissions of inquiry. Though not a policy-making assembly, the Riksdag is thus strategically well placed to influence policy-making. Parliament can also sow the seeds of new legislation by applying concerted pressure on governments to instigate a commission in a desired policy area. It has not been easy for the staple minority governments of recent years to resist such pressure.

Furthermore, by means of private initiatives (*motioner*), the Riksdag articulates a range of demands, especially of a regional nature, which governments may subsequently incorporate into legislative proposals and/or which may contribute to moulding a favourable political climate. The legislative increment of members' initiatives, that is, the extent to which governments make capital out of the 'resource bank' of private measures,

TABLE 6
GROWTH IN THE NUMBER OF PRIVATE INITIATIVES IN THE RIKSDAG, 1960–89

Year	Number of Initiatives
1960	944 (1)
1970	1605
1979/80	2080
1980/81	2218
1981/82	2572
1982/83	2439
1983/84	2985
1984/85	3245
1985/86	3329
1986/87	3767
1987/88	4001
1988/89	4425

1. Figures for the First and Second Chambers excluding identical bills

Source: *Riksdagen i siffror 1989/90*, p.9

is impossible to quantify, but it may not be inconsiderable in the medium term.

The evidence points to an increased legislative entrepreneurialism on the part of Riksdag members. The number of private initiatives has grown almost threefold over the course of nearly two decades of unicameralism (see Table 6). True, the 'freestanding' British-style private member's bill has little chance of success and has become largely an outmoded form of initiative in Sweden. But 'connected parliamentary bills' – usually non-partisan or cross-partisan in character and proposing technical amendments to ongoing government legislation – have had a reasonable success rate. So, too, have 'members' request proposals' (*hemställningsmotioner*), which are relatively easy to formulate and represent a further parliamentary input into the policy process. All private initiatives are ultimately reported on by a Riksdag standing committee and the outcome placed on record.

Since the shift to unicameralism, three factors have combined to make a strong *prima facie* case for increased Riksdag influence in policy deliberation. First, there was the transition in 1971 to a system of small, specialist standing committees – paralleling the government departments – which were vested with the right of legislative initiative as well as the task of scrutinising Cabinet proposals. The reformed committee system replaced the one in the bicameral Riksdag which was based on the constitutional functions of Parliament (passing constitutional laws, the appropriation of taxes, etc.) and was not geared to the effective consideration of (increasingly technical and specialised) public policy measures. The Swedish system of specialist standing committees represents an institutional arrangement possessing considerable *corporate* potential.

Second, there has been the growing incidence of minority governments which has placed a premium on the search – in classical Danish style – for *legislative coalitions* as a means of enacting public policy. Government–opposition deals have been essential to the success of controversial measures. Notable examples include the government's agreement with the Social Democrats on marginal tax cuts in 1981, when the Centre and Liberals made up a bourgeois minority coalition, and the radical tax reform package between the same three parties in November 1989, when the Social Democrats formed a single-party minority cabinet. Deals of this magnitude have usually been preceded by *party leadership talks* bringing together the leaders of all the major parties. Compromises so reached, however, though ultimately dictated by the logistics of the parliamentary arithmetic, may well shift the focal point of bargaining from the Riksdag building to smoke-filled rooms elsewhere.

Finally, there was the belated incorporation into Swedish practice in 1971 of a classical instrument of parliamentarism – the provision formally allowing the Riksdag to express no confidence in the government. This has only been used once so far, in October 1980, when the Social Democrats unsuccessfully tabled a motion of no confidence in a three-party bourgeois coalition which had the slenderest of majorities. Paradoxically, the principal consequence of the introduction of the no-confidence provision appears to have been to consolidate the position of minority governments, since the price of legislative defeat will not be the loss of office unless the matter is specifically designated a 'confidence question'. Equally, this state of affairs has permitted the Riksdag, and not least members on the governing side, greater autonomy in the deliberation of measures. From a Cabinet viewpoint, adverse legislative coalitions have recently exerted significant influence in the deliberative process, routinely modifying and even rejecting major government legislation (the supplementary budget and agricultural policy measures in spring 1989 for example) without ever placing the Social Democrats' tenure of office at serious risk.

It may be helpful to envisage the Riksdag's scrutiny of measures taking place at two complementary levels. There is a superstructure of parliamentary standing committees, many with a long history and tradition. After varying degrees of discussion, the standing committee compiles a report which is subsequently transmitted to the floor of the Riksdag. The increase in cross-cutting issues has meant that after initial consideration, measures may be referred from one standing committee to another. Then there is an infrastructure of party organs embracing policy committees, standing committee groups and full parliamentary group meetings. These two institutional levels form part of a single decision-making system and make generalisations about the precise locus of Riksdag influence in policy deliberation extremely problematical.

Formally at least, the standing committees are the principal arena of legislative deliberation in the Riksdag. Unlike several West European countries, government proposals are usually sent directly to standing committee without the equivalent of a Second Reading debate. The vast majority of Swedish parliamentarians, moreover, perceive themselves as *legislators*, seeking to influence the details of legislation through active participation in the work of standing committees and the linked party organs. Survey evidence indicates clearly that Riksdag members have a strongly positive orientation towards their role on standing committee regardless of their partisan affiliation or committee membership.[29] It follows that standing committee places are keenly sought after and the overall shortage of full committeeships has intensified competition for places.

Consonant with Gudmund Hernes' observation on Norwegian practice, Riksdag members tend to 'end up on the standing committee they are interested in'[30] – former social workers on the Social Insurance Committee, teachers on the Education Committee, farmers on the Agricultural Committee – and which their education, training and previous occupation best equip them for. Committeeships consolidate existing expertise. Moreover, standing committee members will often possess relevant background knowledge of a subject as a result of sitting on the commission which drafted the initial recommendations. When this is not the case, extra information is available via 'hearings' (open or closed) with the minister and/or his senior assistants or from taking unofficial soundings among the relevant ministry officials.

The importance of informal links between legislature and executive cannot be understated. In particular, there have been increased contacts between departmental civil servants and the well-developed staffs of the Riksdag standing committees. These are often at the instigation of the responsible minister with a view to disseminating information and culminate in a luncheon between officials representing Parliament and the political executive respectively.

Some Riksdag standing committees, it may be hypothesised, act as corporate bodies some of the time. The more technical and non-controversial the committee and the subject under consideration, the greater the likelihood of a solidary orientation on the part of members. Even so, most standing committees are animated by partisan behaviour most of the time[31] and, indeed, increasingly by a confrontational government versus opposition mentality. This is especially true in committees such as Taxation, Finance and Economic Affairs which are routinely engaged in resolving high-profile, money-related questions.[32] Each Riksdag standing committee, of course, develops its own culture and this is integrally bound up with the style and approach of the chairman or vice-chairman. Standing committee chairmen appear to act for the most part as conciliators,[33] seeking to achieve broad-based, inter-party compromises, although not always succeeding.

Evidence of the predominantly *permeable* (partisan) nature of the Riksdag standing committees can be gleaned from the growing number of committee reports which contain dissenting statements. Consensus in standing committee appears much harder to achieve than earlier. In the 1988–89 Riksdag session, 68 per cent of committee reports contained a minority statement compared with only 23 per cent in 1976–77. In the first-mentioned session, more than 3,000 dissenting statements were tabled altogether. A large majority of these (69 per cent) emanated from individual opposition parties; 17 per cent involved two parties; 11 per cent three parties; and 3 per cent of them four-party dissent.[34] A handful of dissenting standing committee reports mobilised members on the governing side. Despite the fact that 31 per cent of dissenting reports reflected collective action on the part of two or more opposition party groups, the success rate of these 'reservations', even during a period of minority government, was very low (0.2 per cent).[35] Most, it seems, were demonstrative in character and demonstrated, at very least, the heightened partisanship on standing committees.

Minority governments are inevitably engaged in the search for legislative coalitions to secure a parliamentary majority for the enactment of policy proposals. The introduction of the no-confidence provision, however, has meant that government legislation can be substantially amended or even rejected without this necessitating the fall of the government unless the matter is a confidence question. Government defeats in standing committee and subsequently on the floor of the Riksdag have been relatively commonplace recently, and on occasions Social Democratic standing committee groups have acted independently of their own government. All this has conspired to allow the Riksdag a markedly greater influence in the deliberation of measures than during the one-party majority rule of the late bicameral era.

It is an open question how far a government forced to make substantial concessions in its management of the economy can be regarded as a strong cabinet. This, however, has been the routine fate of the Social Democrats in office in recent years. On 2 June 1989, for example, in the face of united Riksdag opposition, the government was obliged to increase its export support to wheat producers. The Social Democrats in the Agricultural Committee argued unavailingly that this violated the April 1989 GATT agreement on freezing state support to agriculture. When, in connection with the same matter, however, the opposition proposed to double the level of support to the struggling farmers in northern Sweden, the government members on the committee changed tack and followed suit.

Another Social Democratic standing committee group behaved similarly a month earlier when, uniquely, all six parliamentary parties in the Finance Committee opposed a government proposal to raise VAT. This formed part of the revised budget (*kompletteringsproposition*) and was one of a package of measures designed to dampen down an overheating economy. There were also increases in employers' taxes and the abolition of milk subsidies. In the event, in its concern to achieve necessary measures of restraint, the government abandoned its proposed changes in payroll taxes and milk subsidies and reluctantly agreed to a Centre Party scheme for compulsory savings which had been accepted by the Social Democrats in the Finance Committee.

Two main points should be made. First, the compulsory savings scheme, modelled on Danish and West German lines, was the brainchild of the Centre Party's parliamentary group policy committee on Taxation and Finance (a combination of the two standing committee groups) which then successfully lobbied the full parliamentary group and party leader,

Olof Johansson. Second, subsequent negotiations proceeded at two levels: leadership talks involving the Prime Minister, Finance Minister and Centre Party leader, and discussions between the senior personnel of the Finance Committee – the Social Democratic chairwoman Anna-Greta Leijon and Centre Party chief, Gunnar Björk. Significantly, the strategic compromise was reached by the leading standing committee actors and the Social Democratic members of the Finance Committee then fell in line, to the obvious irritation of the Finance Minister who resented the defeat of his original revised budget proposal.[36]

This evidence of the increased influence of standing committee groups in the deliberative process warrants emphasis. In the early 1970s, following backbench disgruntlement, the Social Democrats formulated a rule requesting a Cabinet minister to liaise with his party's representatives on the relevant standing committee – that is, the standing committee group – before introducing an important measure into the Riksdag. The functional logic of this type of legislative–executive dialogue was strengthened with the advent of Social Democratic minority governments between 1971 and 1974 and the so-called 'lottery Riksdag' of 1974–76.

During the interlude of bourgeois government from 1976 to 1982, the Social Democratic standing committee groups spearheaded the attack on proposals, so enhancing their position in the party. By then, standing committee groups constituted special units within the Social Democratic parliamentary group and boasted their own chairman, secretary and whip – the latter to ensure a full attendance of members and deputies at standing committee meetings. This organisation has persisted and vests the chairman with decisive influence as the link with the corresponding government department and the chairmen of other standing committees. Since the Social Democrats returned to office in 1982, the draft of a government proposal has been distributed to the relevant standing committee chairman for his reaction (often informal consultations have already taken place). When the department and standing committee groups have reached agreement, the matter goes to the full Social Democratic parliamentary group where there is rarely any discussion.

As Magnus Isberg has argued, the fact that the Social Democratic standing committee groups and especially their chairmen have exerted more influence on government policy has not been without its benefits for the Cabinet.[37] First, it is an obvious advantage to have the backing of key persons in the party's parliamentary group. In the typical situation of minority government, moreover, it is vital for Cabinets to be able to gauge the likelihood of issue-based legislative coalitions being formed and here standing committee groups can perform a valuable monitoring function. Finally, governments can proceed more confidently with a measure that has the prior approval of the relevant standing committee group(s) rather than having to rely on imposing strict party discipline.

When the three bourgeois parties were in power during 1976–78 and 1979–81, the narrow size of the governing majority dictated a very different style. Cabinet proposals were often a delicate compromise which brooked little or no further discussion in the backbench policy comittees.

Consequently, the main function of the parliamentary group was to show loyalty and discipline in piloting a measure through the assembly.

The Riksdag's influence over the implementation of public policy, and more widely its ability to oversee the workings of the political executive, is relatively weak. This is so both in relation to its role in the formulation and deliberation of legislation and in a wider cross-national perspective. There are, however, some distinctive patterns of influence and some possible evidence of a modest increase in Parliament's (potential) control over central administration. In this sketch analysis, however, four main points must necessarily suffice.

First, the only Riksdag standing committee required to supervise the work of the government and its departments – and then from an essentially legalistic perspective – is the Constitutional Committee (the oldest parliamentary committee dating back to 1809) and this has seen its cutting edge blunted in recent decades by the heightened party politicisation of its activities. Typically, in its much publicised investigation into the controversial Telub scandal in 1981, the non-Socialist majority on the committee closed ranks to shelter its own ministers against a torrent of criticism from the opposition-based Social Democrats. Since then a continuous period of minority government has rendered this type of partisan protection far more problematical and, with the Left-Communists acting independently, the main government players in the protracted investigation of the Ebbe Carlsson 'affair' faced political embarrassment at the hands of an adverse majority in the Constitutional Committee.

Second, although the reformed specialist standing committees of the Riksdag are not constitutionally invested with the task of overseeing the work of the parallel government department – that is, a 'select committee' function – the recent introduction of open committee 'hearings' could well encourage the development of a watchdog role. Standing committee reviews of government policy have been relatively rare, but several parliamentarians believe that the scrutiny function of committees should be given more prominence.[38]

Third, the recent revision of the rules on questions and interpellations have enabled Riksdag members (the Greens have been particularly active) more easily to exact information from ministers, although it should be noted that in the open Swedish system of government, members of Parliament, just like members of the public, are granted ready access to information. Routinely, for instance, a backbench, opposition-party policy committee on Legal Affairs will visit the National Prisons Board where it will be given a full range of information on the treatment of offenders.

Finally, since the shift to unicameralism, it has become increasingly common for Riksdag members to be nominated to the governing bodies of the central boards and agencies which are encharged with the implementation of policy.[39] Appointments may be to large organisations like the Social Welfare Board or much smaller ones such as the Energy Research Council.[40] This is not to imply that parliamentarians can or, indeed, seek to influence the regular operation of central boards – the lack of a party line is felt to be a handicap – although their presence among senior management represents a distinctive pattern of personnel overlap between legislature and executive.

THE RIKSDAG – A 'MORE SUPPORTED' LEGISLATURE?

In a survey in 1987, 62 per cent of citizens expressed 'quite much' or 'considerable confidence' in Parliament as an institution.[41] On this basis, the Riksdag may be presented as a 'more-supported' assembly in Mezey's terms – substantially more so as a social institution than big business, trade unions and the daily newspapers, although significantly less so than the banks and health service (see Table 7). In the case of Parliament, the problem for respondents is always, of course, to dissociate the institution from the (often negative) party political images associated with it. Certainly trust in politicians has been markedly lower than in Parliament itself. During the first decade of unicameralism, for example, an average 59 per cent of citizens 'entirely or largely agreed' with the assertion that 'those who sit in the Riksdag and make the decisions do not pay much attention to what ordinary people feel and think'.[42] In the late 1980s, too, Sören Holmberg's survey work detected a growing cynicism towards party politicians,[43] not least because of the implication of high-ranking figures in a series of major scandals – *inter alia* the Bofors' illegal arms sales and the Ebbe Carlsson affair.

Popular perceptions of the Riksdag are largely moulded by its presentation in the mass media and here parliamentarians themselves have been critical of the tendency to personalise and trivialise matters and to focus comment on the party leaders rather than the real authorities in the standing committees.[44] Equally, it is evident that the Riksdag has let its agenda-setting function largely pass to the media. Formative debate,

TABLE 7

PUBLIC CONFIDENCE IN SOCIAL INSTITUTIONS IN SWEDEN IN 1987

Institution	Confidence%				
	Considerable	Quite a Lot	Quite a Little	Very Little	No Answer
The Government	14	47	29	9	1
Police	11	52	28	8	1
Health Service	30	52	13	4	1
Armed Forces	10	38	36	14	2
Riksdag	12	50	29	7	2
Banks	24	60	11	3	2
Daily Press	3	14	40	13	2
Radio/TV	6	52	31	8	3
Trade unions	5	36	36	18	4
Secondary Education	9	47	30	9	4
Big Business	6	43	34	13	4

Source: Sören Holmberg and Lennart Weibull (eds.), *SOM-undersökningen 1987*, Samhälle Opinion Massmedia 2 (Göteborgs Universitet, 1988), pp.10–11.

in short, is principally conducted on radio, television and in the press rather than in the parliamentary arena. Indeed, notwithstanding some improvement with the advent of open committee hearings, a concern to place the Riksdag more in the forefront of political debate continues to stimulate proposals for procedural reforms.[45] Without doubt, ordinary citizens do not possess a very accurate picture of the routine work of the Riksdag. A number of factors, moreover – particularly the increasingly specialised nature of parliamentary work – have conspired to distance the Riksdag member from his constituents.[46] None the less, there may be evidence of the popular legitimacy of Parliament in the high levels of turnout at the three-yearly Riksdag elections.

In the early 1980s, Elder, Thomas and Arter examined Sweden in relation to an ideal-type *consensual democracy*, broadly defined as one in which the extent of conflict is limited, the intensity of conflict relatively low and there is broad acceptance of the basic rules of the parliamentary game.[47] In many ways it does appear that the recent strains and tensions in Swedish politics have not given way to the partisan conflict and/or protest mobilisation of its Nordic neighbours. Thus, despite a much-publicised stream of tax exiles and (until very recently) a chorus of complaint about high income tax levels, Sweden has lacked a Danish or Norwegian-style anti-tax party.

Since the adoption of a single-chamber system, in fact, only really two issues have threatened the mould of consensual democracy in the scale and depth of political conflict they have generated: the employee investment funds and the future of nuclear energy. The wage-earner funds, which originated in radical trade union circles in the mid-1970s, engaged organised labour against capital; the future of nuclear energy led to a popular referendum in 1980 and prefaced a wider cleavage between the economy and the environment which characterised politics throughout the 1980s and spawned the rise of the Greens. In both cases, however, mass mobilisation ultimately consolidated rather than challenged the centrality of Parliament as the rightful forum of conflict resolution.

In the case of the anti-funds campaign, the Riksdag served as a symbolic outlet for mass-based protest seeking to demonstrate its determination to oppose government legislation within the legitimate framework of decision-making. On 4 October 1983 a demonstration of over 75,000 people – the largest in Swedish history – representing business and industry converged on the Riksdag to transmit a declaration to the Speaker.[48] Petitioning Parliament in this way was at once a public registration of popular dissent and an implicit statement of a readiness to work through conventional channels. Importantly, the opposition coalition against the Social Democratic government's employee investment fund legislation combined parliamentary and corporate-sector élites – precisely as in spring 1989 when the blue-collar federation LO joined the bourgeois parties in rejecting proposed increases in VAT.

Division in the ranks of the bourgeois coalition over the future of nuclear energy[49] led in 1980 to recourse to an extra-parliamentary instrument of conflict resolution in the form of a popular referendum. Environmental questions, however, remained high on the political agenda. Indeed, it was perhaps ironic that representation in the Riksdag became a primary goal, and elections a vital barometer of support for the Greens, the only sizeable anti-system movement in Swedish politics in recent times. Whether this denotes that an integral element in the political culture is an unusually deep-seated internalisation of the legitimacy of the Riksdag in the registration and resolution of political conflict is a matter which could well be taken up in future research.

CONCLUSION

The aim of this analysis has been to present a critical account of the unicameral Riksdag's role, at once bringing out the distinctive features of Swedish legislative practice and the shortcomings of some characterisations of the Riksdag that appear in the comparative literature. It cannot, for example, be regarded as helpful, still less valid, to depict the Riksdag in the words of Hague and Harrop as 'a stable case of an active policy-making legislature' sharing the same legislative pigeonhole as the US Congress with its 'substantial law-making autonomy' and the assemblies in the Third and Fourth French Republics and contemporary Italy which have 'overshadowed political life and the executive'.[50] As Philip Norton notes in the introduction to this volume, it is a real limitation of Mezey-based approaches that they appear to equate policy-*making* with the capacity of assemblies to *break* political executives. Equally, the Swedish Riksdag is not a policy-making body in Loewenberg and Patterson's sense that 'major public policies are initiated within the assembly'.[51] It is, indeed, extremely doubtful if the US Congress or any other West European Parliament approximates to this ideal-type, although the Icelandic Althing until recently did legislate extensively on the basis of private initiatives covering major policy areas.

The Swedish Riksdag belongs to the extended family of policy influencing assemblies in Western Europe, each of which has its own particular institutional features and mechanisms (formal and informal) for exerting a measure of influence over the executive. In Denmark, the evolution of a specialist scrutiny committee like the Market Relations Committee has given the Folketing notable (potential) influence over the implementation of EC policy; the constitutional provision of qualified majorities in Finland has given the Eduskunta opposition unique clout in postponing the final deliberation and resolution of a measure until after a general election. Further examples of the *traits* of individual legislatures could, of course, be presented, but generalisation about the *relative influence* of West European assemblies would remain extremely hazardous. Throughout the region, the policy influence of Parliaments is tied to cultural and constitutional factors together with the structure and dynamics of the party system.

The central thesis of the present account is that the Riksdag is an unusually strong policy-influencing assembly in so far as it is able effectively to participate at all three stages in the policy cycle – formulation, deliberation and implementation. The extensive involvement of parliamentarians on policy-generating commissions of inquiry lays claim to be a singularity of legislative practice in Western Europe. During the periods of stable minority government typifying the unicameral years, moreover, major government policies have been routinely modified in the assembly without this involving the continual threat of 'government-breaking'.[52] In the spirit of the 'open government' for which Sweden is noted, the recent introduction of public standing committee hearings has also enhanced the Riksdag's capacity to scrutinise the implementation of public policy and increased citizens' interest in parliamentary proceedings. All this is not of course to confuse participation and influence. Riksdag participation at all three legislative stages does not necessarily connote the exertion of strong influence. It does, however, signify the opportunity to influence which in circumstances of minoritarian government the Riksdag can exploit to the full.

NOTES

I should like to thank the following persons for interviews and help in connection with the preparation of this study: Olle Svensson, Social Democratic chairman of the Riksdag's Constitutional Committee; Gudrun Schyman, Deputy-Chair of the Left-Communist Party; Margit Gennser, Conservative member for Malmö; Professor Daniel Tarschys, Liberal Party chairman of the Riksdag's Social Affairs Committee; Gunnar Björk, Centre Party leader on the Riksdag's Finance Committee; Bertil Fiskesjö, Third Deputy Speaker of the Riksdag; Per Gahrton, leader of the Green Party; Hans Bergström, political editor of *Dagens Nyheter*; and Ulf Kristoffersson and Magnus Isberg, staff members of the Riksdag's Constitutional Committee.

1. B. von Sydow, *Vägen till enkammarriksdagen: Demokratisk författningspolitik i Sverige 1944–68* (Stockholm: Tiden, 1989), pp.228–80.
2. D. Arter, *The Nordic Parliaments: A Comparative Analysis* (London: Hurst, 1984), p.6.
3. B. O. Birgersson, S. Hadenius, B. Molin and H. Wieslander, *Sverige efter 1900* (Stockholm: Bonniers, 1981), p.286.
4. There have been recent calls for a further reduction in the size of the Riksdag. For a discussion of the issue, see 'Allltför många ledamöter i svenska riksdagen?' *Nordisk Kontakt*, 5/89, p.78.
5. A party polling at least 12 per cent of the vote in a constituency, however, qualifies for parliamentary seats in that constituency.
6. See I. Carlsson, 'Att regera under den nya författningen', *Statsvetenskapliga Tidskrift*, 2, 1989, pp.73–6.
7. L. Lewin, *Ideology and Strategy: A Century of Swedish Politics* (New York: Cambridge University Press, 1989), pp.33–82.
8. D. Arter, 'The Swedish General Election of 1985: increased political influence for the Left Communists', *The Journal of Communist Studies*, Vol.2, No.1 (1986), pp.78–82.
9. For a detailed discussion of strength and weakness in government, see D. Arter, 'Consensus Politics at the Crossroads?' in J. Paastela (ed.), *Democracy in the Modern World: Essays for Tatu Vanhanen* (Tampere: University of Tampere, 1989), pp.115–30.
10. See *Kritiska Europafakta*, 1 and 8 July 1989, p.74. Also 'Centern motsätter sig "total EG-anpassning"', *Nordisk Kontakt*, 10–11/89, p.74, and 'Austria in a Changing Europe', *Itävallan ulkoministeri Alois Mockin esitelmä Paasikivi-Seurassa*, 12 October 1989.
11. 'Valdeltanget högre bland kvinnorna än bland männen', *Nordisk Kontakt*, 10–11/89, p.70.
12. D. Arter, 'A Tale of Two Carlssons: The Swedish General Election of 1988', *Parliamentary Affairs*, Vol.42, No.1 (1989), pp.84–101.

13. Arter, *The Nordic Parliaments*, pp.212–40.
14. See D. Arter, *Politics and Policy-Making in Finland* (Brighton: Wheatsheaf Books, 1987), pp.48–50.
15. D. Arter, 'The Shift to a Unicameral Folketing', in L. D. Longley and D. Olsen (eds.), *Two into One: The Politics and Processes of Bicameral/Unicameral Change* (Westview, 1991). There were admirers of the Finnish qualified majority rules on the Danish constitutional reform commission in the early 1950s.
16. See, for example, M. Gennser, *Motion till riksdagen 1988/89: K 230 Grundlagsfrågor*.
17. von Sydow, *Vägen till enkammarriksdagen*, p. 61.
18. The size of the standing committees was increased from 16 to 17 members in October 1988 to allow the Greens a single delegate on each.
19. G. Loewenberg and S. C. Patterson, *Comparing Legislatures* (Boston: Little, Brown, 1979), pp.206–12.
20. See, for example, H. Hegeland, 'Dra av närvaro på lönen!' *Dagens Nyheter*, 9 Nov. 1989.
21. D. Arter, 'The Nordic Parliaments: Patterns of Legislative Influence', *West European Politics*, Vol.8, No.1 (1985), p.64.
22. U. Christoffersson, 'Riksdagsledamöternas arbetsvecka', i, *Folkets främsta foreträdare*, Tre undersökningar av riksdagsledamoternas arbete i och utanför riksdagen, SOU: 27, 1986, p.23.
23. B. Owe Birgersson, *Riksdagsarbetet i enkammarriksdagen*, Riksdagens protokoll bihang 1975/76, Saml.2. Förslag och redogörelser – 15 Bilag 1 (Stockholm: Gotab, 1976), pp.78–80.
24. B. K. Solvang and J. Moren, 'Partsrepresentasjon i kommitéer: Litt om utviklingen over tid', in J. Moren (ed.), *Den Kollegiale Forvaltning Råd og utvalg i sentraladministrasjonen* (Oslo-Bergen Tromsø: Universitetsforlaget, 1974), pp.33–6.
25. Arter, *The Nordic Parliaments*, p.62.
26. M. Isberg, *The First Decade of the Unicameral Riksdag: The Role of the Swedish Parliament in the 1970s* (Stockholm: Stockholms universitet, 1982), p.48. No less than 61 per cent of all commissions with a parliamentary membership contained representatives of the governing party plus all three opposition parties, the Conservatives, Centre *and* Social Democrats.
27. Arter, *The Nordic Parliaments*, p.63.
28. As Hans Meijer commented in the late 1960s, 'a relatively limited number of individuals within the political parties, who are able to represent several interests, are tapped for many commission appointments'. H. Meijer, 'Bureaucracy and Policy Formulation in Sweden', *Scandinavian Political Studies*, Vol.4 (1969), pp. 108–9.
29. T. Larsson, *Att vara riksdagsledamot*, SOU: 27, 1985, p.55. The workload of standing committees varies a good deal. The Education Committee carries the heaviest burden; others, such as the Defence Committee, are only intermittently busy – the volume of work growing as the completion date of the five-yearly Defence Review approaches. For those delegates not actively involved in an outside organisation, contacts with interest groups can readily grow out of standing committee work.
30. G. Hernes, 'Interest, Influence and Co-operation: A Study of the Norwegian Parliament', PhD thesis, Johns Hopkins University, 1971, p.352.
31. J. Wallenberg, *Den moderna demokratins problem: Om patriarbete och riksdagsarbete* (Doxa: Lund, 1989), p.59.
32. Larsson, p.56.
33. Ibid.
34. *Riksdagen i siffror 1989/90* (Stockholm: Riksdagens Förvaltningskontor, 1989), p.17.
35. Ibid., p.18.
36. Interview with Gunnar Björk, 9 Nov. 1989. See also G. Björk, *Snabbprotokoll från riksdagsdebatterna 1988/89*: 130; Onsdagen den 7 July, especially pp.14–20.
37. M. Isberg, 'Propositionskontakter med Riksdagen – Förr och nu', *Departmentshistorie-kommitten 1989*, pp.19–23.
38. D. Tarschys, for example. *Fakta om folkvalda. Riksdagen 1988–91* (Falköping: Gummersons, 1989).
39. C. Linde, *Departement och Verk*, Om synen på den centrala statsförvaltningen och dess

uppdelning – i en förändrad offentlig sektor (Stockholm: Stockholms universitet, 1982), pp.192–8.
40. Larsson, pp.74–5.
41. S. Holmberg and L. Weibull (eds), *SOM – undersökningen 1987: Samhälle Opinion Massmedia 2* (Göteborgs Universitet, 1988), pp.10–11.
42. E. Lindström, *The Swedish Parliamentary System* (Uddevalla: Svenska Institutet, 1983), p.73.
43. 'Ökat politikerförakt till följd av Boforsaffären?' *Nordisk Kontakt*, 8/87, pp.63–4.
44. Larsson, pp.76–8.
45. Retired Speaker Ingemund Bengtsson suggested in 1987, for example, that there should be more 'second reading-style' debates before a bill was transmitted to standing committee. This is very rare today. See 'Riksdagen måste livas upp', *Nordisk Kontakt*, 1/87, pp.76–7.
46. Larsson, pp.84–5.
47. N. Elder, H. Thomas and D. Arter, *The Consensual Democracies? The Government and Politics of the Scandinavian States* (Oxford: Martin Robertson, 1982), pp.10–11.
48. '75,000 på marsh mot fonderna', *Nordisk Kontakt*, 13/83, p.997.
49. R. Sahr, *The Politics of Energy Policy Change in Sweden* (Ann Arbor: University of Michigan, 1985).
50. R. Hague and M. Harrop, *Comparative Government and Politics: An Introduction* (Basingstoke: Macmillan, 1987), pp.189–90.
51. Loewenberg and Patterson, p.197.
52. Three major conflict lines between the Carlsson Cabinet and the Riksdag look set to dominate the political agenda until the next general election in September 1991. In each case, a *sine qua non* of government success at the crucial parliamentary vote appears to lie in striking a deal with the leading opposition party, the Conservatives, viz the achievement of a left–right legislative coalition. The three are: energy policy and the future of nuclear power; Sweden's relations with the EC and possible moves, following the Austrian example, to reconcile neutrality with an application for membership of the EC; and the implications of the radical tax reform package being implemented over 1990–91, especially the impact of the increased levels of indirect taxation and the broadened VAT base on the poorer households. All three have aligned the government and the political right (Conservatives and Liberals) against a nascent environmental bloc of Left-Communists, Greens and Centre Party. Budgets are also likely to encounter increased opposition. See D. Arter, 'Sweden: Budget Plans', *Oxford Analytica Daily Brief*, 11 January 1990.

Legislatures in Perspective

Philip Norton

The typology of legislatures constructed by Michael Mezey has provided a valuable framework for analysis. That has been demonstrated by the contributors to this volume. Though Mezey categorised the Italian Parliament as enjoying strong policy-making power (hence in the same category as the US Congress), the evidence presented by Paul Furlong suggests that it falls – along with the other six legislatures under review – within the second of Mezey's three types on the policy-making axis: that is, a legislature with modest policy-*making* power. The pressures which forced the legislatures of Western Europe into that category were sketched in the introduction. The maintenance of that position is confirmed by the foregoing articles. The seven – Italy included – also demonstrate the essential characteristics of 'more supported' legislatures. All meet regularly and none appears under threat (now) from élite or public hostility. They are accepted as parts of the constitutional landscape in a way that is not apparent in countries harbouring 'less supported' legislatures. We thus have for analysis seven legislatures falling broadly within Mezey's relatively crowded category of 'reactive' legislatures.

Mezey's work is thus useful in providing a broad analytic framework. Taking us beyond an exclusive focus on policy-making has proved especially valuable in identifying a rich field for enquiry. However, Mezey's broad analytic framework is essentially that – a broad framework. As Ken Gladdish reminds us, it does not help us appreciate differences within a particular category. The contributions to this volume have sought to do that. What emerges clearly from the articles is the difference of degree that exists between the legislatures. Some of the differences may reflect different ways of analysing legislatures; even operating within a common analytic framework, contributors have adopted eclectic approaches. But much of the difference stems from the nature of the institutions themselves and the environments they inhabit. The value of the contributions to this volume is that they give some shape to the differences and allow a number of generalisations to be drawn.

In terms of policy affect, a rough hierarchy of the seven legislatures can be constructed from the evidence offered. We shall attempt such a construction in due course. For the moment, the essential point is that there are differences between legislatures in policy affect. The contributions to this volume are especially valuable in suggesting some of the variables that determine the degree of policy affect. Some of these have already been drawn out by Malcolm Shaw in his analysis of committees in eight, more disparate legislatures.[1] The evidence presented in this volume is insufficient to prove that policy influence is dependent upon these variables – we have too small a sample of legislatures – but it serves to reinforce, and in some areas qualify and go beyond, the principal generalisations drawn by Shaw.

The variables suggested by the articles in this volume can be subsumed under three heads: constitutional, political and procedural. A constitution determines the formal powers and relationships of a legislature in a political system. There are three constitutional constraints that appear significant. The most obvious is where the legislature is denied powers to determine public policy in certain sectors. Such formal constraints are imposed, most obviously, in France. The second constraint exists where a legislative measure may be challenged and overturned, either by recourse to the people (referendums) or to the courts (judicial review). Such constraints variously exist in Western Europe. France, Italy and Ireland are among the countries with provisions for referendums; Holland and Britain are alone in enjoying parliamentary supremacy, enactments of the legislature not being subject to judicial challenge on grounds of being contrary to the provisions of the constitution. The third constraint exists where ministers remain members of the legislature. As was noted in the British example, this may be useful to the legislature in terms of the availability of ministers to answer for their actions, but it also helps the ministry by both providing a 'payroll vote' in the legislature and – where the ministry depends upon the confidence of the legislature – reduces the likelihood of members being willing to defeat a government for fear of forcing an election. This latter constraint is made especially effective by the force of another variable: party. Of the seven legislatures under consideration, in only two (Holland and France) are ministers separate from the legislature.

The political variable is that of party. Whatever the constitutional strength and independence of a legislature, these can be negated in effect by strong political parties. If both executive and legislature are dominated by members of one, partisan party, then party loyalty can ensure the enactment of a party programme, legislators following the directions given by party leaders. As the experience of the United States reveals, it is not sufficient for one party to dominate both branches and, as Malcolm Shaw demonstrates, the number of parties competing in a political system is not the crucial factor. What is needed to ensure party hegemony is one, partisan party enjoying majority support. Partisanship provides the necessary condition for loyalty. A majority allows the party to enact its programme. Where no one party enjoys an overall majority, legislatures generally assume a greater importance in the development of public policy. Thus, on this criterion, Ireland (variously) and the United Kingdom fall at the bottom of the league table.

Under the procedural head, there are two variables that emerge as significant. One is the stage at which a bill is referred to committee for detailed consideration. Shaw's findings suggest that legislatures in which committee stage precedes plenary session are in a stronger position to influence legislation than legislatures where plenary stage comes first. In most West European legislatures, committee stage precedes plenary debate. Again, Ireland and the United Kingdom are the exceptions. Given that both the UK Parliament and the Oireachtas are characterised usually by party dominance, it is possible to argue that committee stage is a dependent variable. However, Shaw's analysis – drawing on a wider range of legislatures – suggests that it is an independent variable and there are plausible hypotheses to support this. In small committees, each legislator carries greater weight than in plenary session; a few cross-votes can affect the outcome of a vote in a way not possible in full session. However, where floor debate comes first, and the chamber has determined the principle and hence the broad contours of the measure, the opportunity for individual legislators to influence significantly the overall shape of the measure is circumscribed. Perhaps most important of all, it is virtually impossible to kill a bill after it has received plenary approval. Where bills are committed first to committee, their survival beyond committee stage is not assured.

The second procedural variable is the degree of committee specialisation. Most of the legislatures of Western Europe have appointed committees to parallel the main departments or sectors of government responsibility. The UK Parliament, before 1979, did not have a specialised committee system. Ireland, too, lacked such system before 1983. Shaw's data lead him to the conclusion that committee specialisation is not an independent variable in determining policy influence. Committee affect, he concludes, is dependent on party strength. However, the evidence presented in this volume suggests that this may not be the case. The departmentally related Select Committees in the House of Commons are clearly constrained by virtue of operating within a strong party system. Despite that, they appear to have exerted some influence in the policy cycle; government has variously acted on the recommendations of committees, recommendations that are usually the product of bi-partisan agreement. The committees are now well established and, according to the Leader of the House in 1989, an indispensable part of the parliamentary system.[2] Not so the Irish committees. As Audrey Arkins has outlined, they have largely atrophied. Yet despite a short and mostly dismal life, they have had, as Arkins shows, occasional influence, their basic failure stemming as much from disinterest on the part of TDs as from asphyxiation by the executive.

If one takes these various constraints, and their apparent importance in each case under review, it is possible to draw up a rough league table of legislatures in terms of policy affect. The list accords with that suggested by the broad tenor of the contributions to this volume. Jockeying for first place – ranking depending on the weight attached to each of the constraints – are Italy, Holland and Sweden; in terms of demonstrable policy affect, Italy probably deserves pride of place. Then come West Germany, Great Britain, France and Ireland. Again, depending on the weighting one gives to particular constraints, France and Britain compete for fifth place. The list, given the difficulties of weighting the constraints, is necessarily hazy, but it has a utility in indicating the relative position of legislatures; it is one to which we shall return.

The contributions to this volume are important also for demonstrating not just certain linkages but, in some crucial respects, the absence of any discernible linkage. There is no obvious correlation between national/local orientations on the part of elected legislators and the electoral system employed to return them. Thus, some degree of local or regional orientation (members seeing themselves as champions of local interests) exists in Ireland (Single Transferable Vote) and – to a lesser extent – Italy (party list system) and Britain (plurality system), but none of note in, say, Holland (party list system). In terms of the relationship of policy affect to electoral systems, it is notable that, of countries employing some form of proportional representation, those using party-list systems tend to predominate at the top of our league table. However, beyond that it is difficult to go. In terms of a simple dichotomy of proportional (PR) systems and those not strictly proportional, the non-proportional systems are hemmed in at the top and bottom by PR systems. Our sample is too small to determine whether Ireland is an exceptional case. Hence, our material will not bear the weight of generalisation.

What is remarkable, and certainly more significant in the context of this volume, is the absence of any discernible relationship between policy affect and how citizens perceive their legislature (and legislators). We have already produced our league table based on policy affect. As Thomas Saalfeld has shown, it is also possible to draw up a league table based on the confidence which citizens have in their national assemblies. One could also employ other indicators – including perceptions of how important the legislature is in the life of the country[3] – in order to produce further tables. Indeed, if one took policy affect, confidence and importance one would get the following contrasts in rank ordering:

POLICY AFFECT	CONFIDENCE[4]	IMPORTANCE[5]
Italy	West Germany	Britain
Holland	Ireland	West Germany
Sweden	France	Holland
West Germany	Britain	(Belgium)
Britain	Italy	France
France		Italy
Ireland		

On the basis of the survey data presented by David Arter and Ken Gladdish, Sweden would probably be at the top of the 'confidence' table and Holland somewhere in the middle. When perceptions of legislators – and the efficacy of making contact with them – are factored in, the picture becomes even more confused. As we have seen, French deputies maintain close local ties. Links between MPs and constituencies are also important in Britain. In contrast, in Holland, as Ken Gladdish reports, a survey in the early 1970s found that over 70 per cent of respondents regarded contacting MPs as an ineffective way of airing problems. Riksdag members, according to David Arter, are becoming further distanced from their constituents.

How citizens assess their legislature thus varies depending on the criteria being employed (confidence, importance, members) and none of these appear to correlate directly with the capacity of the legislature to influence the development of public policy.

What, if anything, does this tell us about legislatures? And what explains it? Why are there these differences? Here it is appropriate to refer back to the introduction and the framework provided by Mezey and Robert Packenham. Packenham's work drew out the importance of legislatures as bodies that are multi-functional: in other words, they have consequences for their political systems other than solely that of allocating values (Packenham's decisional function). The articles in this volume have drawn out those consequences. What is clear from the evidence presented, and what the foregoing data intimate, is the extent to which those consequences vary from system to system. The reason why they vary has been touched upon variously by the contributors. Each legislature has to be analysed in the context of the political culture in which it nestles. That culture affects both the basic place of the legislature in the political life of the nation and the more mundane aspects of its existence. Elite and mass attitudes towards the political system have helped shape (in some instances modify or change completely) political institutions; conversely, the experience of those institutions has influenced attitudes towards the political system. The political culture of each of the seven countries covered in this volume can be distinguished from the others. How people see their national assembly, and what they expect of it, varies from country to country.

Citizens may have confidence in their Parliament for reasons largely unrelated to its capacity to determine public policy. Some national assemblies may – and, on the basis of available evidence, do – fulfil 'symbolic' and not just 'instrumental' satisfactions.[6] The processes – the way in which a Parliament operates as part of a political process – may be far more important than the actual immediate outcome (in policy terms) of those processes. 'Our commitments to democratic processes are essentially commitments to a mode of decision making. The legitimacy of the democratic form of government has never really depended upon the policy outcomes which it is expected to produce.'[7] The modes of decision-making, as we have seen, vary throughout Western Europe. What is important is the extent to which those modes accord with prevailing expectations and national values. Strong leadership by a single national body would be alien to, and generate tensions in, certain political cultures, such as that of the United States. In others, it would not. In Britain and France, the belief that 'government must govern', implicitly without undue interference, is frequently voiced. Periods of coalition government (UK) and 'cohabitation' (France) engender negative responses, albeit not from all, that would find little resonance in several neighbouring states.

The attachment to the different modes of decision-making – to the way the system works – is important in the context of our opening hypothesis. Legislatures in Western Europe appear to have consequences for their political systems which have usually been borne of, and continue to satisfy, national expectations and values. Fulfilling such functions over a period of time has generated mass and élite support which then exists independently of the legislatures' capacity to meet immediate instrumental needs. In short, they enjoy what David Easton has described as 'diffuse support':

> Except in the long run, diffuse support is independent of the effects of daily outputs. It consists of a reserve of support that enables a system to weather the many storms when outputs cannot be balanced off against inputs of demands. It is a kind of support that a system does not have to buy with more or less direct benefits for the obligations and responsibilities the member incurs. If we wish, the outputs here may be considered psychic or symbolic, and in this sense, they may offer the individual immediate benefits strong enough to stimulate a supportive response.[8]

Such supportive responses, it can be suggested, are characteristics of West European polities. The last country to experience a legislature that failed to resonate with national expectations was France under the Fourth Republic. Now, all the legislatures under review enjoy 'more supported' status and the extent of the diffuse support they enjoy underpins the one essential feature of legislatures that emerges from these pages: their resilience. Although one would anticipate some decline in the confidence accorded legislatures at times of systemic stress, the remarkable feature of the past twenty years has been the extent to which they have maintained that confidence. Some decline has variously occurred, as Thomas Saalfeld notes especially in the case of West Germany, but relative to what one might expect that decline has been modest. The maintenance of that support is independent, as we have seen, of policy affect.

Equally remarkable is the position of the legislatures in influencing public policy. The pressures of the past 20 years, as various contributors have recorded, appear to have reduced the level of consensual policy making – but not to have further marginalised, on any significant scale, the policy influence of legislatures. There has been no discernible *trend* of marginalisation. The reasons for this are twofold. One is the very feature we have just identified. At times of stress, governments often need legislatures more than before in order to buttress their legitimacy. The diffuse support enjoyed by legislatures accords them a certain resilience in the domain of public policy. The second reason explains the lack of consistency between legislatures: some have proved more resilient than others. And that is because of country-specific factors. Parliament in Britain, as we have seen, has been cross-pressured as a result of developments peculiar to the institution. David Arter argues that the Swedish Riksdag has expanded its role as an agent of policy influence, as a consequence principally of constitutional developments – the transition to unicameralism. The West German Bundestag has witnessed a relative increase in party cohesion but without altering fundamentally its role as a policy-influencing legislature. In Ireland, the Oireachtas has not so much declined as reverted to the position it held before the 1980s, when it experimented with committees. Thus, to reiterate our opening observation: all the contributors confirm that the seven legislatures remain firmly in Mezey's second category on his policy-making axis. None suggests there has been a major 'decline' since 1970.

This is not to argue that the situation may not change in the future. As Easton observed in discussing the concept of diffuse support, that support is independent of the effects of daily outputs 'except in the long term'. In the long term, support may atrophy. Legislatures may also be subject to other pressures. What then of the future?

THE 1990s?

The decade of the 1990s may prove to be a decade of opportunity for legislatures, though one of challenge for the legislatures of Western Europe. The events of 1989 and 1990 in the Soviet Union and Eastern Europe have given a new significance to legislatures. Previously important primarily if not exclusively for giving formal assent to measures – examples of Mezey's 'minimal legislatures' – the legislatures of Eastern Europe are now beginning to play a more active role in the policy cycle. The basis from which they are starting, in terms of both culture and resources, is essentially weak. The Foreign Affairs Select Committee of the British House of Commons noted the beginnings of change in Hungary when it visited there in 1988. 'Hungarians told us that the roots of democracy were weak in their country compared to the West, as a result of the events of history. Nevertheless, they have an impressive Parliament building on the banks of the Danube, for which they are seeking to create a stronger role.'[9] Hungary is in a better position than certain of its neighbours. For some, the challenge is enormous. Romania in particular has little to draw on, in terms either of experience or political culture, in developing a pluralist political system. The legislatures of Western Europe are giving some assistance. A small example in the British case is the 'Know How' Fund established by the government to assist Poland and Romania, parts of which have been used to help advise Polish politicians on the role and mechanics of the Westminster Parliament. How far Western experience proves exportable, given some of our earlier observations, remains to be seen. The developments in Eastern Europe none the less serve to demonstrate one essential point: the enduring salience of legislatures.

A new form of legislature is not peculiar to Eastern Europe. Western Europe also has one. The European Parliament formally acquired the title of a parliament only in 1987 with the enactment of the Single European Act (SEA) and it constitutes a legislature *sui generis*. Until 1987 it constituted essentially an advisory body in the policy cycle of the EC. Under the provisions of the SEA, it acquired a more central role in the Community legislative process. This new role has been outlined in looking at the position of the UK. It is a role that the Parliament has begun to play with some enthusiasm and effect. The co-operation procedure, applicable in the case of measures necessary to achieve the single market, has resulted in the Parliament achieving a substantial number of amendments to proposed measures at second reading stage.[10] Given the shift of power from the national institutions of the member states to the institutions of the Community, the European Parliament now stands in a position to affect Community legislation in a way no longer possible by the national Parliaments. In certain sectors, legislative competence has passed to the supra-national Parliament.

For the legislatures of the member states, the challenge has been – and remains – one of deciding how to cope with the new situation. The response has been somewhat disparate. At least ten of the twelve have appointed committees to consider EC matters.[11] However, the form which these bodies take, and their remit, varies considerably. Some now allow their Members of the European Parliament (MEPs) to attend meetings as non-voting members. The West German Bundestag gave a lead in this respect, followed by Belgium. Some will call MEPs quite often as witnesses; this is notably so in the case of the sub-committees of the House of Lords' Committee on the European Communities. Most consider draft EC proposals, though only in Denmark is the government obliged to consult the committee (the *Markedsudvalget*) on policy questions of major importance, with the committee having an opportunity to disapprove. The working practices and meeting regularity of the bodies also vary.

There is a recognition in many member states that they have not yet got the balance quite right in dealing with EC legislation and the relations between the national Parliament and European Parliament. There is a tendency in Britain to assume that Parliament is especially ill-equipped, structurally as well as emotionally, to deal with EC issues and that it is, in the words of one observer, 'weaker than . . . its counterparts in other EC states'.[12] In fact, Britain is not quite so exceptional. For example, in the Bundestag – sometimes held up as a model to follow by British reformers – there is a continuing debate as to the adequacy of existing procedures. EC matters are at present dealt with by a sub-committee, itself established only in 1987, of the Committee on Foreign Affairs. In 1983, a joint commission comprising members of both chambers had been appointed – with responsibility to make recommendations on EC policies of fundamental importance – but it was not re-appointed after the general election of 1987. (From 1967 to 1983, the chamber had been largely dependent for information on EC matters on those of its members who were MEPs.) Members of the Bundestag have variously expressed their dissatisfaction with the existing position, most recently in a debate on 13 December 1989 when the Bundestag vice-president, Annemarie Renger, voiced her complaint at the failure of the chamber to establish a permanent committee on EC legislation.[13] The House of Commons at least has such a committee.

It will take some time for national Parliaments to adapt. The attempt by the House of Commons to do so has been sketched already in looking at the UK. The quotation from *The Economist* employed in that article is worth repeating: 'Britain's Parliament is entering a curious constitutional race: if it does not learn, *along with the other national parliaments*, to exercise effective scrutiny over the European institutions, then the Strasbourg parliament will get the job'.[14] In the case of the UK, the potential is there. There is also something to build on. Though obvious limitations exist in the case of the lower houses of the West German and British Parliaments, the upper houses – the Bundesrat and the House of Lords – already have well-established and permanent committees on the European Communities; both are active and influential. These suggest that the potential for influence in the new situation created by the SEA is real. It remains to be seen to what extent it is realised.

Robert Packenham opened his article on legislatures and political development by recording Richard Fenno's observation on studies of Congress: 'These are the best of times, these are the worst of times'.[15] A similar observation may prove appropriate for legislatures themselves in the decade of the 1990s. There is the potential for them to prove, in relative terms, the best of times. There are tremendous opportunities for legislatures in Eastern Europe. There are opportunities for expansion in policy influence by the European Parliament and for the Parliaments of the EC member states to develop and exploit links with that Parliament in order to influence Community legislation. Such linkage may also help counter the perceived 'democratic deficit' in the EC. However, there is also the potential to be the worst of times. Though legislatures in Eastern Europe may be able to exert some independent influence in their respective polities, they are likely to be dependent on other variables; they may yet be submerged in a sea of instability. The concept of diffuse support cannot be applied in societies with no established parliamentary tradition. The legislatures of Western Europe may yet be left behind in the race to establish greater democratic accountability, giving way to the European Parliament; on an even more pessimistic scenario, both the European and national parliaments may lose out to an accretion of policy-making power to the EC Commission. Over time, the diffuse support which has underpinned their legitimacy, and hence their strength, may be eroded.

Given past history, one suspects that the legislatures under scrutiny in this volume will continue to display the resilience that has marked them out in recent years. However, as the parliamentarians of the French Fourth Republic discovered, nothing is certain. The lesson to be learned from the pages of this volume is not one of complacency but of vigilance. For the legislatures of Western Europe, the best way to maintain their policy affect and their support is for them to assume that they will not.

NOTES

1. M. Shaw, 'Conclusion', in J. D. Lees and M. Shaw (eds.), *Committees in Legislatures* (Oxford: Martin Robertson, 1979), pp.361–434.
2. Sir G. Howe, Memorandum to the House of Commons Select Committee on Procedure, 13 October 1989, paragraph 2.
3. See *Euro-baromètre* survey, April 1983, reproduced in D. P. Conradt, *The German Polity*, 3rd ed. (New York: Longman, 1986), p.152.
4. P. H. Merkl, 'Comparing Legitimacy and Values among Advanced Democratic Coun-

tries', in M. Dogan (ed.), *Comparing Pluralist Democracies: Strains on Legitimacy* (Boulder CO: Westview Press, 1988), p.61, as reproduced by Thomas Saalfeld in this volume.

5. Ranked in order of percentage of respondents saying that Parliament was 'very important' in the life of their nation. If the 'very important' and 'important' responses are aggregated, the positions of Britain and West Germany are reversed. *Euro-baromètre* survey, April 1983, reproduced in Conradt, p.152.

6. M. Edelman, *The Symbolic Uses of Politics* (Urbana, IL: University of Illinois Press, 1964), draws out the significance of political symbolism, not least that of political institutions: see especially p.12.

7. T. R. Dye, *Politics, Economics and the Public: Policy Outcomes in the American States*, quoted in J. C. Wahlke, 'Policy Demands and System Support: The Role of the Represented', *British Journal of Political Science*, Vol.1 (1971), p.288.

8. D. Easton, *A Systems Analysis of Political Life*, quoted in Wahlke, p.282.

9. First Report from the Select Committee on Foreign Affairs, Session 1988/89, *Eastern Europe and the Soviet Union*, HC 16 (London: HMSO, 1989), p.xxiii.

10. From July 1987 to March 1989 inclusively, the Commission accepted 67 per cent and the Council adopted 50 per cent of the amendments proposed by the Parliament on first reading (i.e. when giving its first opinion). The figures for the second reading (amendments made under the new procedure) were 60 per cent and 25 per cent. D. Millar, 'The European Parliament', *Study of Parliament Group Newsletter*, No.5 (Spring 1989), p.11.

11. See European Centre for Parliamentary Research and Documentation, *Bodies within National Parliaments specialising in European Community affairs*, National Parliaments Series No.3, April 1989 (Luxembourg: Office for Official Publications of the EC, 1989).

12. J. Lodge, Memorandum of Evidence, House of Commons Select Committee on Procedure, Fourth Report, Session 1988/89, *The Scrutiny of European Legislation*, Vol.II: Minutes of Evidence and Appendices, HC 622-II (London: HMSO, 1989), p.155.

13. I am grateful to Thomas Saalfeld for this information. See also M. Schweitzer, 'Europarat, WEU, NATO, Europäisches Parlament', in H-P. Schneider and W. Zeh (eds.), *Parlamentsrecht und Parlamentspraxis in der Bundesrepublik Deutschland* (Berlin: Walter de Gruyter, 1989), pp.1657–94.

14. 'Europe comes to Westminster', *The Economist*, 16 December 1989, p.33.

15. R. A. Packenham, 'Legislatures and Political Development', in A. Kornberg and L. D. Musolf (eds.), *Legislatures in Developmental Perspective* (Durham NC: Duke University Press, 1970), p.521.

ABSTRACTS

Parliaments: A Framework for Analysis
Philip Norton

Comparative study of legislatures has been limited: in part because of a restrictive paradigm and in part because of methodological difficulties in undertaking comparison. This introductory essay offers a framework for analysis, drawing in particular on the works of Michael Mezey and Robert Packenham. The framework takes one beyond solely that of legislative–executive relations to legislative–citizen relations. It allows contributors to address to what extent legislatures have been further marginalised in the policy cycle since 1970 and to what extent they have become more significant as agents of regime support.

Parliament in the United Kingdom
Philip Norton

Historical and constitutional features of Britain have constrained Parliament as a policy-influencing legislature. Since 1970, the institution has been subject to cross-pressures which have removed the loci of policy-making further from its domain while buttressing its capacity to influence measures placed before it. Regime support functions – especially those of 'tension release' and interest articulation – have assumed greater significance as pressures on the political system have increased. The institution has the potential to enhance support for the political system but is faced by the threat of 'parliamentary overload'.

The French Parliament: Loyal Workhorse, Poor Watchdog
John Frears

The legislative process in France is characterised by executive dominance. Parliament does not initiate legislation, it is largely inadequate as an arena of national debate, and it is not the principal agent of ministerial recruitment. It none the less examines, improves and legitimises legislation. The linkage between constituent and parliamentarian contributes significantly to support for the political system. The working of parties within the political system, the limited legislative activity of the National Assembly and the local attachment of *députés* helps maintain the political stability of the Fifth Republic.

Parliament in Italian Politics

Paul Furlong

Government crises are a feature of Italian politics. Parliament facilitates but is not the principal cause of such crises: party is the independent variable. Parliament is important as an avenue of ministerial recruitment and as a body with strong formal powers in the legislative process. Legislation is considerably amended, though most legislation takes the form of 'little laws' (*leggine*). Parliament retains considerable autonomy and attempts by government to legislate through the use of decree laws have engendered mistrust and resistance.

The West German Bundestag after 40 Years: The Role of Parliament in a 'Party Democracy'

Thomas Saalfeld

The ability of the Bundestag to constrain government is analysed from four different perspectives: the bargaining processes between coalition parties, the relationship between the government and its backbenchers, the strategies of opposition parties, and the inter-action of parties in departmental committees. The most important constraints are found to result from the government's dependence on stable coalitions and cohesive backbench behaviour. Parliament's popular support has grown since the 1950s. However, the recent loss of popular confidence demonstrates that support remains fragile.

Legislative and Executive Relations in the Republic of Ireland

Andrey Arkins

The relationship between the legislature and the executive in Ireland is invariably discussed in terms of subordination of the former to the latter. This study describes recent failed attempts to enhance the effectiveness of the legislature through internal parliamentary reforms. It finds that the Irish parliamentary deputy does not exercise the modest powers available as often or as effectively as he might. This is evidenced by the neglect shown towards the reforms introduced in 1983 which, if nurtured carefully, could have altered legislative-executive relations in Ireland considerably.

Parliamentary Activism and Legitimacy in the Netherlands

Ken Gladdish

The place of the Dutch Parliament in both the constitutional structure and the political system is reviewed and a number of distinctive features identified: the method of national representation, the character of the party system and the dynamics of government. Developments over the past two decades permit the conclusion that parliamentary influence upon policy-making has increased and that, despite continuing qualms over the method of representation, there has been no decrease in parliamentary legitimacy during this period.

The Swedish Riksdag: The Case of a Strong Policy-influencing Assembly

David Arter

Sweden introduced a single-chamber Riksdag, and a revised electoral system, in 1971. The period since then has witnessed a transition to small specialist committees, minority governments, and the introduction of a provision for no confidence votes. A consequence has been a strengthening of the Riksdag as a policy-influencing assembly. Members of the Riksdag also retain an important input in policy formulation through membership of commissions, though the number of commissions has declined in recent years. The Riksdag remains a 'more supported' legislature, enjoying more public confidence as a social institution than big business and the trade unions, though less than the banks and the health service.

Conclusion: Legislatures in Perspective

Philip Norton

The contributions to this volume have allowed a number of generalisations to be drawn. In policy affect, there are constitutional, political and procedural variables that emerge as significant. However, little relationship exists between policy affect and citizen perceptions of legislatures. Expectations differ and each legislature appears to have built up a body of diffuse support, both features serving to explain this lack of relationship as well as the resilience of legislatures. The decade of the 1990s may prove a decade of opportunity for legislatures though one of challenge for the legislatures of Western Europe. Resilience is not guaranteed.